For Teresa: Thank you for giving me the freedom to chase my dream, and for standing by me whenever I needed support. I couldn't have done this without you.

£22·45

UNIX® Program Development for IBM® PCs
Including OSF/Motif™

UNIX® Program Development for IBM® PCs
Including OSF/Motif™

Thomas Yager

Addison-Wesley Publishing Company, Inc.

Reading, Massachusetts   Menlo Park, California   New York
Don Mills, Ontario   Wokingham, England   Amsterdam   Bonn
Sydney   Singapore   Tokyo   Madrid   San Juan
Paris   Seoul   Milan   Mexico City   Taipei

Managing Editor: Amorette Pedersen
Set in 10.5-point Palatino by Benchmark Productions

1 2 3 4 5 6 7 8 9-MW-9594939291
First Printing, August 1991

ISBN: 0-201-57727-5

Table of Contents

Acknowledgments

The examples in this book were developed and tested on an Altos System 5000 80486-based computer running Altos UNIX, a licensed version of SCO UNIX and Open Desktop. The writing, figures and additional testing were done on an Opus Systems System 5000 (no relation to the Altos) SPARC computer running OpusOS (a license of SunOS 4.1) and Open Windows 2.0. The author wishes to thank Altos Computer Systems (now a division of Acer) and Opus Systems for their cooperation and assistance. The systems provided by these companies endured endless hours and merciless abuse without flinching. Because of them, I was able to concentrate entirely on the book and take my equipment for granted.

The author also expresses gratitude to the following companies and individuals:

- The staff and readers of BYTE magazine, and especially Ben Smith, a good friend who convinced me to pursue writing this book, and Jon Udell, who started the process that made me part of the world's best computer magazine
- Chris Williams, Amy Pedersen and the rest of the Benchmark Productions staff, for taking on this project and exhibiting the highest degree of patience and professsionalism throughout
- Ross Oliver, this book's technical editor, for his valuable involvement and input

- David Burnette and other UNIX Review staffers, past and present, for giving me my first assignment and encouraging me to pursue a career as a writer
- The designers, programmers and other creative people at Williams/Bally/Midway, Data East and Premier/Gottlieb for giving me an alternate obsession so I could survive this one. Special thanks to Joe Kaminkow and Larry DeMar for their support and friendship.
- And finally, to David Arkenstone, whose visionary music played constantly during the writing of this book, keeping my head clear and my thoughts focused

Introduction

The writing of computer programs hasn't gotten any easier. In the old days, programmers had to contend with wimpy or non-existent support libraries and tools. There was a lot of inventing going on, but too much of it was directed at creating a foundation on which a program could be built. Too often, building that foundation was such a laborious task that the programmer was left with little energy for the application itself. Later, as libraries and tools began to flourish, programmers found they could concentrate their creativity on the application, depending on an existing infrastructure. As more innovative applications began to appear, users began to *expect* the advanced functionality that the new class of applications brought to solving problems.

These days, users' expectations are higher than ever. In nearly every environment, developers are being forced to find ways to satisfy users' demands, and to keep in step with competitors. DOS programmers quickly discovered that 640K of memory and a single-tasking environment couldn't contain the kind of complex applications that users were spending money to buy. The work-arounds range from the sublime (DOS extenders) to the ridiculous (overlay linkers). Even though DOS has been around seemingly forever, only now is it being reshaped to make a suitable foundation for advanced applications.

In ever-growing numbers, users are turning to another environment in which virtual memory, multitasking and other desirable attributes are not wedged-in layers, but part of the base operating system. UNIX also plays most frequent host to the most widely-implemented graphical user interface, the X Window System, whose ease of use and visual appeal attract still more converts.

Where users go, developers are bound to follow, and that means that lots of programmers who earned their wings in environments like DOS, Windows, and even VMS and MVS, are now expected to transfer their skills to the unfamiliar domain of UNIX. My first experience as a UNIX programmer was like that of so many of my colleagues. I became buried under a mountain of documentation, and hurried to complete projects by writing code that clearly reflected my incomplete understanding of my new environment. Later, as it does for all of us, time and study tied up the loose ends, but I shudder to think of the atrocities I committed and the corners I cut for not taking the time to grasp some crucial concepts. But I got away with it, mostly because UNIX wasn't much known back then. In today's increasingly competitive market of UNIX applications software, there is little room for poorly-written code, and worse, no forgiveness for applications that fail to take best advantage of their environment.

This book, then, is a guide for developers who may be unacquainted with some of UNIX's more advanced facilities. Even if you're programming with UNIX for the first time, you'll find this book a good fit. It starts easily, with basic concepts like shell programming, and works into the advanced topics of user interfaces and client/server programming. It's something of a natural progression, but each chapter (after the first two) fairly stands alone; you can effectively skip to the material you need to get started on a specific project.

I wrote this book because I had never seen one like it, and as such, it defies description to some extent. Simply stated, it is a book of examples and explanations. If you leaf through this book, you'll find a considerable portion of it is filled with source code. This emphasis on practical examples is thanks to my discussions with numerous programmers who have indicated that a concise, well-written, *working* example is worth a pile of theoretical discussions and wordy dissertations. All of the examples contained here, over 7,000 lines in all, were created especially for this book, and are profusely commented and formatted for easy reading. Nearly all of them are directly executable; there are very few cases of code snippets that don't really work. I made some effort to contain the size of the examples so that you could type them in, but some topics demanded more code. To save you time, I have collected this book's examples, as they appear here, on diskettes that you may order through a form in the back. Because the source code is so much of this book, the code itself is a copyrighted, licensed product that may not be redistributed except under the terms described in the brief license in the back. I know this will grate on some readers and critics, but like every author, my goal is to get as many copies of this book into people's hands as I can. If huge hunks of the book can be picked up for free from bulletin boards and public computer networks, I will have wasted nearly a year's worth of effort. Please abide by the terms of the license.

The examples depend on two additional sources to make their points. First, there's the explanatory text that accompanies each example. I avoid line-by-line walk-throughs of the code—that's tedious and often puts the reader to sleep before the important portions are highlighted. Instead, I focus on those concepts that might be difficult to grasp quickly. My intent is to help you "over the hump" of those issues that might slow your progress. The other resource that works hand-in-hand with this book's example code is not found between the covers of this volume, but rather on your shelf: your own programmer's guide and reference manuals. I purposely littered this book with references to existing UNIX documentation (standard manuals, not other "third-party" volumes) for two reasons. First, with so much ground to cover, I wanted to avoid duplication of material. And second, I believe firmly in the "teach a man to fish" principle. By being directed to the UNIX manuals, you'll gain the ability to locate topics there and to understand the format in which the information is presented. Once you've completed this book, you should be ready to set it aside and rely solely on your UNIX and X Window manuals.

Thanks for purchasing this book. I hope you'll find it useful.

—*Tom Yager*

NOTE: *This book is written with the PC developer in mind. But it is not strictly limited to Intel-based systems. Many of the examples were also tested in other environments, including Interactive UNIX, SunOS and System V, Release 4. Extensive testing was performed only under Open Desktop/SCO System V UNIX, but I've tried to keep the material as general as possible. Any machine running System V, release 3.2 or later (or which offers facilities compatible with this release) should have no trouble with the examples and concepts contained herein.*

Chapter 1

UNIX Basics

A lot of UNIX's complexity is hidden in various "black boxes", pockets of functionality that we needn't concern ourselves with in the writing of applications. This chapter deals with those elements which are essential to program design: The shell, the editor, and the compiler.

If you have been experimenting with UNIX already, you may be able to skip sections of this chapter. If you've worked with UNIX but don't quite know where you stand, read this chapter anyway; it will help you gauge your experience. If you are a beginner, now is the time to find an introduction to UNIX and pick up some required skills. You will need to understand these basics before you begin this chapter:

- Logging in and out
- UNIX file system organization
- File access: Permissions, users, and groups
- Creating and changing to directories
- Displaying the current directory
- Using the UNIX command line (editing characters, etc.)
- Commands, options, and arguments
- UNIX editors

An excellent introduction to UNIX, including these topics, is AT&T's *User's Guide* (Part number 307-231). The complete document includes everything mentioned in the list in its first portion.

The Bourne Shell

A good deal of what users recognize as the "personality" of UNIX is not the operating system per se, but the command interpreter, or *shell*. Modern PC UNIX systems include either two or three shells. In this case, we will concern ourselves with the universally-implemented Bourne shell.

You usually don't need to start the shell manually; one is loaded for you when you log in to UNIX. The question is, which one are *you* running? Unless you are certain that you are running the Bourne shell (the default prompt, a "$" character, is a fair tip-off), you will want to start one manually so the following examples will work properly. To do that, simply type sh at your shell prompt, and press Return.

Your system may run the Korn shell by default. Since the Korn has the same standard prompt as the Bourne shell and contains a superset of Bourne shell functionality, examples in this book should work.

If your shell prompt is #, or if you know you are logged as root (or superuser, as it is sometimes called), switch to an account which does not have superuser privileges. While there are no examples in this book which intentionally guide you to do damage to your system, the potential always exists. Logging in as an ordinary user is an excellent safeguard against this.

Shell Parsing: Wildcards, Variables and Escapes

Like all operating systems, UNIX at its most basic level simply runs programs. You request commands by name; the shell locates the executable file that matches the name you entered, and executes it. During the process of evaluating, or *parsing*, the command line, the shell looks for certain characters which trigger special handling. For example, the command

```
$ ls /dev/f*
```

is a request for a list of files in the /dev directory whose names start with "f." Rather than require that every command understand how to process this and other filename wildcards, the shell expands the wildcards into full filenames *before* the requested command is loaded. So, when the ls program is loaded by the above command, rather than being passed /dev/f* as an argument, it is handed the full names of all files which match that wildcard. So, no matter what language you work in, even if you are writing simple shell scripts, all of your commands inherit the ability to accept file wildcards. This capability also imposes some requirements on the way your programs handle arguments. Whenever possible, you should write your programs to accept an unlimited number of file name arguments.

Shell Variables

You are accustomed to using variables to store data in programs you have written. The UNIX shells allow you to use variables in the traditional sense for the symbolic representation of data, and for internal purposes as well.

Ordinary variables in the shell are local to that particular copy of the shell; sub-shells (launched by some applications or by running another shell manually) and other users' shells cannot see them. In the Bourne shell, setting a variable is a simple assignment:

```
$ month=October
```

All variables are stored as strings, so they can represent any data type.

Variable values can be drawn from the shell with the special character, $. So, to verify the success of the assignment above,

```
$ echo $month
October
```

echo is a command which simply displays all of its arguments. You can also use variable names in expressions like this:

```
$ day=12; year=1990
$ echo $month $day, $year
October 12, 1990
```

The semicolon in the first line of the example above allows multiple statements on a single line. It saves space here, and saves time during manual entry of commands, but don't overuse the semicolon in your shell programs—it makes them harder to read.

In addition to the traditional use of variables, the UNIX shell has a special class for housekeeping purposes: the *environment variable*. The environment is a buffer (maintained by UNIX) which contains a group of strings. These strings are usually in a familiar "variable=value" format. They are used for many things, from modifying the behavior of the shell to telling applications what kind of terminal you have.

Any ordinary variable and its contents can be placed in the environment with the export command:

```
$ export $month
```

What value does this have? Only "exported" variables can be used by programs launched from your current shell. As an example of this, try this sequence:

```
$ localvar=tofu; globalvar=dragon
$ export globalvar
$ echo $localvar $globalvar
tofu dragon
$ sh
```

The next prompt is from a sub-shell, a separate process:

```
$ echo $localvar $globalvar
dragon
```

The following command returns you to your original shell:

```
$ exit
```

Note that the value of an unassigned variable is the null string; that's why there was no error generated by the above statement which requests the value of localvar. Because it was not exported by the first shell, it had no value in the second shell. This also serves to illustrate the parent/child relationship of UNIX processes.

Each process has its own environment, and they neither cooperate nor interfere with each other, with one exception: Child processes (programs launched from the current shell, and the programs *they* launch) inherit their parent's environment. There is no way for a parent process to read or change a child's environment once that child is running. Similarly, a child cannot alter its parent's environment without some serious wrangling by the programmer.

Shell Escapes

To pass an argument that contains spaces or other special characters, you need to *escape* them, that is, prevent the shell from interpreting them. There are several ways to do this. The ugliest and most direct method is to precede the character you wish to escape with a backslash (\). If you had escaped the $ in the earlier command, it would have looked like this:

```
$ echo \$globalvar
$globalvar
```

The escape character tells the shell to ignore any special meaning for only the first character following the backslash. In this case, the dollar sign is escaped, preventing the shell from interpreting $globalvar as a variable name.

Another level of shell escape is offered by apostrophes, or single quote marks ('). Enclosing a group of characters in quote marks causes the shell to pass that entire string unmodified to the command. The command

```
$ echo '$PATH $TERM $HOME'
```

offers up quite a different response if the apostrophes are removed. Try it.

There is a third level of shell escape, provided by double quote marks ("). These permit the shell certain operations on the quoted string (such as variable substitution and command substitution, covered in Chapter 2).

A Word About Options

If arguments were made up of just words, the words would always have to be presented in a predictable order so that the receiving command would know what each argument meant. This is impractical, so most UNIX commands have special arguments that serve as identifiers and switches.

Hyphens   By convention, these special arguments are set off from the rest of the command line with a hyphen (-). When used as switches to turn program options on or off, these arguments typically use a single letter to identify the option to enable. For example, the command

```
$ ls /bin
```

will list the names of files in the /bin directory, but in a single column. You can enable the command's tabular format option by adding an option:

```
$ ls -x /bin
```

(By the way, when you choose options for your own programs, try to have them make more sense than this.) Most commands also allow you to combine options following a single hyphen. To create a tabular file listing which includes file sizes, you could either enter

```
$ ls -x -s /bin
```

or

```
$ ls -xs /bin
```

Not all commands permit this, but users expect it. Consider this when designing your own command's syntax.

Identifiers   The hyphen can also precede an identifier, a single character which informs the program that a special argument follows. Later in this chapter, you will see a command which resembles

```
$ cc foo.c foo1.c foo2.c -o foo
```

The -o in this command line tells the cc command that the argument which follows, namely foo, should be taken as the name of the output file. Since any number of source file names could be supplied, there would be no way to know which was the output file name without the -o.

When considering the command-line interface to your program, resist the urge to spell out your options. While it might have been clearer to exchange the above command for

```
$ cc foo.c foo1.c foo2.c -output_file foo
```

it would not follow UNIX option formatting guidelines. If you're curious, see the rules laid out in the Intro(1) manual page at the head of your UNIX *User's Reference*.

Pipes and Redirection

Let's imagine that you want to maintain a list of names and phone numbers. Think of the things you will need. First, of course, you need a way to create the file, and to get the names into it. You will need to create special subdirectories for this and other exercises in this book. To ensure that the exercise is created under your home directory, type cd and press Return. Then, enter mkdir exer1, replacing exer1 with a name of your choosing if you like. This creates the new subdirectory. Then, enter cd exer1 (or whatever name you chose, of course) to make that your current directory.

The quickest way to get data into a file is not very intuitive:

```
$ cat > phone.list
```

If you typed this command, your cursor should now be sitting at the start of a blank line; no shell prompt. Go ahead and enter a few lines of a phone directory list, names first, like so:

```
Louis B. Mayer 408-123-4567
The Broadway Arcade 212-555-1234
Zeppo Marx 888-1511
```

Don't worry about errors at this point. Enter five or six names and then terminate the entry by pressing Control-D at the beginning of a new line. This is UNIX's default end-of-file character (EOF), and you should now be back at the shell prompt. If you are not, someone changed the EOF character on you, and you need to ask your administrator what it was changed to.

Redirection   The command you used to put data in the file illustrates a crucial shell facility: I/O redirection. Every program has three standard I/O channels, often called stdin, stdout and stderr. The first two are used to provide the program with default input and output channels. The third is a special channel used to display or log error messages.

Unless redirected, the shell opens your keyboard as the default input device, and your display as both the output and error device. You can redirect any of these devices without affecting the others. Less-than and greater-than signs (<, >) are used for redirection because they illustrate the flow of data. Less-than, which points *toward* the command, indicates input, and greater-than (pointing *away*) is output. Redirecting the error output is more complicated, and not immediately useful to us; we will skip that for now.

The command used to load the phone number file should be clear once you know what cat does: It sends everything it inputs (from stdin) straight through to its output (stdout). In our example, we left the input alone, so the default, your keyboard, was used. We redirected only the output (remember, the error output does not follow) to a file called phone.list. So, if you want to display the file you've just created, what do you do?

```
$ cat < phone.list
```

In this case, phone.list could also have been supplied as an argument. That statement may surprise you; perhaps it seemed to you that phone.list *was* an argument. It wasn't. Like the shell file and variable parsing described earlier, all traces of redirection requests are scrubbed from the command line before the command is loaded. The cat command, and your commands as well, will not know whether redirection has been applied (and, in most cases, they shouldn't care).

Whenever you redirect your input or output, I/O always starts at the beginning of the file. Your keyboard and display do not have beginnings and ends (although the keyboard can simulate an end-of-file with Control-D), but when you redirect I/O to ordinary files, you need to consider the consequences. When redirecting output, the shell will either create *or erase* the file. If the file already exists, its contents will be discarded. With input, the shell will give you an error if the input file does not exist, and unless the application manipulates the file, input will always start on the first character and continue until the last character is read.

There is one special kind of output redirection. By using *double* greater-than signs (>>), you direct the shell to skip to the end of an existing file before starting to output. For example if you wanted to add a few numbers to your phone list, you could do so with

```
$ cat >> phone.list
```

The new entries would be tacked onto the bottom of the file you created earlier.

Pipes   A pipe is a communication channel between two separate programs. It connects the standard output of the first command to the standard input of the second:

```
$ cat < phone.list | grep Marx
```

(grep searches for a string in a file, or its standard input). Instead of sending its output to the display, cat had its standard output redirected by the shell to a pipe, which sends the data to the grep program's standard input. Several pipes can appear on a command line, and using them is the only way to unleash the power of many UNIX commands. A command which is meant to be part of a pipe is called a *filter*.

These are the basics for the shell. A later chapter will be devoted to shell programming; what you've read here will leave you prepared for that.

The vi Editor

To write a program, any program, you need to place the source code in a file. You could use cat and type very carefully, but most programmers use a more convenient solution, a full-screen editor.

There are many editors for UNIX, ranging from public-domain hacks to fancy, expensive third-party tools. Like the Bourne shell, however, only one full-screen editor is found consistently across all versions of UNIX: the vi editor. If you read through a reasonable introduction to UNIX, you probably came across a section on vi. If you only skimmed it, you may wish to read it again. This chapter groups together the most commonly-used commands, and shows you some shortcuts that might take you longer to find on your own.

Getting Around the File

You should still have that phone.list file you created for the previous section. The primitive methods used to create and extend the file lacked one crucial ability: editing. Once you pressed Return, there was no way to change the data except to delete the file.

The vi editor uses the System V "curses" display library. (Chapter 3 will show you how to use this library in your own applications.) To display full-screen text, curses needs to know what kind of terminal you have. Each type of terminal responds to different character sequences which move the cursor, clear the screen, and perform other control functions.

An environment variable, TERM, informs curses applications of your terminal type. There is no magical way to determine what kind of terminal you have. Ask the system; chances are, your terminal type is already properly set. To find out what terminal the system thinks you have, do this:

```
$ echo $TERM
```

If the answer comes back "unknown," or you don't think it matches the terminal you're using, you may need to set it manually.

If you're using an SCO or Interactive UNIX text console (the display attached to the computer), you can probably use AT386 as a terminal type:

```
$ TERM=AT386; export TERM
```

If you are running under Open Desktop or some other flavor of the X Window system, your terminal type is most likely xterm.

If you are not using the console, ask someone who knows to help you determine and set your terminal type. The names are not arbitrary. They are stored in configuration files (terminfo files), and the names must match exactly for curses to work. To find out what terminal types are available on your system, you can use:

```
$ ls -xR /usr/lib/terminfo | pg
```

The long path names (which start with /usr/lib/terminfo) are directory names. The tab-separated short names are the valid terminal types for your system.

To feed the phone.list file to the full-screen editor, use this command:

```
$ vi phone.list
```

(To save space, we will avoid using large boxes which simulate screens. They will be described, or the relevant portion of the screen will be shown.) The screen will clear, and, assuming you've set your terminal type properly, your phone list will appear. If you have fewer lines in your phone list file than there are lines on your display, empty lines will be filled by the editor with tilde (~) characters. This distinguishes between truly blank lines (lines containing only white space and an end-of-line character) and lines falling past the end of the file.

You should be able to move around the file. Your cursor starts out positioned in the upper left over the first character in your file. The arrow keys should move the cursor. (If you're running under X Window, be aware that the mouse does *not* move your editor's cursor.) If they don't, you haven't set your terminal type properly.

At any time during this discussion, you can quit the editor by typing esc, then :q!, and pressing Return. This will not save the file you've been working on—any changes will be lost—but it will force a rapid exit from the editor.

vi is a *modal* editor. That means there are distinct modes for executing commands, editing, and inserting text. Moving between modes is managed with these characters:

Table 1-1: vi Mode Switching

From edit to insert:	**i**
From edit to overstrike:	**R**
From insert/overstrike to edit:	**Esc**
From edit to command:	**:**

Although some transitions have alternate switch characters, these are the only direct transitions available. To get to command mode from insert mode, for instance, you must press Esc first to get to edit mode.

Edit mode is the time to position the cursor in the file, and to delete text. In addition to the arrow keys, the following keys position the cursor. There are others, but these are the most common:

Table 1-2: vi Cursor Movement

Up one line:	**k**
Down one line:	**j**
Left one character:	**Backspace**
Right one character:	**Space**
Left one word:	**b**
Right one word:	**w**
Find character on:	
current line:	**f***char*
Up one screen:	**^B**
Down one screen:	**^F**
Up one half screen:	**^U**
Down one half screen:	**^D**

If you are not using the console or another super-fast text display, you should compare the speed of moving up and down by half and full screens (^U and ^D vs. ^B and ^F). Half-screen moves are usually done with line-at-a-time scrolling, while full-screen travel is handled by erasing and repainting the screen.

Depending on the display device you use, one method may be considerably faster than the other.

Text deletion is handled by several edit mode commands including:

Table 1-3: vi Text Deletion

Delete character under cursor:	x
Delete charter to left of cursor:	X
Delete to end of line:	D
Delete line:	dd

In edit mode, most commands can be repeated by entering a number prior to the command. To delete eight characters, starting at the current cursor position, type 8x. To delete 12 lines, type 12dd. Similarly, type 4^B to scroll up four screens. Neither the number nor the command will display as you type it; edit mode commands are "blind."

Command mode opens up access to the core of the vi editor, a UNIX line editor called ex. In fact, you will find an executable called ex on your system (it is really just a link to vi) which brings up vi in a command-oriented, line edit mode.

One common shortcut to command mode is specifically used for searching. You can press the / key in edit mode, and follow it with a search string. The string can be a full regular expression, discussed in Chapter 2. Regular expressions use special characters, however, so if you are searching for a string which contains them, they must be escaped with backslashes, like so:

```
/Press \*B for
```

Search commands position the text cursor at the first match in the file. Pressing the "n" key in edit mode will move to the next match.

Pressing ":" to get to command mode will move the cursor to the bottom of the screen, and the colon character will be echoed. This colon signifies command mode. Text cannot be edited, and the cursor cannot be moved within the file using the edit mode keys. In command mode, however, you have a powerful editing language at your disposal. This is where the real strength of vi shows through.

Edit mode commands are generally written:

```
[range] command [options]
```

A range can be expressed in several ways; special characters are employed to help abbreviate some range expressions. In the following examples, remember that these are not commands, just ranges:

Table 1-4: vi Text Addressing

Single line (line 12 of file):	**12**
Up seven lines from current position:	**-7**
Current line:	**.**
Current line to end of file:	**.,$**
Top of file to current line:	**1,.**
Lines eight through 14:	**8,14**
Line four through first line containing "foo":	**4,/foo/**
Entire file:	**%**

Range expressions are combined with commands to alter the file. Here are some common commands, with typical range expressions:

Table 1-5: vi Command Mode Commands

Delete:	**:.,$ d**
Copy:	**:4,/foo/ co .**
Move:	**:3,18 m 23**
Write (to file):	**:1,. w phone.list**
Substitute (change):	**:% s/old stuff/new stuff/**

When editing a large file, it can be inconvenient to remember line numbers or use search strings to identify ranges. vi allows you to mark a line in a file with an alphabetic character. In edit mode, you mark a line with two characters: "m" for mark, and any character a-z. You can then use the letters you've chosen to refer to the marked lines in a range expression in command mode, like this:

```
:'a,'b m .
```

Incidentally, in edit mode, pressing apostrophe and a line mark letter will move the cursor to that line.

Marked lines also combine well with text holding areas, called *yank buffers*. These are also identified alphabetically (their identifying characters are not related to those for marked lines), and can make manipulating blocks of text much easier. To place text into a yank buffer, use the yank command:

```
:'a,'b ya a
```

Yanking text into a buffer replaces any previous contents. The buffer's text can be inserted into the file at any location with the put command:

```
:pu a
```

This inserts the contents of buffer "a" at the current location in the file. Using put on a buffer doesn't erase the buffer; you can put it as many times as you like.

Working With Files

vi is particularly adept at dealing with files. You can specify a number of files on the command line, and switch among them during a single edit session. The editor is also loaded with commands that make it easier to bring in and store text.

All file manipulation is done in command mode (don't forget the ":"). Here are the most important vi file commands:

Table 1-6: vi File Commands

Save entire file to phone.list:	:w phone.list
Overwrite existing file:	:w! phone.list
Write file using original name:	:w
Append to existing file:	:w >>phone.list
Use text as command input:	:w !sort
Insert file at current line:	:r phone.tmp
Insert output of command:	:r !ls -x
Display current file name and size:	:file
Discard changes since last save:	:e!
Edit next file in list:	:n
Edit first file in list:	:rew
Edit previous file:	:e#
Save and quit:	:wq
Quit without saving:	:q!

Wherever it makes sense, range expressions can be inserted in front of these commands. Experiment with a few.

Advanced Features

Working on any software project generally means spending most of your time in the editor. vi has several programming-specific features that make coding go more smoothly. Even the editor itself is programmable to a point.

For any structured program that doesn't fit on one screen, it is common to improperly match braces and parentheses. The editor can help you keep these straight. Position the cursor on one of these characters, and press the percent (%) key. The editor will locate the matching character, if any, and it will beep if there is no match. The matching operation works in both directions; pressing "%" again after a match is found will put you back where you were.

Structured code is much easier to read if it is properly indented. vi doesn't enforce sensible indentation, but can help you maintain it yourself. The first such method is through an editor variable called "autoindent." Like the shell, the editor maintains a set of variables which track its current state and allow you to change it. By using the command, :set autoindent (you can abbreviate that to :set ai), any new line being inserted into the file will be indented the same distance as the line preceding it. To back off an automatic indent by one tab stop, use ^D in insert mode. To cancel automatic indent, use :set noai.

Another editor variable which affects formatting is tabstop. The default on most systems is eight spaces. You can change it like this: :set tabstop=4. Complex structured programs with deeply nested constructs can be made much easier to read this way. You should mark any file containing a non-standard tab width with a comment informing the reader of the correct setting.

If you are curious about vi's other internal variables, the command :set all lists them. Any changes you make are discarded when you leave the editor, so feel free to experiment. The ex(1) manual page describes some of the variables, but your implementation will almost certainly include variables not discussed in the manual.

There is no way to save the current state of the editor's variables, but you can create a file which automatically sets them for you when the editor is loaded. This file is named .exrc, and you can load it with commands (minus the leading ":") for initializing your default editing environment. If .exrc does not exist in your current directory, your home directory will be searched. This way, any directory can have editor settings which override the defaults set up in your home directory's .exrc. Here is an example .exrc file:

```
set tabstop=4
set autoindent
```

This file will be read until the end, and the editor will then enter edit mode as it normally would. The .exrc file is not limited to variable definitions; it can contain any number of valid command-mode commands.

Aside from variable options, there are two editor commands that affect the indentation of program (or other) text. As editor commands, less-than (<) and greater-than (>) shift a specified range of text left or right one tab stop, respectively. Let's say you just enclosed a block of C code in a while loop. The contents of the new block should be indented. Move the cursor to the top of the block and mark it: ma from edit mode. Then move the cursor to the bottom of the block, and use the following command to indent the block:

```
:'a,. >
```

Note that if you've changed the tab stop value, there is an independent variable called "shiftwidth" that needs to be set to the same number so operations like this will match your changed tab setting.

vi has a host of other features which you should explore once you've gotten through some of the chapters to come. It is a very capable editor, and well-suited to the editing of source code. Through the use of variables, multi-file editing, and other features not discussed here (like macros), vi can be tailored to your preference.

Take some time now to work a bit with the editor. You might move to one of the source-code snippets a few pages ahead and try entering it. Toggle the autoindent mode as you go, and decide which you prefer. You will save considerable time later if you teach yourself the editor now.

The C Compiler

If any of the terms used in this section are not clear, then you may need to brush up on your C knowledge. Some C books are UNIX-specific, and are a good match with this text. The definitive text is *The C Programming Language* by Kernighan and Ritchie (Prentice Hall, 1988). It is dense, and may be difficult for beginners, but it is still the fastest way to learn the language.

Most professional software development in UNIX is done in C. As a result, it is by far the best supported language. In order to run any of the code in this book, you must understand how to operate the compiler. The UNIX C compiler serves precisely the same purpose as a compiler in any other environment, and it requires the same elements. In addition to your C source code, the compiler needs to know where to find the appropriate header files and libraries.

The UNIX C compiler's front-end is usually given the name cc. This program kicks off several others, each of which handles a portion of the compilation process. On most systems, this process includes preprocessing, compiling, optimization, and linking. You can launch each of these steps by hand, but cc makes it much easier to manage. This single command combines and routes command-line arguments to the appropriate component.

Because there are several steps involved, the list of compiler options can be lengthy and confusing. Luckily, there are a few predictable options which can generally be used regardless of the operating system version or compiler. These options are:

Table 1-7: Compiler Options

Name output file:	**-o** *name*
Compile only—don't link:	**-c**
Apply optimization:	**-O**
Generate debugging info:	**-g**
Link with library:	**-l** *name*
Alternate include file path:	**-I** *dir;*
Alternate library path:	**-L** *dir;*

Let's examine each of these briefly. Create a program, and call it example1.c. Use the source code below:

```
#include <stdio.h>

main()
{
    printf("Yo!\n");
}
```

This is about as simple as a C program gets. To compile it, you would use the following command:

```
cc -o example1 example1.c
```

This is the minimalist's cc command line. It specifies a source file and output file (executable), and the compiler will follow the steps needed to translate one to the other. It may seem redundant to specify an output file name so similar to the source file name, but UNIX tradition holds that the default name for any executable should be a.out; if you don't supply a name of your own (using -o as above), the linker will call it that. After compiling, you should be able to directly execute the command you have created by typing its name: example1.

Note that the above source code references a header (or include) file called stdio.h. By enclosing the name in angle brackets (less-than and greater-than), you instruct the compiler to use the normal include file directory. On System V systems, this is generally the tree which starts from /usr/include.

If your program uses a header file from a directory outside the standard set, there are two ways to proceed. First, you can specify a full pathname, enclosed in quotes, following the #include directive, like so:

```
#include "/usr/include/stdio.h"
```

On most systems, this is equivalent to #include <stdio.h>.

Another, more versatile, way to handle custom header files is to place them wherever you like, reference them in your programs with angle brackets, and use the -I compiler option to add the location to the search list. Change example1.c so that it reads:

```
#include <stdio.h>
#include <example1.h>

main()
{
    printf(MESSAGE);
}
```

Then create a header file, example1.h, that contains this text:

```
#define MESSAGE "Yo!\n"
```

If you try using the compiler command given earlier, you should get an error message that your include file cannot be found. If you placed example1.h in your current directory, you need to add it to the compiler's include file search path:

```
cc -I . -o example1 example1.c
```

If you have other directories to add to the path, you should specify additional -I arguments:

```
cc -I . -I $HOME/include -I /project/include -o example1 example1.c
```

As for the other switches, short explanations will suffice for now:

The library path option works just like the include path option. The UNIX C compiler normally looks for its library files in /usr/lib. Each library file is specified with a separate -l option, and if any of the requested libraries are anywhere but /usr/lib, you need to tell the compiler:

```
cc -L /project/lib -L $HOME/lib -o example1 example1.c -lm
```

This command specifies the linking of a single library, called m (actually, the library name is translated to libm.a before searching starts). Searching will take place in the directories specified by the -L options. libm.a is the UNIX math library, which example1.c doesn't require; it is superfluous but harmless in this example.

The optimization and debug info options are mutually exclusive; don't ever use them both. Optimization runs the intermediate code through a program that checks for patterns of executable instructions which don't perform as well as they could. The optimizer rearranges things, sometimes moving or eliminating chunks of code. Some optimizers (like the one in the Microsoft compiler supplied with SCO UNIX) can be told to optimize for size, performance, or even for tuning their operation to include or exclude certain specific optimizations. The -O option is generally defined as "maximum safe optimization," with performance improvement being the goal.

Optimization is a tricky issue, because some compilers do it better than others, and also because not all code benefits from it. Our own example1.c, for instance, would gain nothing at all from being optimized; the longer and more complex your program is, the more reason you have to request optimization. An optimizer's job is to modify your code. There is, therefore, room for the resulting code to be "broken" in some way. Unfortunately, there is no way to predict whether optimization will have an adverse effect on your program. Only rarely does it create problems, but this is one more reason to ensure that your software is thoroughly tested before its release.

The debugging info option, -g, inserts information into your executable file which the debugger, sdb, requires. It is primarily a map which links symbol names to storage locations. Debugging information takes up considerable space at the beginning and more as your programs grow larger; always strip it out before your programs are shipped. The strip command handles this. In the section on make, we'll discuss strip in more detail.

It might seem counter-intuitive to ask the compiler *not* to create an executable, but it is quite handy. In a large project, considerable time is saved by retaining the intermediate object (.o) files. Then, when recompiling, only those modules whose source code has changed need to be compiled. The -c switch only generates the object file. It takes far less time to link object files and libraries than it does to compile. Again, make manages this process for you, tracking source changes and determining the quickest way to build an executable.

Lastly, you should know that, while the order of arguments on the cc command line is not important, organizing it with the options first is the best way. This allows any number of source file names to be specified at the end of the command, and makes it easier to add file names later.

A Shortcut to make

While the compiler's simple command-line interface is enough for projects involving only one C language file, any serious work is (and should be) split into multiple files. Imagine the time you would waste recompiling every module in a large project when, in fact, you had only made changes to one or two.

That's where make comes in. By comparing the dates of source files against the most recently produced executable, make determines which modules need recompiling, and which can simply be linked in object form. make is really a complex language of its own, containing much more functionality than most programmers ever use. If you want to become a make expert, I advise you to read the *Programmer's Guide* and *Reference* volumes. For our purposes, and possibly for 90% of the projects you will run into, a simple boilerplate serves the purpose. Enter this and save it under some sensible name, so you can use it in the C language projects which appear in Chapter 3 and beyond:

```
# boilerplate Makefile
# Assign the executable's name to PROGNAME, supply
```

```
# a space-separated list of object files as OBJS,
# and set the CFLAGS and LIBS variables to reflect
# the options you want passed to the C compiler
# and linker, respectively

PROGNAME=example1
OBJS=example1.o
CFLAGS=-O -I .
LIBS=-s

all:    ${PROGNAME}

${PROGNAME}:    ${OBJS}
    cc ${LIBS} ${OBJS} -o ${PROGNAME}

clean:
    rm -f ${OBJS} ${PROGNAME}
```

An entire chapter could be devoted to the wizardry behind make, but the tiny Makefile above is enough to get you through all of the projects in this book, and most projects in general. If you trouble to learn more about make, you can enhance this script as you like.

Using the script is straightforward. Make a copy of the boilerplate, and plug your program name, a list of object files (all of the .c files with their extensions changed to .o), and switches for the compiler and linker into the appropriate variables. The compiler switches that go into CFLAGS can include: -O for optimization, -g for debugging (remember not to combine these two), -I directives for include file searches, and any other compiler switches listed on the cc reference manual page. The LIBS variable is usually just used to hold -L and -l library directives, but any switch appropriate for the linker (see the ld page) can go here. I used -s as a default; this strips the symbol information from the output file in the interest of conserving space. If you put -g in CFLAGS, take -s out of LIBS.

The C projects in this book are accompanied by a description of the settings to plug into the Makefile boilerplate. Once the settings are in place, you can kick off a make with this simple command:

```
$ make -f makefile_name
```

If you set aside a special directory for the project (one which will have only one makefile), give your makefile the name "Makefile" (with a capital M—that makes it appear first in a directory listing so you can see it more easily), and a complete build can be kicked off by just typing make.

There will be times when you want to force a complete rebuild, such as following a change to a local header file that is included in several C source files. (A makefile can be built that handles this automatically, but it would add considerable complexity to our boilerplate). To do this, a make *rule* (that's a makefile statement) called clean is included which erases the executable and all of the object files, forcing recompilation from scratch. Use make clean to execute this rule.

Summary

By now you should have a grasp of the basic skills needed to operate the editor, shell and compiler. Before you move on, please make sure you understand the basics as they've been presented. If you need additional information, try looking in the UNIX *User's Reference* and *Programmer's Reference* manuals for the manual pages covering these commands: vi, ex, sh, and cc.

Chapter 2

A Quick Tour of Shell Programming

Since UNIX programming is done almost exclusively in C, most of the following chapters will focus on that language. We'll pause briefly to learn some shell programming basics because, as you build yourself a comfortable environment, you will find knowledge of the shell as a *language* increasingly valuable. It's also likely that any application you release to the outside world will be accompanied by shell scripts to handle configuration, installation, and other tasks that must be portable across different types of systems.

Perhaps it seems a little strange to you to think of the shell in those terms. If you come from an MS-DOS background, you know that the programming facilities provided by the COMMAND.COM shell are slow and all but worthless. UNIX, on the other hand, has had a robust shell language for years.

The Bourne shell is good for more than just executing lists of commands. It is fully functional, with structured elements and flow control befitting a proper language. While it isn't appropriate to write entire performance-dependent applications in the shell, many tasks are best delegated to this simple interpretive environment. This chapter will give you a basic understanding of the shell, certainly enough to help you build some useful tools for yourself and others. It will also help prepare you for what lies ahead: Many of the same design principles useful for UNIX programming in general can reasonably be learned in the shell. You should not expect, however, to get all the facts here; much is left out in the interest of hurrying you toward "the good stuff," the chapters on C programming which follow.

The shell's most primitive facilities lie in the domain of user interfaces. Most modern users expect their programs to precede input requests with detailed prompts, and to offer lists of choices in the form of menus. The shell has nothing built in for these or the many other niceties that users have every right to expect, so we'll create a few of our own by way of education.

An Interface From The Ground Up

Even if we weren't working on a set of interface routines, the interface would be a good place to start. Working from the interface "inside" toward the non-interface code lets you (and others) see what the project will look like at a very early stage. No matter how precious and elegant your algorithms and data structures, users will fail to appreciate them if they are forced to deal with an unpleasant interface.

Sometimes the interface is time-consuming because it is so tempting to overdo. In the case of the shell, however, there is little opportunity to drape applications with superfluous interface adornments. In fact, living within the limits of the shell can be a little frustrating. Most commercial software takes advantage of direct display control, and accepts single keystrokes and function keys to trigger actions. These are things the shell cannot do unaided. Later chapters will discuss building fancier (even graphical) interfaces, but for the shell, we will stick with a simple "glass TTY" interface. Both input and output will be done a line at a time.

A more detailed discussion of defined functions will follow, but an introduction is in order here. Functions in the shell are not like those in the compiled languages you're used to. Most of what you would take for granted simply doesn't exist; named arguments and typed return values, for instance, are both missing. Despite its shortcomings, the shell's function facility is useful.

The basic definition for a shell function may look familiar:

```
function_name()
{
    ...function code...
}
```

The parentheses following the function name are little more than a prop. Actually, it's what the shell uses to recognize that you are defining a function.

You can't specify argument names or calling sequences inside the parentheses; all of the argument processing is done by hand, inside the function itself.

Arguments come into a function the same way they enter a shell script, as numbered variables. This first example is a quick lesson in shell argument handling:

```
# showargs.sh: display arguments to shell
# Note: This program is formatted with tabs every 4 spaces

count=1          # initialize argument count
while [ "x$1" != "x" ]; do  # loop until we get a null arg
echo "$count:" $1        # display arg number and content
count=`expr $count + 1` # add one to count variable
shift       # move all args left by 1 ($2 becomes $1,
        #   $3 becomes $2, and so on)
done        # end of while/do loop
```

Before you can run this, or any of the shell examples in this chapter, you need to mark the script file as executable: chmod u+x showargs.sh.

This script is useful for showing how the shell breaks input into words, and how quotes and backslashes affect that processing. After you have run the program several times with different kinds of arguments, take some time to examine the program itself. Based on its output and the comments, can you understand what each line does? Don't grade yourself too harshly.

The first line of the executable portion (count=1) is plain enough: a variable assignment. Because shell variables are not typed, you do not declare them in advance as you do in C and most other typed languages. This is convenient, but lack of typing can also be a hindrance, as we will see when we step down a few more lines.

Take a look at the while statement. The foreign-looking stuff between the brackets may put you off a bit, but look closely at each element and think it through. The first ("x$1") makes a quoted string built from tacking an "x" onto the front of the first argument passed to the shell program. If you call showargs.sh like this:

```
$ showargs.sh and now for something
```

The first time "x$1" is evaluated, it will be reduced to "xand".

The next element, !=, might be familiar to you as "not equals" from some other language. That's exactly what it means here, except that it can only be applied to character strings in this context. What follows it is simply the quoted "x". So, now you know that a test is being performed, and what we're testing. But what are we looking for? For a clue, imagine that $1 was unassigned, a null string. The test would be false because "x$1" would reduce to "x", which *is* equal to the right side of the expression.

Now that the meaning of the expression inside the brackets is a bit clearer, the brackets themselves need some explaining. Things are not quite as they appear. The "[" character is actually the name of a program, an alias for the program test. Because it is a program name, the space following it is essential. test evaluates a conditional expression, up to a closing "]" character, and sets a return code indicating the test's result: true or false.

A moment's digression: Every UNIX program can, when it completes execution, pass a single integer return code to its caller. The norm is to return a zero for successful execution, and non-zero for some error condition. Based on this, test's return value seems backward: zero for true (success), non-zero for false (failure). Don't let this throw you; shell statements which expect condition codes understand this scheme. You should avoid building dependence on the specific numeric values of "true" and "false" into your scripts. Aside from being bad practice, the numeric values of true and false may not always be predictable from one system or shell to another.

Not all programs can be counted on to pass a valid success/failure return code. The reference manual page for any standard UNIX command will discuss the significance of its return codes, if any. The programs you write should use success=0/error!=0 return values whenever possible. UNIX supplies a code of zero whenever a program doesn't return one itself. The special shell variable $? holds the return code of the previously executed command. Be careful with it, though: if you use echo $? to display a program's return value, and then use $? again after the echo command, you'll get the return value from echo. If you plan to use a program's return code more than once in a shell script, assign it to a variable immediately.

test is such a shell necessity that I'll set off a few of its more common operations on the next page:

Table 2-1: test Command

test *expr*

[*expr*]

Where *expr* is built using the following components:

File Tests

(all file tests return *false* if file doesn't exist)

r *filename*	File is readable
w *filename*	Writable
x *filename*	Executable
f *filename*	Regular file
d *filename*	Directory
s *filename*	Not empty (size > 0)

Examples

```
$ if [ -d /bin ]; then echo "true"; else echo "false"; fi
true
$ if [ -f /bin ]; then echo "true"; else echo "false"; fi
false
```

String Tests

z *string*	*string* is null (length 0)
n *string*	*string* is non-null (length > 0)
str1 = *str2*	Two strings are the same
str1 != *str2*	Two strings are not the same

Examples

```
$ if [ "foo" = "bar" ]; then echo "true"; else echo "false"; fi
false
$ if [ -n "" ]; then echo "true"; else echo "false"; fi
false
```

Numeric Tests

num1 -eq *num2*	Two numbers are equal
num1 -ne *num2*	Not equal
num1 -lt *num2*	*num1* less than *num2*
num1 -gt *num2*	*num1* greater than *num2*
num1 -le *num2*	*num1* less than or equal to *num2*
num1 -ge *num2*	*num1* greater than or equal to *num2*

Example

```
$ a=8; if [ $a -lt 9 ]; then echo "true"; else echo "false"; fi
true
```

Conjunctives

!	Negation: turns true to false, false to true

Table 2-1: test Command (Continued)

expr -a *expr*	Expressions "anded" together
expr -o *expr*	Expressions "ored" together

Examples
```
$ if [ -f /bin/date -a -x /bin/date ]; then echo "true";\
  else echo "false"; fi
true    # /bin/date is both a regular and executable file
$ a=12; if [ $a -eq 4 -o $a -eq 12 ]; then echo "true";\
  else echo "false"; fi
true    # variable "a" is either equal to 4 or 12
```

If you look carefully, you will see an expression which more simply tests for the condition that "x$1" != "x" seeks. For some reason, the expression used in the example is very common in shell scripts. It is important that you recognize it and its purpose.

Now, go back to the next unfamiliar statement in the code. count='expr $count + 1'. This one line illustrates two features which, if removed, would cripple the shell. First is the grave accent ('). These are an odd form of redirection, and they are used to enclose a command line. That command is executed, and the entire expression between the accents is replaced by the *output* of the command. Notice that this is output, not return code. To illustrate: If you want to get the current user's name, you can use the who command:

```
$ who
johnboy     ttyp00      Dec 25 16:47
```

That is not very helpful, however, if what you wish to do is use that output elsewhere. To capture it in a variable, use:

```
$ username=`who`
$ echo $username
johnboy     ttyp00      Dec 25 16:47
```

Any valid UNIX command line can be used inside the accents, even multiple semicolon-separated commands and pipes. If the command kicks back more than one line of output, you still get it all. As an example, try the following sequence of commands (output is not shown):

```
$ cmdout=`date; ps`
$ echo $cmdout
$ echo "$cmdout"
```

Now let's focus on what's inside the grave accents: expr $count + 1. We noted earlier that the shell's lack of data typing presented problems. Because it doesn't know numbers from strings, it cannot (or, more correctly, *won't*) do math. That responsibility is pushed off to the expr command. In this capacity, expr is limited to integer calculations. You can use any of the four basic operators, but remember to use a backslash in front of "*" so the shell doesn't interpret it as a wildcard. Spaces around operators and numeric values are not optional. Each operator and value must be passed as a separate argument.

Note that expr also has facilities for comparing numbers, strings, and evaluating complex regular expressions, a standard UNIX pattern-matching language. The reference manual entry for expr describes its other capabilities in more detail.

expr is most commonly used in shell scripts precisely as shown above. The command is all but useless without the grave accents which allow its output to be sucked into a variable. Again, note that while UNIX provides for an integer return code, expr does not use that mechanism to provide the result of the expression. It sends the result to its standard output, and that is what the grave accents capture.

Note that the assignment to "count" is outside the expr expression. It might seem more natural to say expr count = count + 1. Unfortunately, expr cannot do assignments to shell variables; only the shell can do that. You *can* use variables in expr expressions by extracting their values by preceding them with dollar signs, because the shell replaces variable references with their values before executing the command.

The shift statement in our first example speaks for itself, but you might not understand why it is so important. The shell is limited to ten argument variables, named $0 through $9. $0 is always set to the name of the running program, so you really only have room for nine arguments. That might seem like enough, but imagine that a user supplies a filename wildcard as an argument:

```
$ showargs.sh /bin/*
```

The shell expands this to a list of all the files in your /bin directory. On my system, that amounts to 151 arguments. showargs.sh is able to handle this because of its repeated shift commands. If it had used direct numeric references to the arguments without shifting instead (e.g., $1 $2 $3 $4 ...), it would only be able to display the first nine arguments. To say it again: If your program is written to accept filenames as arguments, you should write it to accept an unlimited number of them whenever it is logical to do so.

Because shift is used, the program never needs to refer to anything but the first argument variable, $1. That's because shift, as its name implies, moves everything in the argument list one argument to the left. The current $1 is discarded and replaced with the current $2, and so on until the last argument.

While the example above works, there are three other, simpler, ways to process all of the arguments coming into a shell script or function: The $* and $@ variables, and a special form of the for statement. All of these will be discussed in the next section.

Shell Flow Control Statements

In showargs.sh, a while loop is used to keep scanning the argument list until a null argument, indicating the end of the list, is reached. The while statement is only one of several keywords which can affect the flow of execution through a script.

There is no goto. The way the shell works with script files makes it all but impossible to implement. Arguably, its absence forces you to write good structured programs. Some shell scripts, however, prove this not to be the case.

Since while is in our example program, it is a good place to start. The syntax looks like this:

```
while condition; do
    ...statements...
    done
```

while, do and done are all keywords, so they must appear at the beginning of a statement. That means, for example, that the do keyword must be preceded either by a new line or a semicolon. (The layout I use reflects my own preference. Keeping do with while seems more readable to me, but it would have been just as correct to put it on the next line.) You should also notice that, unlike C, it is not necessary to enclose the statements between do and done in braces or other containers.

The *condition* following the while keyword is commonly satisfied with a test (a.k.a. "[") command, but any command or function that returns a valid code can be used. As long as "success" (0) is returned, *...statements...* will be executed.

while conveniently checks a condition at the top of every new loop, but there are often times when some condition within the loop requires a change in flow. You have two options here: First, you can force the loop to repeat immediately by using continue. The next statement executed is the enclosing while, so the condition is rechecked. Second, continue is often used to skip over discarded input, and to end the loop after a condition flag is set.

There is another way to bring a premature end to a while loop: break. This will cause execution to resume at the statement following the done keyword.

Both continue and break will accept a single numeric argument. With the argument, you can ask to reiterate or break out of a specified number of nested while statements. Crossing several nested levels with a single command can be a debugging nightmare, leaving you wondering "How did I get *here*?" when your script exhibits some odd behavior. Specifying a number of levels assumes that your statements will always be nested at the same depth. If you add or remove a level, your multi-level break or continue will put you in the wrong place. Avoid crossing several nesting levels at once.

A structured statement closely related to while is for. This command loops once for each word in a specified list, assigning each "current" word to a variable. A group of statements is then executed, which presumably perform some kind of processing on the current word. Here is the syntax:

```
for variable [ in word1 word2 ... ]; do
    ...statements...
    done
```

By convention, the brackets signify an optional portion of the command. You don't type them in.

for is most commonly used to process arguments and lists of files. The *word1 word2 ...* is filled in nicely by a file or argument wildcard which expands to a space-separated list of words. If the portion in brackets (the in keyword and the corresponding list of words) is done away with, the shell supplies its own list of words, the arguments to the current script or function. This abbreviation is not used very frequently, and is not at all obvious.

The most sensible way to feed the entire argument list to a for statement is with either the $* or $@ variable. If you look at the sh reference manual page, it might appear that these two variables are identical in function. They're not. They differ in the way they handle quoted arguments.

If you recall, enclosing portions of a command's argument list in quotes causes the shell to ignore spaces (and, optionally, special characters) in those portions. If you use this command line with showargs.sh:

```
$ showargs.sh word1 word2 "word three" word4
```

you'll see that "word three" is interpreted by the shell as a single word. If you use $* or $@ in a for construct, however, they both cause the quotes in an argument list to be discarded. If you rewrote showargs.sh to use one of these variables, it would see five arguments ("word" and "three" would be split) instead of four. The solution is simple enough, but far from intuitive. To preserve quoted arguments in a for statement, use the $@ variable enclosed in quotes:

```
for a in "$@"; do
```

for is most closely related to while for two reasons: First, both are iterative. The statements they contain are executed until some condition is satisfied (in the case of for, the condition is the end of the word list). Second, both can be modified through the use of break and continue.

We've already seen a simple example of if, but it, too, falls under the flow-control heading. It supports a couple of syntactical twists that haven't been discussed:

```
if condition; then
... statements1 ...
[ elif condition; then
... statements2 ... ]
[ else
... statements3 ... ]
fi
```

The *condition* is the same type used with while: either a test statement or any program or function which sets a predictable return code can be used. The elif keyword is short for else if (but don't use it spelled out), a construct which appears frequently when making decisions which have several possible outcomes.

Among the more complicated and useful statements of the shell is case:

```
case word in
    pattern)
```

```
      ... statements1 ...
      ... last statement;;
[ pattern2)
      ... statements2 ...
      ... last statement;; ]
   esac
```

case checks a string against a list of patterns. A segment of code (*statements1* and *statements2* above) is attached to each pattern. If the word matches one of the patterns, that pattern's associated code is executed up to the first occurrence of a pair of semicolons (*;;*). Each test starts with a pattern which must be followed by a right parenthesis, and ends with statements terminated by double semicolons.

The patterns follow the same scheme as shell filename wildcards. The shell uses a modified *regular expression*, the great and powerful (and hideously complicated) pattern-matching language which is part of the UNIX function library. See the ed (1) manual page for a summary of regular expressions. The patterns in the case statement (and also shell filename wildcards) are limited to the following special characters:

Table 2-2: Case Statements Patterns

Symbol	Description
*	Match any number of characters (or none at all)
?	Match any one character
[... *characters* ...]	Match any of the enclosed characters. A range can be specified by the form *char1-char2*, and bracketed characters can be *excluded* from a matching pattern by using "!" as the first character inside the brackets.
pat1 | *pat2* [| ...]	Not usable in shell filename wildcards. Allows match to occur against any one of a number of patterns.

In the case of case, the code attached to the *first* matching pattern is executed. To handle the equivalent of a "default" or "otherwise" clause (any condition not explicitly matched by another pattern), use the "match everything" wildcard: "*".

Look over the definitions in this section and make sure you understand them. You may want to place a bookmark at the section's start so you can refer back to it as we move on to the first real code segment in our project.

Building The Function Library

When you write C programs under UNIX, you have the benefit of massive function libraries, hundreds of routines which make your life easier *because you didn't have to write them.* This luxury does not exist in the shell, which has a total vocabulary of fewer than 40 keywords. This sparseness conserves memory, but it makes a programmer's life more difficult. Even the simplest support functions often need to be hand-written before you can get started.

Remember that when you design shell functions, you will not be able to return directly anything but a single integer result to the caller. Working around the shell's limitations builds character, though, so let's dive right in to the first code module.

You should treat all of the code examples in this book in the same way: Get it into your system, run it (all examples are directly executable unless otherwise specified), and study it to understand as much as possible on your own. The explanatory text which follows each example should clear up any questions you have. Then, if you have time, make a copy of the example, modify it, enhance it. This exercise is the greatest test of your understanding of the concepts being presented.

Here we go...

```
# funcs.sh
# Shell function library for chapter 2 example
# Tabs in this program are set 4 spaces apart.

# kbpause: Ask user for permission to continue
# Args: 1:prompt (optional)    Returns: None.
kbpause()
{
    if [ "x$1" != "x" ]; then
        echo -n $1
        else
        echo -n "Press Return to continue: "
        fi
    read a
}

# yesno: Put up prompt, accept verified yes/no input
#    from keyboard
# Args: 1:quoted prompt    Returns: 1=yes, 0=no
yesno() {
    while true; do  # set up loop; keep asking until
                    #    they get it right
        echo -n $1 "(y/n): "      # -n means no c/r; $1
                            #    is func argument
        read a        # grab kb input into variable a
        case $a in  # compare contents of "a" against
```

```
                     #    following patterns
          [yY]*)   return 1;;       # "yes"
          [nN]*)   return 0;;       # "no"
          *)       echo "Please respond with 'y' or 'n'"
                   continue;;       # do while loop
                                    #    again
          esac     # end case statement ("case"
                   #    backward)
       done     # end while/do statement
}    # end function yesno

# function tests go here
yesno "Does your dog have fleas?"    # call yesno(), pass
                                     #    prompt as arg
if [ $? = 1 ]; then      # test return value if it is
                         #    equal to 1 ("yes")...
    echo "true"
    else                 # if it is anything but 1...
    echo "false"
    fi

kbpause "Testing the custom prompt (press Return)..."
kbpause
```

Even though this is a shell script, the execution path doesn't start with the first line. Function definitions, as in other languages, are not executed when they first appear.

Because shell functions cannot be exported to other shells, it is not possible to call on functions defined in other files. That is why the test code is tacked onto the bottom of the file. If it weren't part of the same file in which the functions were defined, there would be no functions to test.

A function, once defined, is called as though it were a regular UNIX program. This may seem a bit odd at first. After all, the word "function" brings to mind a keyword followed by a comma-separated list of arguments enclosed in parenthesis. Even BASIC functions follow this protocol. But again, shell functions are special. Because they are handled like ordinary shell and UNIX commands, the same internal routines that parse and separate command arguments can be used on functions. This also makes it much easier for you to turn stand-alone shell scripts into functions, and vice-versa. In most cases, all that is needed is to add the function definition itself, and maybe change the names of a few variables.

Why change variable names? If you recall, variables, unless exported, are local to a *file*. There is no concept of function-local variables. Any variable used inside a function definition is available to any other code in the same file. If you are accustomed to using variable names like "a" and "i", here is another reason for switching to names that make sense: It is much less likely that you will collide with another shell variable of the same name.

In looking at the example, you'll notice a keyword we haven't covered yet: read. This is the shell's most direct method for bringing keyboard input into a shell variable. Because read modifies the value of the variable(s) passed to it, make sure you leave the dollar signs *off*.

If you call read with a single variable name, as in the code example, an entire line of input is taken from the keyboard and assigned to the named variable. If you specify more variables, each variable gets one word. If there is more input than there are variables to hold it, the remainder of the input is discarded. Likewise, if there are more variables than input, the unfilled variables will have null values.

Adding Menus to Shell Scripts

When it comes to presenting a list of choices, there are probably more ways to structure those choices than you can imagine. Since the formatting capabilities of the shell are limited, however, it is wise to keep things simple. Keeping that in mind, we will create a function that displays a numbered list of choices in a familiar vertical style.

To create a menu *function*, we need to think a bit about how the arguments will be passed. Unless the menu is incredibly brief, the arguments will run well off the end of the command line used to call the function. There is nothing we can do in the writing of this function to solve that problem; argument parsing is handled for us before the first line of the function is executed. Instead, we need to remember one of the great shortcuts of the shell: If input will extend past the end of a line, it can be split with a backslash followed *immediately* by a Return.

Every time you press Return, UNIX translates it to a linefeed character. Each line in a UNIX text file ends with a linefeed (ASCII code 10), so if you are passing text files between systems, you may need to convert the line-ending characters. MS-DOS, for example, uses carriage return (ASCII 13) followed by linefeed at the end of each line.

A side note: This function definition should be added to the "funcs.sh" file started above. Add the new function after the end of the last one, but before the first line of test code. Then add the new test code at the very end. That way, the other tests will still be intact, and you can quickly ensure that you haven't damaged your script entering the new lines. Here's the new function:

```
# shell_menu: display a menu and accept a user's choice
# args: 1-n:menu items      returns: selection number
# choice string is returned in menu_choice_string

shell_menu()
{
    while true; do
        choice=0        # init counter
        for menu_s in "$@"; do   # loop through args
            choice=`expr $choice + 1`  # increment count
            echo "$choice: $menu_s"    # display item
            done
        echo -n "\nSelect: "               # display prompt
        read menu_choice                   # accept choice
        if [ -z "$menu_choice" ]; then # cover invalid selection
            menu_choice=0                  #   with default of 0
            fi
        if [ $menu_choice -lt 1 -o $menu_choice \
            -gt $choice ]; then            # Out of range?
            echo "\nPlease select a number between 1 and $choice\n"
            continue                       # Yes--ask again
            fi
        menu_choice_string=`eval echo "\\$$menu_choice"`
        return $menu_choice     # bug out with result
        done             # makes shell happy--never executed
} # end function shell_menu

# test shell_menu function

shell_menu "Option 1" "Option 2" Three "This is option 4" \
    "Option 5" "Option number six"
echo "choice: $?    String: $menu_choice_string"
```

It may seem unnecessary to include the done that closes the while loop in the example above. After all, it is never executed. The flow either jumps back up to while, or out of the function completely, before done is ever reached. Besides being good programming etiquette, the done statement is a shell essential. If you leave it off, your script will fail. This is not the shell being finicky and reading ahead to check your syntax. It is a by-product of the way the shell necessarily handles structured statements.

None of the functions provided are "bullet-proof," that is, they can be crashed with bad input (try using "a b c d" or "1foo" as a response to shell_menu's prompt), or terminated by interrupts. If you are distributing shell scripts as part of a package of software, you should take care that an inexperienced user, or someone looking for trouble, can't easily crash your script. Then too, you should always assume that your script *can* be crashed; keep that in mind when you are creating temporary files and making other changes. Programs shouldn't leave debris lying around, or make the operation of the system or your software more difficult because some event resulted in an abnormal termination.

You have not been provided with any programs (except snippets of test code) that use the functions created here. That exercise is left to you. Don't just enter these functions and say "Mm-hmm;" enhance them, and apply them in programs of your own design. Using these functions, and any others you write, is as simple as calling them from within your shell script, as shown in the test code. Remember to tack on all of the function definitions (minus the test code) to the *top* of any script that uses them.

Chapter 3

Textual User Interfaces

Even in the complicated new world created by graphical user interfaces (GUIs), developers must still present the majority of information to users in a seemingly uninteresting form, the character. True, GUIs do tend to generate more excitement than do old-fashioned text interfaces, but GUIs have problems of their own which have not yet been solved. For example, they still cannot be operated from inexpensive serial terminals. They are also horribly inefficient over dial-up lines, but technology is advancing to change that. Most importantly, even though the urge is strong to represent *everything* graphically on a system that is capable of it, most managers would prefer not to see their inventory reports laid out in columns of icons. Interesting or not, the world spins on text, and there's no escaping it.

When programming a textual interface for an application, you do not have as much flexibility as you do with a graphical one. But then there isn't as much to learn, either. The terminal control and text interface routines which are part of PC UNIX systems have evolved over many years. As a result, they are, with some exceptions, mature, efficient, and easy to implement. This chapter will give you the knowledge you need to write effective UNIX text-based applications. Use your imagination; there's no rule that says it *has* to be boring.

A UNIX Text Interface Primer

Before launching into this chapter's project, we need to define a few terms and gain a basic understanding of how System V UNIX handles text interfaces.

There are several levels of interfaces available to System V programmers. Aside from doing read and write calls directly to the tty (terminal I/O) devices, the simplest and most commonly used method of text I/O is through the "standard I/O" mechanism. You can't get far in C without knowing how to format output with printf and its cousins. Yet as versatile as printf's formatting capabilities are, the output is still very primitive. The standard I/O library treats every display device as if it were an old-fashioned Teletype.

For years, terminals have had the ability to place characters at specific positions on their screens. It wasn't always so, but now, as UNIX programmers, we can expect that every user of our applications has at least these functions available through his or her terminal:

- Position cursor
- Clear entire screen
- Highlight character (color, reverse video, etc.)

This may not seem like much, but it is just enough to make any application much easier for the user to work with. Because these functions have been available in terminals for so long, terminal emulators have picked them up as well. Your PC UNIX text console is a terminal emulator, as is the xterm program under X Window. Most DOS communications packages can do terminal emulation as well, making it possible for your UNIX applications to interface with just about any device the user chooses.

Unfortunately, each type of terminal defines its own character sequences for controlling the formatting of output. If you knew exactly what kind of environment your application would be running in, then you could code specifically for certain kinds of terminals by placing the special sequences directly in your code. This would not allow your customers any room for change.

System V UNIX gives you, the programmer, three layers of libraries whose functions keep you from having to remember and manage all those special sequences. The first such layer is terminfo, a function library that uses a database filled with the sequences needed to drive a great many different kinds of terminals. The user or system administrator sets the term environment variable (discussed in Chapter 1) in each user's shell to match the terminal type being used. This name matches an entry in the terminfo database. A corresponding function library allows you to call out terminal capability strings by name, allowing you to build full-screen applications without targeting them for a specific flavor of terminal. terminfo is rather primitive, however, because you have to manage the interface yourself.

The next layer, curses, adds functions which call terminfo to make things happen, but these functions provide the programmer with an easier way of dealing with the display. In curses, an image of the entire screen is maintained in memory. You modify the image to your liking, and then make calls that update the physical screen to match the stored image. This "batched approach" is an efficient way to code text applications. curses also makes judgments about the quickest way to get data to the display. Only data which changes is output, so dial-up and slow serial terminal users can still make use of curses applications. All users, even those on fast terminals, benefit from curses' efficiency, though. This efficiency is lost when coding directly to the terminfo level, so we'll pass over that and cover curses in the chapter's first programming example.

The highest level of text interface available to System V programmers is ETI, the Extended Terminal Interface. This obviates the necessity for programmers to create their own libraries of routines to handle things like menus and input fields. ETI is a layer on top of curses, and nearly all applications will need to use a mix of curses and ETI calls. Only very rarely does an application need to dabble in the lower-level terminfo calls.

curses Concepts

Initial contact with the curses library goes more smoothly if you understand a few key things about it first.

The most important point has already been mentioned: Everything you output through curses is buffered, and sent to the real display only when you specifically request it. The buffer is really a copy of the screen, with special attributes (like reverse video) marked where appropriate. A text cursor position and other housekeeping information is also maintained.

In addition to a copy of the entire screen, curses buffers the contents of individual windows, and another construct called a *pad*. A window is what you would expect it to be, a rectangular region of the screen which contains text. The limitation of windows is that they must be no larger than the dimensions of the screen. If you have a scrolling form, squeezing it into a window is a dicey affair; you must add lines manually to the top and bottom as the user scrolls. The pad solves this problem by allowing you to create windows which are larger than the screen, vertically, horizontally, or both. You adjust the viewable region of a pad by positioning a viewport on top of it. As the viewport moves around the pad, the text in the included region is made visible.

Placing text in a window or pad is simple. curses has a broad set of functions that place a character, a string, or a printf-formatted list in a window or pad. Most functions have variants that include arguments for placing the output at a specified position, or in a certain window. curses conveniently defaults to sending its output to a window that covers the entire screen. Many applications can use this default window throughout, simplifying things considerably.

A curses Example

We'll be moving on to ETI rather quickly from here, but understanding its curses foundations is important. curses is not at all difficult to use, provided you are familiar with C. Here is an example which makes use of some of the concepts described above. This example is a standalone executable. Copy your boilerplate makefile to cursesex.mk (or some other unique name of your choosing), and edit it to add the following parameters:

```
PROGNAME=    cursesex
OBJS=        cursesex.o
LIBS=        -lcurses
```

The following example, as with the other C program examples in this book, lacks proper checking of function returns and error handling. The simplest exercise involving these examples is to look up the error return values in the *Reference Manual* and work checks into the code. While these examples may have educational value here, don't ever release anything this ruthless to users.

If you enter this program incorrectly, it's possible that it may fail while curses still has control of the screen. If this happens, you will get an error message followed by the shell prompt, but keys you press will not echo, and Return may not work. The simplest fix for this mode is to use the following sequence:

```
^Jstty sane^J
```

The first ^J clears any "leftover" keys. stty sane is a command that sets a reasonable group of options for an interactive terminal. The second ^J is needed to execute the command because curses usually turns off the default Return-to-linefeed conversion.

After executing stty sane, your interrupt, backspace, and erase-line keys may be changed back to the system defaults (which usually don't come close to what most people use).

```
/* cursesex.c: Chapter 3 curses sample program */
/* replacement for shell menu program from chapter 2 */
/* tabs in this example are 4 spaces apart */

#include <stdio.h>
#include <curses.h>

main(argc, argv)
int argc;
char **argv;
{
    int     choice;

    if (argc < 2) {      /* no command line arguments */
        fprintf(stderr,
            "usage: %s [ -t title ] item1 item2 ...\n", argv[0]);
        exit(0);
    }

    init_screen();       /* get things started */
    choice = show_menu(argc, argv);      /* parse the args and
                                        put up the menu */
    close_screen();      /* back to normal mode */
    exit(choice);        /* kick back the result */
}

/* init_screen: initialize curses library, set up screen for menu */
init_screen()
{
    initscr();  /* start curses, set up screen buffer */
    wclear(stdscr);      /* clear the default window */
}

close_screen()
{
    endwin();
}

show_menu(argc, argv)
int argc;
char **argv;
{
    int     items, current, choice, title = 0, longest = 0;
```

```
int     left, top;
char    str1[100], *center_text();

/* parse the input */
items = argc - 1;
current = 0;

while (++current < argc) {  /* loop through all args */
    if (*argv[current] == '-') {    /* look for option char */
        --items;            /* don't count option as menu item */
        if (*(argv[current] + 1) != 't') { /* allow only 't' */
            fprintf(stderr, "%s: invalid argument\n", argv[0]);
            return(0);
        } else {
            if (++current >= argc) {    /* ran out of args */
                fprintf(stderr, "%s: missing title\n", argv[0]);
                return(0);
            }
            --items;    /* don't count title as menu item */
            title = current;    /* save index of title */
        }
    } else if (strlen(argv[current]) > longest)
        longest = strlen(argv[current]);    /* set max str len */
}

/* arguments all processed -- display the menu */
mvaddstr(0, 0, center_text(argv[title], COLS)); /* title at top */
longest += 4;   /* add room for item # */
left = (COLS - longest) / 2;    /* center for longest item */
top = (LINES - items) / 2;  /* center vertically, too */

/* item loop--display as item only if not option or title */
current = choice = 1;
for (current = 1; current < argc; current++) {
    if ((*argv[current] != '-') && (current != title)) {
        mvprintw(top + choice, left, "%2d. %s",
            choice, argv[current]);
        ++choice;
    }
}
wrefresh(stdscr);   /* flush to display */

while (1) { /* input loop */
    move(top + choice + 2, 0);  /* position for prompt */
    clrtoeol();     /* erase entire line (old input) */
    mvaddstr(top + choice + 2, left + 1, "Select: ");
    wrefresh(stdscr);
    getstr(str1);   /* grab line from keyboard */
```

```
        if (sscanf(str1, "%d", &current) != 1) { /* bad input */
            show_error("Bad input: numeric input expected");
            touchwin(stdscr);    /* refresh entire screen */
            wrefresh(stdscr);    /* put menu back */
            continue;            /* repeat input loop */
        }
        if ((current < 1) || (current > items)) {
            show_error("Selection out of range");
            touchwin(stdscr);
            wrefresh(stdscr);
            continue;
        }
        break;  /* good input; set up for return to caller */
    }
    wclear(stdscr);
    wrefresh(stdscr);    /* clear screen before leaving */
    return(current);     /* holds user's choice */
}

char *center_text(str, len)
char    *str;
int     len;
{
    char    tmp[255];
    int     space_count;

    *tmp = 0;        /* set initial space to prepare for appends */
    space_count = (len - strlen(str)) / 2;
    if (space_count <= 0) {
        strcpy(tmp, str);
        return(tmp);
        }
    sprintf(tmp, "%*s", space_count + strlen(str), str);
    return(tmp);
}

/* show_error: display error message in pop-up, wait for input */
show_error(str)
char    *str;
{
    WINDOW  *popup;
    int     top, xsize, left, i;
    char    *message = {"Press Return to continue"};

    top = (LINES - 5) / 2;  /* center five-line window vertically */
    xsize = (strlen(message) > strlen(str)) ?
        strlen(message) : strlen(str);
    xsize += 4;      /* leave two spaces on sides */
```

```
    left = (COLS - xsize) / 2;
    popup = newwin(5, xsize, top, left);
    mvwaddstr(popup, 1, 0, center_text(str, xsize));
    mvwaddstr(popup, 3, 0, center_text(message, xsize));
    revbox(popup, '#');
    wrefresh(popup);
    wgetch(popup);
    delwin(popup);
}

/* draw reverse-video box in a window */
revbox(win, c)          /* draw reverse-video box */
WINDOW  *win;           /* the window to be boxed */
char    c;                /* border character to use */
{
    int     i;
    int     row, col;

    getmaxyx(win, row, col);
    wattron(win, A_REVERSE);        /* set reverse video */
    for(i=0; i<row; i++) {
        mvwaddch(win, i, 0, c);
        mvwaddch(win, i, col-1, c); /* vert */
    }
    for(i=0; i<col; i++) {
        mvwaddch(win, 0, i, c);
        mvwaddch(win, row-1, i, c); /* horiz */
    }
    wattroff(win, A_REVERSE);       /* unset reverse */
}
```

Since this is the first complete C application in this book, we will digress for a bit to explain some of its finer points. It is hardly a perfect example of a UNIX program, but it's a good start.

Working from the top, you will notice that main() was put first. This makes the code easier to follow, and also drives home the point that the main() function should be the shortest, least-busy function of all. This is no less true in UNIX than in any other environment.

The init_screen and close_screen functions do not seem to do much; indeed, close_screen contains only one function call. Purists will chafe at the thought of adding one unnecessary function call because it impacts performance, but we are not splitting atoms here (or hairs). Imagine that you built a huge application on top of this code, opening and closing the display in several places. Functions which start or terminate communications with some device are a good place to leave room for future changes. There are plenty of other such worthy cases, and it is wise not to be miserly in putting wrappers in your code where they make sense.

show_menu() is where all the *real* work gets done. The command-line argument variables are passed to it so that argument processing doesn't have to be done in main(). This might be a little more conservative than necessary, but it seems appropriate for this example. A couple of global variables could have been assigned and the show_menu() call made without any arguments, but globals are a hindrance. Overuse makes code harder to read and debug.

There must be a million ways to process arguments, and in UNIX there are at least twice that many. The 17 lines in show_menu do the job, but they are not very portable. There are two requirements: Accept a large number of arguments, and permit one option ("-t" followed by a title string), which may occur anywhere on the command line. The parsing loop was used to count the total number of menu items, and to find out for purposes of formatting how many characters were in the longest item. Here, reusability was sacrificed for expediency. This argument parsing routine may not be usable in another application, but it came together much more quickly than a more general-purpose parser.

The menus displayed in this example are not fancy, but they are clear and readable. Centered blocks represent a simple approach to formatting. Centering as decoration can be overdone, but in this case, the menu looks much better centered vertically and horizontally than it would have looked backed up against the left margin. As for what constitutes "overdoing" with regard to centering, imagine this menu with each item individually centered on its line. Centering everything against the longest item is cheap to implement, and has a little more class than a left-justified list.

The curses output routines used in the example are simple and few, but the calls used here include most of what you will need for average applications. The format of the argument list for each call should be clear from the variable names used, but have your *Programmer's Reference* handy in case you get lost. The curses calls are grouped together in the manual under curses; they are not listed individually by function name.

An important thing to remember when using curses is this: Because of the changes it makes to your display I/O settings, you should not use the standard I/O functions (like printf() and gets()) while curses is active. The result of a raw printf() on a curses-controlled screen is undefined, but it will certainly mess things up. Unless it has been redirected, even outputting to the STDERR channel will trash your display. The safest way to collect debugging and logging information is to open a text file at the beginning of your application, and use fprintf(logfile, ...) to save messages to it. If you are running under X Window, or you have a spare terminal nearby, you can use a tail -f logfile command from another window or terminal to watch the messages as they are output. Using standard I/O input functions with curses active is even more dangerous.

Input in curses is simple by default. Character and string input requests alike cause the application to block, waiting for either a keypress or a Return, respectively. The getstr function pulls in a full line of input from the keyboard, echoing it, and permitting command line-type editing. This is the easiest way to bring in a field of input, but it does offer the user boundless opportunities to shoot down your application. There is no argument for the maximum size of the string, and 200 characters of input into a 40-column field will not only mess up your screen, but probably crash your program. Try it. The obvious alternative is to roll your own string input routine, a replacement for getstr(). Luckily, ETI has a whole set of field input functions, so we can skip over input device control, the most convoluted, unpleasant part of programming in curses! By the way, there is a scanw function which could have handled the input and conversion in one step; they were separated for clarity.

center_text() shouldn't need any explaining, except that it makes use of the global LINES (the associated COLS is used elsewhere) to determine the width of the screen. This variable is set by curses at initialization time, based on the setting of the TERM environment variable, and the environment variables LINES and COLS, if they exist. Some terminals have predictable screen dimensions, others don't. Terminal emulator windows under X Window are good examples of terminals with unpredictable sizes.

If you're running the full-screen examples from an X Window environment (such as Open Desktop) and they behave erratically, try typing this to correct it:

```
$ eval `/usr/bin/X11/resize`
```

If implemented properly, this command will correctly set the values of the LINES and COLS environment variables to match the current size of your terminal window.

The show_error function displays a pop-up window, and it is here that you will find what you need to create a curses window. New windows are created with a fixed size, and at an initial position which is specified relative to the upper-left corner of the screen, with the upper-leftmost character at row zero, column zero. curses doesn't deal with stacking your windows as you want them. You might think that deleting the pop-up window would appropriately remove the pop-up's contents from the display. You will notice, however, that a call to touchwin() in show_menu() is included; this marks the entire window as "dirty," and redraws it. This is because curses has no concept of overlapping windows, and it doesn't know that the pop-up clobbered the text in the underlying window. The ungainly touchwin(), wrefresh() sequence is a common way to simulate overlapping windows.

ETI Basics

Before ETI came along, curses was the best you could do (at least, using the standard tools) for full-screen textual interfaces under UNIX. Now there is ETI, but things still haven't advanced all that far. ETI is considerably better than raw curses, but it is still weak enough to be only a building block on which you layer your own interface routines.

ETI is three pairs of library/header file combinations with specific purposes: Menus, panels and forms. The names are a little deceptive; it makes one think of text interface tools that approximate their graphical counterparts. This has been done; there are some excellent toolkits that let you migrate text programs to GUIs with no more than a compile, but not in ETI. Even though many of your users will probably have fancy color graphics displays and mice, ETI will leave them stuck with the keyboard. Remember that as you set out to design your application, if you progress too far down the text interface route, you make it difficult to migrate up to a GUI later. That is why the coverage of curses and ETI in this chapter is very light. It is possible to write eye-popping, colorful, complex interfaces using the text tools described here, but if you do that, your effort will be wasted on users who expect movable, resizable windows, and mouse support. At some point, we can reasonably expect users to have graphical displays available, just as we expect advanced text terminals today, but for now, the text device is the more common.

With these caveats in mind, let's take a closer look at ETI.

ETI Menus

The ETI menu library provides a set of functions for building, displaying and collecting results from text menus. As noted earlier, there is much that ETI menus cannot do. There is no conception of menu bars and pull-down menus; ETI menus are best suited to static and pop-up use, and, of course, you can't point and click on your selection with a mouse. That's not to say there is no versatility at all. ETI menus can be organized into either vertical or horizontal, "Lotus-style", formats, and you can even scroll a long list of choices in a window of limited size.

It seems appropriate to rebuild this chapter's earlier command-line menu example using the ETI menu library. This is not the best possible demonstration of ETI menus; there are countless things you can do to this program to improve it. If you want to learn more about ETI, you'll need the *Programmer's Reference* pages titled "menu" and "item" to go beyond the scope of this example. The *Programmer's Guide*'s coverage of this topic are not recommended, or of any of ETI for that matter. The ETI documentation in the *Programmer's Guide* is, at best, convoluted.

What follows is the full text of the functions you need to change in the earlier example. The show_error function can be removed entirely. The condition covered by show_error, the invalid user input, is now not possible.

Here are the makefile template parameters for this example:

```
PROGNAME=      etisample1
OBJS=          etisample1.o
LIBS=          -lmenu -lcurses
```

```
/* etisample1.c: Chapter 3 ETI menu and panel sample */
/* replacement for shell menu program from chapter 2 */
/* tabs in this example are 4 spaces apart */

#include <stdio.h>
#include <menu.h>
#include <curses.h>

/* define a token value to represent leaving the menu without
    making a selection */
#define INTR    (MAX_COMMAND + 1)

/* init_screen: initialize curses library, set up screen for menu */
init_screen()
{
    initscr();  /* start curses, set up screen buffer */
    nonl();     /* don't do newlines */
    raw();      /* no line input */
    noecho();   /* don't echo input characters */
    wclear(stdscr);     /* clear the default window */
}
```

```
int process_key(c)
int c;
{
    switch(c) {
        case 3:      return INTR;      /* ^C exits */

        /* up-arrow, 'k' key, backspace move to prev. item */
        case KEY_UP:
        case 'k':
        case 'K':
        case 8:      return REQ_PREV_ITEM;

        /* down-arrow, 'j' key, spacebar move to next item */
        case KEY_DOWN:
        case 'j':
        case 'J':
        case ' ':    return REQ_NEXT_ITEM;

        return c;    /* default case--kick back orig. character */
    }
}

show_menu(argc, argv)
int argc;
char **argv;
{
    int     items, current, choice, title = 0, longest = 0;
    int     left, top, input_key;
    char    str1[100], *center_text();
    MENU    *menu0;
    WINDOW  *menu0_window;
    ITEM    *menu0_items[25];    /* increase this to allow for more
                                    menu items */

    /* parse the input */
    items = argc - 1;
    current = 0;

    while (++current < argc) {  /* loop through all args */
        if (*argv[current] == '-') {     /* look for option char */
            --items;          /* don't count option as menu item */
            if (*(argv[current] + 1) != 't') {  /* allow only 't' */
                fprintf(stderr, "%s: invalid argument\n", argv[0]);
                return(0);
            } else {
                if (++current >= argc) {    /* ran out of args */
                    fprintf(stderr, "%s: missing title\n", argv[0]);
                    return(0);
```

```
        }
        --items;    /* don't count title as menu item */
        title = current;    /* save index of title */
    }
    } else if (strlen(argv[current]) > longest)
        longest = strlen(argv[current]);    /* set max str len */
}

/* arguments all processed -- set up for the menu */
revbox(stdscr, ' ');    /* border around window */
wattron(stdscr, A_REVERSE);    /* so title & prompt blend in
                                   with border */
mvaddstr(0, 0, center_text(argv[title],
    COLS)); /* title at top */
/* add prompt at bottom */
mvaddstr(LINES - 1, 0,
    center_text("(Press ^C to exit)", COLS));
wattroff(stdscr, A_REVERSE);    /* cancel reverse video */
left = (COLS - longest) / 2;    /* center for longest item */
top = (LINES - items) / 2;   /* center vertically, too */

/* item loop--add as item only if not option or title */
current = choice = 1;
for (current = 1; current < argc; current++) {
    if ((*argv[current] != '-') && (current != title)) {
        /* add item to list */
        menu0_items[choice - 1] = new_item(argv[current], "");
        ++choice;
    }
}
menu0_items[choice - 1] = (MENU *)0;    /* mark end of list */
menu0 = new_menu(menu0_items);  /* create menu */
/* create subwindow to hold menu */
menu0_window = subwin(stdscr, items + 2, longest + 2,
    top, left);
/* enable keypad mode so arrow keys will work */
keypad(menu0_window, TRUE);
set_menu_sub(menu0, menu0_window);  /* attach menu to window */
post_menu(menu0);
touchwin(stdscr);
touchwin(menu0_window);
refresh();
wrefresh(menu0_window);

while (1) { /* input loop */
    /* get a key and translate it to a menu action */
    input_key = process_key(wgetch(menu0_window));
    menu_driver(menu0, input_key); /* let the driver have it */
```

```
            if (input_key == 13) {   /* use return as item select */
                current = item_index(current_item(menu0)) + 1;
                break;
            }
            if (input_key == INTR) {     /* leave without choosing */
                current = 0;
                break;
            }
            continue;
        }
        wclear(stdscr);
        wrefresh(stdscr);     /* clear screen before leaving */
        return(current);      /* holds user's choice */
}
```

You will notice that the changes were not all that traumatic; up to a point, a menu is a menu, and the way we did it by hand earlier in the chapter was not unlike ETI's way. ETI gets much higher marks for elegance, however; the other program looks rather ugly and weak by comparison.

The sequence of events is pretty simple, and is mostly spelled out in the comments. The changes to init_screen() are needed because the keyboard input that drives the menu works best in single-character mode. It would be awkward to require the user to press Return after each request. The automatic character echoing is turned off as well, so that only input drives the menu; it never appears as characters on the screen.

The process_key function translates an input character, which is held in an int because it can be larger than eight bits, into an action token. These tokens are interpreted by the ETI menu_driver function, which changes the display to reflect the requested action. As an example, consider this chain of events: The user presses Space. This is picked up by the curses wgetch function, and passed to our process_key(). There, a case statement determines that the matching action token is REQ_NEXT_ITEM, a pre-defined ETI menu token meaning "skip to the next menu item." That token is passed to ETI's menu_driver(), which moves the menu bar down one row to indicate that the current selection has changed. Then the input loop goes around again, and it continues until either ^C or Return is pressed.

You may have noticed that there is no explicit refresh() call in the input loop. The menu_driver() doesn't do it, wgetch() does. The output buffer is routinely flushed prior to taking keyboard input. This prevents synchronization problems.

There are many other menu tokens not listed here which control scrolling menus, pattern matching (shortcut by typing the first few letters of the desired option), and other features. Not that they are unimportant; if this topic interests you at all, experiment on your own. We will see a different kind of menu in the next section, and wrap up this chapter by showing a complete application that uses a combination of curses and the ETI libraries. It's a big one, so now might be a good time to take a break.

curses and ETI: The Whole Enchilada

Most full-screen UNIX applications will use a combination of curses and higher-level ETI calls. The next example illustrates this, and also introduces you to another useful ETI element, the form.

ETI forms are implemented in a fashion very similar to menus. Whereas a menu is a collection of items, a form is a collection of fields. Each field's data structure holds information on placement, length, type, and other parameters. Even if you never use fields and forms in the manner of the following example, you should be aware that ETI fields are the most elegant method UNIX has to offer for collecting input on a text display. The versatility of this mechanism extends far beyond the simple use shown in the example; there is elaborate support for everything from varying field types to automatic field verification.

The following example is a *very* primitive card database. The focus is on the interface; the database portion works, but only well enough to help drive the interface. This example was written, as are the other examples in this book, to explain itself through comments as much as possible. After the program text is completed, we'll shine some light in the darkest areas, but wherever something is unclear, you should consult your *Programmer's Reference*. The relevant sections are "curses," "field," "form," and "menu."

Here's the example. The makefile boilerplate should be copied, then modified thus:

```
PROGNAME=    eticards
OBJS=        eticards.o show_error.o
LIBS=        -lmenu -lform -lcurses
```

The show_error.c file is taken from our earlier example. The show_error and revbox functions were copied to a separate file, and a single directive added at the top:

```
#include <curses.H>
```

The source code for the main program module follows:

```
/* eticards.c: Card file application using ETI functions */
/* for chapter 3 */
/* tabs in this file are four spaces apart */

#include <unistd.h>
#include <fcntl.h>
#include <stdio.h>
#include <curses.h>
#include <menu.h>
#include <form.h>

#define INTR    (MAX_COMMAND + 1)

/* create structures and lists of menu items and fields */
typedef struct {
    char    *item, *desc;
} menu_item;

typedef struct {
    int     rows, cols, rowpos, colpos, options;
    char    *data;
} field_def;

menu_item main_menu_list[] = {
    "Open", "Open an existing card file",
    "New",  "Create a new card file",
    "Quit", "Exit",
    (char *)0, (char *)0,
};

menu_item card_menu_list[] = {
    "Next", "",       /* horizontal menu, so no descriptions */
    "Previous", "",
    "Clear", "",
    "Search", "",
    "First", "",
    "Last", "",
    "Update", "",
    "Add", "",
    "Delete", "",
    "Quit", "",
    (char *)0, (char *)0,
};
```

```
#define FIELD_OPTS O_VISIBLE | O_ACTIVE | O_PUBLIC | O_EDIT
#define LABEL_OPTS 0

field_def card_field_list[] = {
    /* rows, cols, rowpos, colpos, options, data */
    1, 40, 4, 15, FIELD_OPTS, 0,         /* key field */
    1, 40, 6, 15, FIELD_OPTS, 0,         /* data field 1 */
    1, 40, 7, 15, FIELD_OPTS, 0,         /* data field 2 */
    1, 40, 8, 15, FIELD_OPTS, 0,         /* data field 3 */
    1, 40, 9, 15, FIELD_OPTS, 0,         /* data field 4 */
    1, 0, 1, 0, LABEL_OPTS, "Card File Entry",  /* title */
    1, 0, 4, 3, LABEL_OPTS, "Search key:",      /* prompt */
    1, 0, 6, 3, LABEL_OPTS, "Data:",            /* data prompt */
    1, 0, 11, 0, LABEL_OPTS, "[press ESC for menu]",
    0, 0, 0, 0, 0, (char *)0,
};

/* structure of database record */
union dbrec_s {
    char    key[41], data[4][41];
    char    array[5][41];
} dbrec, *dbptr = &dbrec;

main(argc, argv)
int     argc;
char    **argv;
{
    init_screen();  /* initialize the display system */
    /* call main application routine */
    /* pass default card file name if provided on command line */
    do_cards(argc > 1 ? argv[1] : (char *)0);
    close_screen(); /* shut down display system */
    exit(0);
}

init_screen()    /* curses/ETI initialization */
{
    initscr();
    nonl();
    noecho();
    raw();
    wclear(stdscr);
}

close_screen()
{
    wclear(stdscr);
    refresh();
```

```
    endwin();
}

do_cards(first_file)
char    *first_file;    /* first card file to open */
{
    MENU    *main_menu, *card_menu;
    ITEM    *main_menu_items[4], *card_menu_items[11];
    FIELD   *card_fields[11];
    FORM    *card_form;
    WINDOW  *main_menu_win, *card_menu_win, *card_win;
    char    temp[80];
    int     inkey, i, rows, cols, top, left;
    int     state, dbfd, recnum;

    /** build main menu **/
    for (i = 0; main_menu_list[i].item != (char *)0; i++)
        /* load menu field array */
        main_menu_items[i] = new_item(main_menu_list[i].item,
            main_menu_list[i].desc);
    main_menu_items[i] = (ITEM *)0; /* mark end */
    main_menu = new_menu(main_menu_items);  /* create menu */
    scale_menu(main_menu, &rows, &cols);    /* get menu size */
    top = (LINES - rows) / 2;
    left = (COLS - cols) / 2;
    /* create centered subwindow for menu */
    main_menu_win = subwin(stdscr, rows, cols, top, left);
    keypad(main_menu_win, TRUE);    /* enable arrow keys */
    set_menu_sub(main_menu, main_menu_win); /* attach menu to win */

    /** build card form **/
    for (i = 0; card_field_list[i].rows != 0; i++) {
        /* if it's a label, we know the length of the field */
        if(card_field_list[i].cols == 0)
            card_field_list[i].cols =
                strlen(card_field_list[i].data);
        /* if the column position is 0, center the field */
        if(card_field_list[i].colpos == 0)
            card_field_list[i].colpos =
                (65 - strlen(card_field_list[i].data)) / 2;

        /* create field, add to array */
        card_fields[i] = new_field(card_field_list[i].rows,
            card_field_list[i].cols, card_field_list[i].rowpos,
            card_field_list[i].colpos, 0, 0);

        /* set the field options--disable edit for labels */
        if(card_field_list[i].options != 0) {
```

```
            set_field_opts(card_fields[i], card_field_list[i].options);
        } else field_opts_off(card_fields[i], O_EDIT | O_ACTIVE);
        /* set the label string */
        if(card_field_list[i].data != (char *)0) {
            set_field_buffer(card_fields[i], 0,
                card_field_list[i].data);
        } else set_field_back(card_fields[i], A_UNDERLINE);
    }
    card_fields[i] = (FIELD *)0;     /* mark end of field list */

    card_form = new_form(card_fields);  /* create form */
    top = (LINES - 12) / 2;
    left = (COLS - 65) / 2;

    /* subwindow to hold form */
    card_win = subwin(stdscr, 12, 65, top, left);
    keypad(card_win, TRUE);      /* enable arrow keys */
    set_form_sub(card_form, card_win);  /* attach */

    /** create card menu **/
    for (i = 0; card_menu_list[i].item != (char *)0; i++)
        /* load menu field array */
        card_menu_items[i] = new_item(card_menu_list[i].item,
            card_menu_list[i].desc);
    card_menu_items[i] = (ITEM *)0; /* mark end */
    card_menu = new_menu(card_menu_items);  /* create menu */
    /* don't show description field */
    menu_opts_off(card_menu, O_SHOWDESC);
    /* change format to horizontal: max 2 rows, 6 cols (of items) */
    set_menu_format(card_menu, 2, 6);

    /* create top-left subwindow for card menu */
    card_menu_win = subwin(stdscr, 2, 65, 1, 1);
    keypad(card_menu_win, TRUE);     /* activate arrow keys */
    set_menu_sub(card_menu, card_menu_win); /* attach */

    state = 0;  /* start with main menu (see table below) */

    /* open default db if user requests it */
    dbfd = open_db(first_file);
    if (dbfd >= 0)  /* sucessful open */
        state = 2;  /* skip right to card data screen */
    else {          /* open failed */
        show_error("Could not open database");
    }
    recnum = 0;      /* we haven't read a record yet--no updates */

    /** main processing loop **/
```

```
/* state assignment map:
    0   main menu, not posted yet
    1   main menu posted & active
    2   card data entry screen, not posted yet
    3   card data entry screen posted & active
    4   card menu, not posted yet
    5   card menu, posted & active
    255 exit program */

while (1) {
    /** main menu loop **/
    while(state == 0 || state == 1) {
        if (state == 0) {    /* main menu needs posting */
            wclear(stdscr);
            /* create border outside menu window */
            do_border(main_menu_win, "Card Filer--Main Menu",
                "from chapter 3");
            post_menu(main_menu);    /* display menu */
            refresh();
            state = 1;
        }

        /* grab a key and run it through our translator */
        inkey = process_menu_key(wgetch(main_menu_win));
        /* hand translated key to menu driver for action */
        menu_driver(main_menu, inkey);
        /* clear match pattern so it works more intuitively */
        menu_driver(main_menu, REQ_CLEAR_PATTERN);
        if(inkey == 13) {    /* select */
            /* process main menu selection */
            switch(item_index(current_item(main_menu))) {
                case 0:          /* Open */
                    unpost_menu(main_menu);
                    state = 2;   /* activate card data entry */
                    break;
                case 1:          /* New */
                    beep();
                    break;
                case 2:          /* Quit */
                    state = 255;
                    break;
            }
        }
    }

    /** card form loop **/
    while (state == 2 || state == 3) {
        if (state == 2) {    /* init form window */
```

```
            wclear(stdscr);
            do_border(card_win, "Card Create/Examine/Modify", "");
            post_form(card_form);
            refresh();
            state = 3;
        }
        /* turn on instructions ("ESC for menu") */
        field_opts_on(card_fields[8], O_VISIBLE);

        /* get and process user input */
        inkey = process_form_key(wgetch(card_win));
        form_driver(card_form, inkey);
        switch (inkey) {
            case INTR:      /* ESC: card menu request */
                /* turn off instructions--menu will be active */
                field_opts_off(card_fields[8], O_VISIBLE);
                state = 4;
                break;
        }
    }

    /** card menu loop **/
    while (state == 4 || state == 5) {
        if (state == 4) {   /* put up card menu */
            post_menu(card_menu);
            refresh();
            state = 5;
        }

        /* get and process user input */
        inkey = process_menu_key(wgetch(card_menu_win));
        menu_driver(card_menu, inkey);
        menu_driver(card_menu, REQ_CLEAR_PATTERN);
        switch (inkey) {
            case    INTR:   /* ESCape back to card form */
                unpost_menu(card_menu);
                state = 3;  /* no need to recreate it */
                refresh();
                break;

            case    13:     /* selection */
                /* actions based on menu item selected */
                switch (item_index(current_item(card_menu))) {
                    case    0:  /* Next */
                        ++recnum;
                        if (read_rec(dbfd, (char *)&dbrec,
                            recnum) < 0) {
                            --recnum;
```

```
            beep();
      } else {
            load_fields(&dbrec, card_fields);
            refresh();
      }
      break;
case    1:   /* Previous */
      if (recnum > 1) {
            --recnum;
      } else {
            beep();
            break;
      }
      if (read_rec(dbfd, (char *)&dbrec,
            recnum) < 0) {
            ++recnum;
            beep();
      } else {
            load_fields(&dbrec, card_fields);
            refresh();
      }
      break;
case    2:   /* Clear */
      recnum = 0;
      for (i = 0; i < 5; i++)
            *dbrec.array[i] = '\0';
      load_fields(&dbrec, card_fields);
      refresh();
      break;
case    3:   /* Search */
      break;
case    4:   /* First */
      recnum = 1;
      read_rec(dbfd, (char *)&dbrec, 1);
      load_fields(&dbrec, card_fields);
      refresh();
      break;
case    5:   /* Last */
      recnum = read_rec(dbfd, (char *)&dbrec, 0);
      if (recnum > 0) recnum /= sizeof(dbrec);
      load_fields(&dbrec, card_fields);
      refresh();
      break;
case    6:   /* Update */
      if (recnum == 0) {   /*no read, no update*/
            beep();
      } else {
            store_fields(&dbrec, card_fields);
```

```
                                    write_rec(dbfd, (char *)&dbrec,
                                        recnum);
                            }
                            break;
                    case    7:   /* Add */
                        store_fields(&dbrec, card_fields);
                        write_rec(dbfd, (char *)&dbrec, 0);
                        break;
                    case    8:   /* Delete */
                        break;
                    case    9:        /* Quit to main menu */
                        unpost_form(card_form);
                        unpost_menu(card_menu);
                        state = 0;
                        break;
                }
            }
        }
        if (state == 255)   /* exit */
            return;
    }
}

/* translate menu keystrokes to action tokens */
int process_menu_key(c)
int c;
{
    switch(c) {
        case 27:    return INTR;    /* ESC exits */

        /* up-arrow, 'k' key, backspace move to prev. item */
        case KEY_UP:
        case 'k':
        case 'K':
        case 8:     return REQ_PREV_ITEM;

        /* down-arrow, 'j' key, spacebar move to next item */
        case KEY_DOWN:
        case 'j':
        case 'J':
        case ' ':   return REQ_NEXT_ITEM;

        return c;   /* default case--kick back orig. character */
    }
}

/* key translations for form */
int process_form_key(c)
```

```
int c;
{
    switch(c) {
        case KEY_LEFT:      return REQ_LEFT_CHAR;
        case KEY_RIGHT:     return REQ_RIGHT_CHAR;
        case KEY_HOME:      return REQ_LAST_FIELD;
        case 13:                                    /* c/r */
        case KEY_DOWN:                              /* down arrow */
        case 9:             return REQ_NEXT_FIELD;  /* tab */
        case KEY_UP:                                /* up arrow */
        case KEY_BTAB:      return REQ_PREV_FIELD;  /* back tab */
        case 27:            return INTR;            /* ESC */
        case 8:             return REQ_LEFT_CHAR;   /* backspace */
        case 127:           return REQ_DEL_CHAR;    /* delete */
        case 21:                                    /* ^U */
        case 24:            return REQ_CLR_FIELD;   /* ^X */
    }
    return c;
}

char *center_text(str, len)
char    *str;
int     len;
{
    char    tmp[255];
    int     space_count;

    *tmp = 0;       /* set initial space to prepare for appends */
    space_count = (len - strlen(str)) / 2;
    if (space_count <= 0) {
        strcpy(tmp, str);
        return(tmp);
        }
    sprintf(tmp, "%*s", space_count + strlen(str), str);
    return(tmp);
}

/* draw border, with title and caption, around a subwindow */
/* draws in parent window (assumed to be stdscr) to avoid changing
    chars in subwin */
do_border(sub, title, caption)
WINDOW  *sub;           /* the window to be boxed */
char    *title, *caption;   /* top and bottom labels for border */
{
    int     i;
    int     rows, cols, top, left;

    getbegyx(sub, top, left);   /* get window position and size */
```

```
        getmaxyx(sub, rows, cols);  /* macros--no need to pass pointers */
        wattron(stdscr, A_REVERSE); /* set reverse video */
        for(i = top - 2; i <= top + rows + 1; i++) {
            mvwaddch(stdscr, i, left - 2, ' ');
            mvwaddch(stdscr, i, left + cols + 1, ' '); /* vert */
        }
        for(i = left - 2; i <= left + cols + 1; i++) {
            mvwaddch(stdscr, top - 2, i, ' ');
            mvwaddch(stdscr, top + rows + 1, i, ' '); /* horiz */
        }
        mvwaddstr(stdscr, top - 2, left - 2, center_text(title,
            (left + cols + 1) - (left - 2)));
        mvwaddstr(stdscr, top + rows + 1, left - 2, center_text(caption,
            (left + cols + 1) - (left - 2)));
        wattroff(stdscr, A_REVERSE);     /* unset reverse */
}

/* open a database (close current one if open), return handle to it */
int open_db(filename)
char    *filename;
{
    static int  dbfd = -1;  /* remember whether db is open */

    if (dbfd >= 0)  {   /* database is currently open--close first */
        close(dbfd);
        dbfd = -1;
        }
    return(dbfd = open(filename, O_RDWR));
}

/* read a record from the database */
int read_rec(fd, buf, recnum)
int     fd, recnum;
char    *buf;
{
    long    result, pos;

    pos = (long)((recnum - 1) * sizeof(dbrec));
    /* seek to record position */
    if (recnum != 0) {
        if ((result = lseek(fd, (long)pos, SEEK_SET)) < 0L) {
            return((int)result);
        }
    } else {
        if ((result = lseek(fd, (long)(-sizeof(dbrec)),
            SEEK_END)) < 0L) {
            return((int)result);
        }
```

```
    }
    pos = result;   /* save byte position to report on return */
    /* read record at that position */
    if (result = (long)read(fd, buf, sizeof(dbrec)) <= 0)
        return(-1); /* bad read */
    return((int)pos);
}

/* write record to database. if recnum == 0, append to end of file */
int write_rec(fd, buf, recnum)
int     fd, recnum;
char    *buf;
{
    long    result, pos;

    if (recnum != 0) {
        if ((result = lseek(fd, (long)(--recnum * sizeof(dbrec)),
            SEEK_SET)) < 0)
            return((int)result);
    } else {
        if ((result = lseek(fd, OL, SEEK_END)) < 0)
            return((int)result);
    }
    pos = result;
    if (write(fd, buf, sizeof(dbrec)) <= 0)
        return(-1);
    return((int)pos);
}

/* load the fields--assumes current database structure */
int load_fields(buf, fields)
union dbrec_s   *buf;
FIELD           **fields;
{
    int     i;

    /* copy the data into the display buffer (buffer 0) for
        all fields */
    for (i = 0; i < 5; i++)
        set_field_buffer(fields[i], 0, buf->array[i]);
}

int store_fields(buf, fields)
union dbrec_s   *buf;
FIELD           **fields;
{
    int     i;
```

```
    /* haul field buffer 0 into our structure */
    for (i = 0; i < 5; i++)
        strcpy(buf->array[i], field_buffer(fields[i], 0));
}
```

This program could have been broken up into smaller pieces. The do_cards function is entirely too bulky, but it was left in one piece so that its flow could be followed with a minimum of page-flipping.

The behavior of this program is affected by a few things I chose *not* to do. Completing this program is your exercise for this chapter; we'll discuss some of the missing elements at the close. As it stands now, entering the name of the program (eticards, unless you chose something different), followed by the name of an *existing* file, will bring up the card data entry form. Pressing the ESC key on that form will call up the card menu, which lets the user choose the action that should be taken relative to the currently displayed card. Pressing ESC in that menu will return to the card entry form. Selecting "Quit" from the card menu backs out to the main menu. "Quit" from the main menu is wired to exit the program. The other two entries on the main menu (Open and New) aren't wired to anything important.

The behavior of the form used in this example is straightforward. An array of structures (card_field_list) is defined that holds the definitions for both the data entry (editable) and label (non-editable) fields in the card entry form. Code in do_cards() translates this array into an array of FIELD * elements (card_fields). This array is then bound to a new form through the new_form function. The resulting form, card_form, is then assigned to a window with set_form_sub(). Following that, the form is ready to be used.

Data in any form field can be changed on the fly with set_field_buffer(). See load_fields() in the example. A field can have multiple data buffers, but buffer zero is the default display buffer. If a form is active, copying new data into a field's display buffer changes the virtual display. refresh() can be called to update the physical display after changing fields.

There are some interface "tricks" performed in eticards that could use calling out. There is a prompt, defined in the card_field_list array, at the bottom of the card entry form that directs the user to "press ESC for menu." This prompt doesn't make sense while the menu is displayed, so it is hidden while the menu is active. The do_border function draws borders around subwindows, but note that the border characters are not written to the menu or form subwindows; those windows are, and must remain, under the control of the menu and form routines. Instead, do_border gets the placement and dimensions of the sub-window passed to it as an argument, and draws the border on its parent window (stdscr).

The process_form_key and process_menu_key functions include references to key value macros like KEY_UP and KEY_DOWN (for the up and down-arrow keys, respectively). This is another gift from curses and terminfo, but it comes with a catch. Most modern terminals use "escape sequences" to pass arrows, HOME, and some other special keys to applications. They're called escape sequences precisely because the first character is an ESC. There are very few keys you can expect to be present on every keyboard that runs your program and if you write applications that use keys like DO and HELP, some users won't stand a chance. Even the ubiquitous arrow keys pose problems in some environments, including SCO UNIX, on which Open Desktop is based. Arrow keys generate escape sequences, and sometimes the curses input routines stop listening after the first character, passing an ESC to the application instead of a KEY_UP or KEY_DOWN. There is no magic fix; you have to work around it. It isn't wise to leave arrow keys out of your application: They are very intuitive for users, and there are times when they function perfectly. However, you should always have an alternate key available for any action that would require a special key like an arrow or function key. You might assign ^U as a synonym for KEY_UP, for example. This also means you need to be careful about how you use ESC. In the example, the worst it will do is pop a menu up or down; you certainly would not want to have "press ESC to erase card file" there instead.

The menus are "unposted" when moving to the card form. This effectively removes their data from the curses buffer so that a subsequent refresh() makes them disappear. If you look at the state transitions in do_cards(), you will see the unpost_menu() and refresh() calls. If you look closely at the switch from the card form to the card menu and back, you will notice that things are handled a little differently. The card form is *not* unposted when the card menu is brought up; it remains on-screen for reference, and to avoid having to redraw the whole screen when the menu is dismissed. Pressing ESC while the card menu is posted will unpost the menu, and return to the form *in the exact place* where it was left. This is a feature of ETI that some might consider a flaw. You can have multiple interface elements, forms, and menus posted on the same screen at the same time. eticards doesn't do much with this, but it wouldn't be difficult to work it so that the menu and the form were active *at the same time*, just driven by different keystrokes. One of the marvelous things about the design of ETI is that the programmer has minute control over the handling of input. If you want certain keys to act on the menu, and everything else to act on the form, they can.

This example has some holes in it. There are menu options with no associated code, and poor notification of error conditions. Sometimes the program just beeps. Your task is to make eticards.c into a real program. Plug the holes. Doing this properly will involve creating a pop-up form or two. Other touches that might not be so obvious include adding a record number field a "modified" flag to the data entry screen. Check the documentation for the field_status function.

Avoid making changes to the database I/O functions for now. We'll be revisiting this example in later chapters, and modifying those functions. If you feel confident that you can merge your changes with those that will appear later, be my guest.

The Wrap

Does that cover everything there is to know about UNIX text applications? Hardly, but working through the examples and using the *Programmer's Reference* as a resource should leave you in excellent shape to tackle a project, even if that project is just learning more about curses and ETI. We will come back to the foundations laid here in later chapters, though, so be sure you feel comfortable with this material before moving on.

The next chapter deals with some UNIX-specific issues that can help you build more versatility and efficiency into your programs. You will still need to keep the *Programmer's Reference* nearby. Don't lose this chapter's last example; we'll be modifying it in Chapter 5 to add some interesting capabilities. You might spruce up the interface—do more key mappings, add help text, whatever you like—but don't change the menus or the disk I/O. If you rearrange these things, it won't be impossible for you to use the changes in the coming chapters, but it will be more difficult.

## Chapter 4

Processes and Inter-Process Communications

When a UNIX executable program is loaded, it doesn't just run. The operating system first makes preparations, setting aside room for the program and its memory-bound data, initializing an environment, and preparing for access to files and devices. Even more than this takes place between the time you take your finger off the Return key and the appearance of your application's first character. UNIX handles it all for you, quietly; all you have to do is know the name of the program you want to run.

There is more to running a UNIX program than just loading a binary image and jumping to its entry point, which is the pattern of most single-tasking operating systems. There is a need for a place to hold information about open files, environment variables, accounting statistics, and the like. In UNIX, every running program is allocated a *process* to track its resources, and to hold the operating system's "housekeeping" data. A process, at least in most versions of UNIX, is little more than a collection of memory: The program and its data, plus the system's housekeeping.

It is not possible for a single UNIX process to run multiple execution paths simultaneously. For example, to handle a task like printing while you continue to type, your program must start a new process to handle the printing. Once your program starts a new process, that process separates completely from the one that spawned it. Because of this, you must resort to some unusual means to open and maintain lines of communication between your application and its "child" processes.

This chapter deals with these topics, starting with a look at ways to start new processes (and why you would even want to), and moving on to the basics of communicating between disjoint processes.

Getting The Process Down

All kinds of greasy things happen inside UNIX when you ask to run a program, and you can get along very well without understanding much of what's happening under the covers. UNIX provides a set of functions that let you create multi-tasking applications, and you needn't be a genius to use them.

There are two basic calls you can use in your application to create new processes: system() and fork(). Any C program can request the running of another program by including a call to system():

```
system("ls -l");
```

This call creates a new process, loads a shell, and passes the argument ls -l to it. There is more going on than that, but you will be doing it all by hand soon enough. Your program will then "block," or halt execution, until some event takes place. In this case, when the shell created by the system() call exits, your program's execution will resume. Blocking until the command completes is often useful, but it hardly makes the best use of UNIX's multitasking. Your program stops, another runs to completion, then your program runs again. There is a better way, but things immediately become more complicated.

The fork function is an application's only way to create a new *asynchronous* process. system() uses it internally. Unlike system(), fork() does not require the name of a program as an argument. In fact, it takes no arguments at all. How does it know what to execute? Simple. It executes the program that made the call.

You see, when you make a call to fork(), a copy of the current process is made, leaving two processes with identical executable and data memory images. After the copy, *both* copies of the program start and execute at the same time and at the same instruction, the statement following the fork() call.

You might wonder what purpose there is in running two copies of the same program simultaneously. True enough, and if you're not paying attention, that's exactly what you'll get. Both programs will try to communicate with the same screen, open the same files, and generally play havoc with everything. The trick is in fork()'s return code, an integer process ID, or PID. The fork() call helps you discern the parent from the child by passing a return code of zero to the new child process (the copy), and the child's process ID to the parent. Your program, based on fork()'s return code, must send the child on a different execution path. In essence, you need to build a sub-program for each child process into your application.

Here is a quick, self-running, example:

```
PROGNAME=       fork1
OBJS=           fork1.o
LIBS=

/* fork1.c: example of the fork() system call (for chapter 4) */
/* tabs in this program are four spaces apart */

#include <stdio.h>

main()
{
    int     pid, a;

    a = 55;         /* set a variable that we can check later */
    printf("Your current process list:\n");
    system("ps");   /* display this user's processes */
    printf("\n\nNow starting child process...\n");
    pid = fork();
    if (pid < 0) {  /* error--couldn't fork */
        perror("fork failed"); /* display error text and leave */
        exit(1);
    }

    /* at this point, there are now two copies of this program running
        exactly the same code, side-by-side. We must identify the child
        and send it along a different execution path. */
    if (pid == 0) {
        /* only the child executes this */
        printf("child: started, a == %d\n", a); /* we exist */
        sleep(5);   /* give the parent a chance to do its thing */
        a = 99;     /* change the variable; does my father know? */
        printf("child: changed value of a to %d\n", a);
        sleep(5);   /* make dad wait */
        printf("child: leaving now\n");
        exit(0);    /* go away */
    } else {
        /* only the parent runs here */
        sleep(1);   /* let the kid talk */
        printf("parent: fork() returned %d, process list is:\n", pid);
        system("ps");
```

```
        sleep(7);    /* wait for the child to change the variable */
        printf("parent: a == %d\n", a);
        wait(&a);        /* block until child exits */
        sleep(1);
        printf("parent: child exited\n");
    }
    exit(0);
}
```

Executing this program will result in a running dialogue which illustrates how fork() behaves. Run it and look over the results. See what conclusions you can draw on your own before reading on.

The first thing that should be apparent to you is that the PID is not just some random number thrown at you by fork(). As its name implies, a process ID is the distinct identification of a process. PIDs are used throughout UNIX in utilities, including ps (the process lister), to tell processes apart. The example's second call to ps shows that a new process *with the same name* has been started after the child reports that it is running. Note that the process ID reported by ps for the child process corresponds with the value returned by fork().

As the example shows, it is not uncommon to have multiple processes with the same name, and the program name cannot be used by the system to identify a process. To keep things running smoothly, each process is *guaranteed* a unique PID, different from every other process running on that machine.

Another point illustrated by the example is the sharing of data between parent and child. When the copy is made, both the program and all its data in memory are copied. The child process knew about the integer variable "a", but once the child started running, it had its own complete, separate, memory image, including a separate copy of the storage allocated for "a". Therefore, when the child changed that variable's value, the change was not reflected in the parent program. Reversing the test—having the parent change the value and testing for that change in the child—would have shown that the separation of data storage works both ways. Now, perhaps, you can begin to see why inter-process communication is needed. There is no way to declare a C variable "common", and have it shared between parent and child.

Two quick side notes about this example before we move on: The fork() call works fast, much faster than this example makes it appear. This program is loaded with sleep() calls to synchronize the output of the parent and the child. Because of the way UNIX buffers its output, the parent might have displayed "child exited" before the child told us it was leaving. Second, notice that the program checked for a less-than-zero return value from fork(), calling the function perror in that condition. By convention, UNIX system calls (not all function calls, just the low-level ones) return something less-than-zero to indicate an error condition. perror(), when called *immediately* after such an error is detected, will output a description of the error, prefixed by text you provide as an argument, to the STDERR output. There will be other examples of error handling throughout this book, but again, making the examples bullet-proof is mostly your job.

The Simplest Connection: Pipes

You already know the word "pipe." It appeared in Chapter 1's introduction to the shell. In that context, it referred to the use of the pipe character, "|", to connect the stdout of one program to the stdin of another. Pipes are not the exclusive domain of the shell, however. As this section demonstrates, they are immensely useful in C applications as well.

The most recent example showed the split between parent and child processes following a fork(). While no data exchange path is automatically opened at fork() time, the pipe is the most commonly-used means of creating such a path. Here is how it starts:

```
int    ends[2];
err = pipe(ends);
```

There are two ends to every pipe, just as there are with the real thing, and there is direction of flow from source (writer) to sink (reader). A call to the pipe function creates the pipe, and provides us with a very comfortable way to access it: a pair of file handles, one for each end of the pipe. One read-only (sink), and one write-only (source). Because the pipe "ends" are file handles, ordinary UNIX I/O calls can be used to shuttle data back and forth.

You don't fork *prior* to creating a pipe, any more than you turn the water on before installing your plumbing. The parent creates the pipe first, then calls fork(). It is the nature of fork() to have file handles among the data passed from parent to child. A direction of communication is chosen, parent to child or child to parent, and the writer outputs data into the pipe. The reader needn't be constantly listening; the data is buffered and delivered in the order written.

One thing that catches some programmers off-guard is the idea that a pipe is bi-directional. Can't a single pipe, with its read and write handles, be used to run from both parent to child *and* child to parent? It can, at least there's nothing to keep you from doing that, as long as you read from and write to the proper file handles. Remember: one pipe uses two file handles. The problems with doing bi-directional I/O through a single pipe are several: First, output from multiple writers flows into the pipe without control. Messages from one writer will inter-mingle with those from another, and they will have to be sorted out. Another issue is the dreaded *deadlock,* a frequent cause of headaches among developers of multitasking software. It goes like this: Writer 1 outputs a large block of data into the pipe. Writer 2, without first reading from the pipe (which would drain it), also tries to write data. Result: The pipe's buffer fills, and both processes block until a reader comes along. That's the catch: The blocked processes *are* the read-ers, which now cannot read because they are blocked. And they won't become unblocked until one of them can read. And so on. Lastly, even if you could syn-chronize and pace your output, every read from a pipe is destructive: The data is removed. Any process reading a message intended for some other recipient will have to put that message back in the pipe—*at the rear*. The moral of the story is that attempting bi-directional traffic on a single pipe is a lost cause. The solution is to open *two* pipes, and that's exactly what our example illustrates.

A common use for pipes is to put fancier or friendlier interfaces on existing applications. The ed editor, for instance, is a powerful line editor, but it has been blessed with a face that even its mother couldn't love. We could rewrite ed, but let's assume we don't have the source code. Can we give it a new look without changing the original program? Thanks to pipes, we can.

The shell makes I/O redirection easy, but it is a bit more complicated in C. Since we cannot rewrite ed and move its I/O from stdin and stdout to our pipes, somehow we have to remap its stdin and stdout channels from the outside.

Here is what to expect from the example: The parent opens two pipes, then forks. The child closes the stdin and stdout passed to it by the parent. This is OK, and remember, it doesn't affect the parent. The child then uses the dup() system call to "clone" its pipe channels, first the one from which it reads, then the one to which it writes. The order is important, and it is dependent on one of those ancient, arbitrary tenets of UNIX: The first two file handles, numbers zero and one, are stdin and stdout, respectively, and 2 is stderr. Closing them frees them up, and dup() always stashes its duplicated file information under the first avail-able handle. After that, every printf() unwittingly writes to one pipe, and every gets() reads from the other. The child's I/O has been effectively rerouted to the parent's pipes. That takes care of the child, but ed is still not involved. There's one more step: exec().

exec   There are six flavors of exec(), but all of them do the same thing, they load and run a program. Unlike system(), exec() loads the requested program *over* the one that called it. The requesting process stops running the current program, and starts running the new one. The combination of fork() and exec() keeps UNIX alive; every time you ask the shell to run a program for you, it clones itself with fork(), prepares things, perhaps by redirecting the standard I/O channels if you requested it, then uses exec() to clobber its cloned self with the requested program.

The six variants of the exec call offer different methods of handling arguments, environment variables, and the use of the PATH environment variable. Specifically, arguments can be passed to an exec()-spawned program in two ways: as distinct, char * arguments with the list terminated by a zero pointer, or as the familiar array of char * elements, just as argv[] comes into the main function of a C program. An array of environment variables can also be passed to certain forms of exec(). Finally, you can either pass a fully-qualified file name, or use a form of exec() that looks in all the directories named in the PATH environment variable for the name you specify.

Having the parent's environment passed down is more manageable than creating one from scratch. Similarly, using the PATH variable to automatically search for the program is easier than requiring that it be installed in a fixed directory. With these elements in mind, there are only two of the six exec() calls worth remembering: execvp() and execlp(). The syntax for these calls looks like this:

```
execlp(progname, arg_0, arg_1, arg_2, ..., (char *)0)
execvp(progname, argv)
```

For the purposes of our example, we'll use execlp(). The other form is most useful for those cases where you want to build an argument list on the fly. Since we know in advance what the arguments to ed will be, we needn't go through the hassle of plugging them into an argv array.

One last point worth mentioning before moving on. You'll notice that arguments are numbered from zero. As with the earlier shell examples, argument zero is reserved for the name of the program. This is usually the same as the filename (with any path specification stripped off), but you can use any string you like. That string will show up in ps listings as the name of the program.

That's enough preparation. On to the code:

```
PROGNAME=       edfront
OBJS=           edfront.o

/* edfront.c: Chapter 4 pipes example */
/* tabs in this program are four spaces apart */

/* Syntax: edfront filename */

#include <stdio.h>
#include <fcntl.h>
#include <signal.h>

int child_exited = 0;   /* global flags */
int parent_terminate = 0;

child_exit()    /* called when child process exits */
{
    printf("\n\nChild process exited.\n");
    child_exited = 1;   /* set flag so loop in main() exits */
}

terminator()    /* parent received termination signal */
{
    printf("Parent signalled to terminate\n");
    parent_terminate = 1;
}

main(argc, argv)
int     argc;
char    **argv;
{
    int     parent2child[2], child2parent[2];   /* pair of pipes */
    char    request[80], reply[255];    /* outgoing & incoming */
    int     pid;    /* process ID for child */
    int     flags;  /* file flags */
    int     i;      /* in case we need it */
    char    *translate(), *command;

    if (argc < 2) {     /* bad arg count */
        fprintf(stderr, "usage: %s filename\n", argv[0]);
        exit(1);
    }

    /* open pipes */
    if ((pipe(parent2child) < 0) || (pipe(child2parent) < 0)) {
```

```
    /* one or both wouldn't open */
    perror("Pipe open failed:");
    exit(1);
}

/* make sure parent is notified when child exits */
signal(SIGCLD, child_exit);
/* set up local signal handler so we can clean up when asked
    to leave */
signal(SIGHUP, terminator);
signal(SIGINT, terminator);
signal(SIGQUIT, terminator);
signal(SIGTERM, terminator);

/* spawn new process */
pid = fork();
if (pid < 0) {  /* error */
    perror("Pipe open failed:");
    exit(1);
}

if (pid == 0) { /* child */
    /* map pipes as STDIO channels */
    close(0);
    close(1);    /* close current STDIN and STDOUT */
    dup(parent2child[0]);    /* new STDIN */
    dup(child2parent[1]);    /* new STDOUT */
    close(parent2child[0]); /* no need to waste */
    close(child2parent[1]); /*   file handles */
    execlp("ed", "ed", argv[1], (char *)0); /* run ed */

    /* a successful exec never returns */
    perror("execlp failed");
    exit(1);
} else {     /* parent */
    fcntl(child2parent[0], F_GETFL, &flags);
    flags |= O_NDELAY;  /* so read() won't block */
    fcntl(child2parent[0], F_SETFL, flags);
    while(1) {
        /* check to see if parent has been asked to quit */
        if (parent_terminate != 0) {
            kill(pid, SIGTERM);     /* terminate child */
            child_exited = 1;   /* set flag for cleanup */
        }
        /* if flag is set, parent was signalled that child
            terminated--clean up and quit */
        if (child_exited != 0) {
            close(parent2child[0]);
```

```
                    close(parent2child[1]);
                    close(child2parent[0]);
                    close(child2parent[1]);
                    exit(0);
            }
            printf("edit: ");    /* put up prompt and get input */
            gets(request);        /*    from keyboard */

            /* make an extra check of flags so we don't
                get garbage output on the way out */
            if ((parent_terminate != 0) || (child_exited != 0))
                continue;

            /* call translator, then copy result back so newline
                can be added */
            command = translate(request);
            strcpy(request, command);
            strcat(request, "\n");

            /* send request to ed */
            write(parent2child[1], request, strlen(request));
            sleep(1);    /* let ed think about it */

            /* loop on input--call read() until it returns 0 (empty
                pipe) */
            while((i = read(child2parent[0], reply, 254)) != 0) {
                reply[i] = 0;    /* null-terminate (read() doesn't) */
                printf("%*s", i, reply);
                reply[0] = 0;    /* clear for next pass */
            }
        }
    }
}

/* simple translation of user command to "ed" command */
char *translate(cmd)
char    *cmd;
{
    static struct {        /* create translation table */
        char *mycmd, *edcmd;
    } cmdtable[] = {
        "quit",        "q",
        "exit",        "q",
        "save",        "w",
        "list",        "1,$p",
        "top",         "1",
        "bottom",      "$",
        "up",          "-",
```

```
        "down",      "+",
        "page",      ".,.+20p",
        (char *)0,  (char *)0,
    };

    int     i;

    for (i = 0; ; i++) {      /* find match in table */
        if (cmdtable[i].mycmd == (char *)0)
            return(cmd);      /* no match--give original arg back */
        if (strcmp(cmd, cmdtable[i].mycmd) == 0)
            return(cmdtable[i].edcmd);
    }
}
```

Depending on how much UNIX programming you've done, there should be more unfamiliar things in the preceding example than just the code related to pipes.

Signals   This example is the first code we have created that responds to *signals*. A signal is a sort of high-priority interrupt that is directed at a specific process. Whenever you use ^C, or DEL, or whatever your interrupt key is set to, to interrupt an executing program, you are really sending it a signal. There are several types of signals, each one tagged with a different integer identifier. These integers are mapped to symbols in the header file signal.h.

What happens when a signal is sent to a process depends on the signal, and whether that process has a *signal handler*. All signals have default actions. Most terminate, or kill, the program. Others dump core first, creating a file image of the program's data memory at the time the signal was received. Using the signal function, you can override the default action for a signal, and arrange to have a function called whenever the signal is received. In the example, we define two signal handlers, child_exit() and terminator(). In main(), calls to signal() set these functions up as signal handlers. child_exit() is called in response to a SIGCLD signal, which indicates that a child process has exited. This way, if something happens to terminate ed, we can have the parent exit instead of writing to a pipe that will never be read. This works so well that edit commands are never checked for the instance of quit; when a "quit" command causes ed to terminate, the parent process is notified (through SIGCLD), and it exits.

When a signal handler is defined, a signal causes the execution of the main program code to stop. The handler runs to completion, and then the main program resumes at the next statement. Because execution is diverted, it's a good idea not to make your handler do too much. In the example, both handlers display strings to show they have been called, but even this is not good practice. In general, a handler should set a flag and return, so that the user's perception of program flow is disrupted as little as possible. Similarly, your code should handle signals immediately. Although you have the power to do so, or even to ignore a signal completely, the receipt of a signal may be the last chance your application has to close its files and exit cleanly before a power failure or a shutdown.

There is no way to predict *where* in your program a signal might take place. Indeed, they can occur almost anywhere, but you won't, for instance, get a SIGCLD signal before you've spawned any child processes. A blocking call, such as the gets() in the example will be interrupted when the signal arrives. You cannot ask an I/O request to pick up where it left off, but that's of little concern. All the signals the example is built to handle result in termination. Because the gets() can be interrupted, and blocking calls have a much higher likelihood of being interrupted than other code, the signal flags are checked immediately after the call. Without this check, the program will try to process one more command, the possibly incomplete string brought in by the interrupted gets(), and probably display some garbage as a result.

When you are expecting signals, check for them frequently. The only other alternative is to have the signal handlers clean up and exit directly, but that approach has two problems. First, there is no clear exit path in the code. Simply by reading main() through, every exit point can be identified. Second, since a signal handler cannot be called with arguments, you would have to load up on global variables so the handler would know which files to close and such. Messy.

This is also the first example that has performed file I/O, even though the files in this case are pipes. Being familiar with C, the business of read() and write() should not be foreign to you; most non-UNIX C compilers have standardized on the UNIX syntax and behavior for these, and other, I/O calls. You may not have encountered the O_NDELAY flag, as set in the fcntl() call in main(). The "N" in NDELAY means "No", and no delay means no blocking. Ordinarily, a read from a pipe's file handle will block if there is no data in the pipe. In the case of our example, some ed commands like "substitute" create no output; the pipe read() following the passing of the command to ed would block forever. By setting the O_NDELAY flag on the parent's read pipe, the read() call simply returns a zero when there is no data in the pipe. A one-second sleep() prior to the pipe read() is a primitive attempt to ensure that ed has had sufficient time to say everything it wanted to. On a slow or heavily-loaded system, this might not be enough, and this approach is not recommended for use in commercial code. The right approach would involve either a tighter coupling of the front-end with ed, sifting through the output looking for clues to the end of each block of it, or the use of background processing to collect input from the keyboard while blocking reads were done on the incoming pipe. Do a little head-scratching over these options, and maybe come up with some of your own. Then make some changes.

The next section deals with a more complex and sophisticated method of inter-process communications.

The Best There Is: Shared Memory

When you think of linking two processes together, there is nothing more desirable than shared memory. Its use requires careful preparation and clean-up, but it is such an easy and elegant answer to inter-process communications that it spoils you for anything less.

In moving to shared memory, we will purposely skip over two other forms of UNIX inter-process communications, semaphores and messages. Shared memory may render semaphores and messages obsolete. There may be cases when shared memory is not the best solution, but such encounters are rare to non-existent. Of the methods available, shared memory is the fastest by virtue of its reduced overhead.

The term "shared memory" brings to mind the simplicity of the "common area" featured in some other environments. The basic concept is the same: Allocate a block of memory that can be accessed by a number of users and processes. Access is not a matter of read()s and write()s; rather it is the manipulation of pointer variables. UNIX shared memory is accessed much like regular memory, except that it is not part of the general pool managed by functions like malloc().

The versatility of shared memory lays the foundation for the discussion of a class of application that forms the basis of this book, the client/server application. You are probably familiar with the term, but the following definition maps directly to the material to come: A client/server application is one that is split into (at least) two parts, a provider of a service, and a consumer of that service. Many modern UNIX database managers (like the one included with SCO Open Desktop) are client/server applications. When a client needs data from the database or wishes to make a change, it does not access the database directly. Instead, it uses some kind of command language or other shorthand to formulate a request message, and uses some method to send that message to the server.

The server, in turn, processes the request and performs some action *asynchronously*, sometimes returning a response message of its own. The X Window system is an excellent example of this concept, and offers some of the best evidence available that it *works*.

What are the advantages of client/server applications? The most obvious one is among the least important, asynchronicity. A database client could, for example, take in a request from the user, ship that request to the server, and ask for another request before the server was finished processing the preceding one. People aren't accustomed to working that way; most of us expect to see a dialogue with a computer carried out in a "question, answer, question, answer" format.

Perhaps the most compelling reason to use client/server techniques is *central control*. A single server queueing requests from multiple clients allows the server to control every aspect of access to the data. A server might have global read and write privileges to all files in the database, but each client would have to qualify for the right to access a particular file. The single-server approach also ensures proper—by the developer's definition, at least—handling of concurrency and locking problems. If all requests go through a single server, the chances of overlapping modifications to a file are reduced to zero.

What does it take to cash in on this wondrous capability? As you were warned, there is some setup and takedown involved, but before slamming into an example, let's get some basics down.

You cannot use shared memory by just declaring an array of type "shared char". Would that it were that simple. Instead, a request must be made of the operating system though the shmget function. A server sets aside a block of shared memory by calling shmget() with certain flags set, like so:

```
shmid = shmget(key, size, IPC_CREAT);
```

Each segment of shared memory has a *key* associated with it. Once the server allocates a segment with a particular key, clients can access that same segment by providing a matching key, and by passing access permission tests. A successful call to shmget() returns a segment ID, a cousin to the integer file handle. The process must use this segment ID in all future calls relating to that memory segment.

A server that spawns all its own child processes, and that can therefore pass the value of segment ID to its children, doesn't need to worry about the value of the key. For these cases, the key argument can be replaced with the constant IPC_PRIVATE, that more or less indicates that the caller does not need a key.

Keys are called for in the case of the independently-launched client process, one that is *not* a child of the server. Clients need a way to know which segment to attach to, and a "widely-known" key is one way to handle this. You simply settle on a certain key value, and use that same key in your server and all its clients.

After calling shmget(), you are still not ready to access the shared memory segment you have created. All that's left is to *attach* it. Attaching a segment is the step that makes it look like regular memory. Well, almost. As noted, it doesn't become part of the central pool. The only way to get to a shared memory segment is through a base pointer. Of course, among the great strengths of C is its handling of data pointers, so this is hardly a restriction.

Attaching a shared memory segment is easy:

```
char_ptr = shmat(shmid, NULL, 0);
```

The last two arguments, with values other than those shown, let you pick the address to which the segment will be mapped. There are significant limitations to the range of addresses that may be used; specifying the argument list as above lets the system choose for you. If you are successful, shmat() returns what you have been waiting for, a pointer to the first character of the shared memory block. From here, it can be read and modified as though it were ordinary memory.

A client process needs to know the segment ID, but knowing the key, it can obtain the ID with shmget(). A call to that function without the IPC_CREAT flag as the third argument will return the segment ID associated with the passed key, if any. The advantage is that, while the key can be a preset value known in advance, the segment ID can, and probably will, change from one invocation to another.

Shared memory has a set of access permissions based on the user and group IDs associated with the calling process. Each segment is stamped with the user ID (UID) of the user associated with the process that allocated the segment. Subsequent shmget() calls do not change the segment's ownership. A nine-bit flag holds the permission bits that control the read and write access for users matching the segment owner's UID, group ID (GID), or neither ("other").

Setting the initial access permissions for a segment is as simple as passing a properly-coded bit pattern as the third argument to shmget(). The server process, instead of passing IPC_CREAT, passes this *plus* the ORed-together values reflecting the desired initial permissions:

Table 4-1: Shared Memory Access Rights

Access Rights		Octal Flag Value
User:	Read	0400
	Write	0200
Group:	Read	0040
	Write	0020
Other:	Read	0004
	Write	0002

A shmget() call that sets initial access permissions looks something like this:

```
shmid = shmget(key, size, IPC_CREAT | 0644);
```

This is a common arrangement: Read/write access to users matching the owner's ID, and read-only to members of the group and all others. Of course, being the whiz at octal math that you are, you were way ahead of me on that one.

To close this chapter, we will construct a short example of a client/server application that uses shared memory. This case will be a simple one, but it will bring into play most of the facets of managing shared memory. Among the most important is that shared memory is *not* deallocated when all the processes using it are terminated. It hangs around until the system is reset, or until it is explicitly destroyed. Only a super-user, or a process with a UID matching that of the segment's creator, may remove an allocated segment. The example uses what we have already learned about signals to try to keep the program from exiting unexpectedly. If these safeguards fail, you will have to resort to the ipcs and ipcrm commands to list and remove the shared memory segments. See the *Reference Manual* pages on these commands if it comes to that.

The example programs are only skeletons, but they do run as is. The server and client are separate executables; the server is run once, and it can tell if you try to run it again. It places itself in the background, and waits for a client to connect and pass a request. The client program can be run and exited as many times as you like; the server waits quietly for the next connection. To terminate the server, use ps to get its process ID, and the kill command to send a signal to it. The server will acknowledge the receipt of the signal, and terminate. The server will *not* terminate itself when you log out. Be sure you kill the process before leaving. Of course, if you should leave one running, there is no harm done; you can kill it anytime.

Here is the example. There are three files: shmexam.h, shmserv.c, and shmcli.c. They are presented in that order, and must be separate files:

```
/* shmexam.h: Header for shared-memory example for chapter 4 */
/* tabs in this example are four spaces apart */

#include <stdio.h>
#include <sys/types.h>
#include <sys/ipc.h>
#include <sys/shm.h>
#include <signal.h>

/* client request codes */
#define CONNECT_REQUEST 1
#define SEARCH_REQUEST 2
#define MODIFY_REQUEST 3
#define DELETE_REQUEST 4
#define NEXT_REQUEST 5
#define PREV_REQUEST 6
#define SEEK_REQUEST 7
#define DISCONNECT_REQUEST 8

/* server response codes */
#define REQUEST_REFUSED_RESPONSE 1
#define REQUEST_ACCEPTED_RESPONSE 2
#define NO_MATCH_RESPONSE 3

/* common shared memory block key (value is meaningless) */
#define KEY_VALUE 13760

/* define some basic structures, shared by both the server and client
    modules */
typedef struct {            /* general purpose request block */
    int     pid, request, reply;
    char    data[205];
} shm_block;
```

Modify the makefile boilerplate with these settings for shmserve:

```
PROGNAME=       shmserve
CFLAGS=         -I .
OBJS=           shmserve.o
```

```
/* shmserv.c: Shared-memory server example for chapter four */
```

```
/* tabs in this program are four spaces apart */

#include <shmexam.h>

/* unavoidable globals */
int     terminate_request = 0;

terminator()    /* set flag to shut server down on signal */
{
    fprintf(stderr, "shmserv: Terminate request received\n");
    terminate_request = 1;
}

main(argc, argv)
int     argc;
char    **argv;
{
    int     pid;

    if (argc != 2) {    /* db file argument required */
        fprintf(stderr, "usage: %s dbfile\n", argv[0]);
        exit(1);
    }
    if (access(argv[1], 4)) {   /* check for read perm on file */
        perror("Can't access database");
        exit(1);
    }

    /* fork and detach--parent doesn't need to wait */
    if ((pid = fork()) < 0) {
        perror("fork failed");
        exit(1);
    }
    if (pid == 0) {     /* child--the work gets done here */
        setpgrp();          /* so we don't get signals from parent */
        run_server(argv[1]);    /* start server */
        exit(0);
    }
    /* no parent process code--parent exits, child is adopted by
        process 1 (init) */
}

run_server(dbfname)
char    *dbfname;
{
    int     req_block_id;   /* shm seg ID */
    char    str1[255], str2[255];
    void    *shmptr;
```

```
shm_block   *blockptr;  /* pointers to shm areas */

/* initialize the shared memory */
req_block_id = shmget(KEY_VALUE, 256, IPC_CREAT | IPC_EXCL |
    0600);  /* limit access to calling user */
if (req_block_id < 0) {
    /* this is why we kept our stderr link */
    perror("Can't create shared memory segment");
    exit(1);
}
shmptr = shmat(req_block_id, NULL, 0);  /* attach shared mem */
if ((int)shmptr == -1) {    /* this is strange, */
    perror("Can't attach shared memory segment");
    exit(1);               /* but only way to check error */
}

/* wire in signal handler */
signal(SIGHUP, terminator);
signal(SIGINT, terminator);
signal(SIGQUIT, terminator);
signal(SIGTERM, terminator);

/* set up pointer, initialize data in the shared segment */
blockptr = (shm_block *)shmptr;
blockptr->pid = 0;
blockptr->request = 0;
blockptr->reply = 0;

/* request loop */
while (1) {
    if (terminate_request != 0) {   /* got a signal */
        /* a real server should notify its active clients, if
            possible, before exiting */
        shmdt(req_block_id);    /* detach the segment */
        shmctl(req_block_id, IPC_RMID, NULL);   /* remove it */
        exit(0);
    }

    /* see if a request came in */
    if ((blockptr->request != 0) &&
        (blockptr->reply == 0)) {   /* got a live one */
        /* stubs to handle requests */
        switch (blockptr->request) {
            case CONNECT_REQUEST:
                blockptr->reply = REQUEST_ACCEPTED_RESPONSE;
                strcpy(blockptr->data, "Connect OK");
                break;
```

```
            case SEARCH_REQUEST:
                blockptr->reply = REQUEST_ACCEPTED_RESPONSE;
                strcpy(blockptr->data, "Search request");
                break;

            case MODIFY_REQUEST:
                blockptr->reply = REQUEST_ACCEPTED_RESPONSE;
                strcpy(blockptr->data, "Modify request");
                break;

            case DELETE_REQUEST:
                blockptr->reply = REQUEST_ACCEPTED_RESPONSE;
                strcpy(blockptr->data, "Delete request");
                break;

            case NEXT_REQUEST:
                blockptr->reply = REQUEST_ACCEPTED_RESPONSE;
                strcpy(blockptr->data, "Next request");
                break;

            case PREV_REQUEST:
                blockptr->reply = REQUEST_ACCEPTED_RESPONSE;
                strcpy(blockptr->data, "Prev request");
                break;

            case SEEK_REQUEST:
                blockptr->reply = REQUEST_ACCEPTED_RESPONSE;
                strcpy(blockptr->data, "Seek request");
                break;

            case DISCONNECT_REQUEST:
                blockptr->reply = REQUEST_ACCEPTED_RESPONSE;
                strcpy(blockptr->data, "Disconnect request");
                break;

            default:
                blockptr->reply = NO_MATCH_RESPONSE;
                strcpy(blockptr->data, "Unknown comand");
            }
        }
        sleep(5);    /* we're in no hurry */
    }
}
```

Modify the makefile boilerplate with these settings for shmcli:

```
PROGNAME=    shmcli
CFLAGS=      -I .
OBJS=        shmcli.o
```

```
/* shmcli.c: Skeleton shared-memory client for chapter 4 */
/* tabs in this example are four spaces apart */

#include <shmexam.h>

main()
{
    int      shmid, request, trycount;
    void     *shmptr;
    shm_block    *blockptr;

    shmid = shmget(KEY_VALUE, 256, 0);  /* must already exist */
    if (shmid < 0) {
        perror("Can't attach to server");
        exit(1);
    }
    shmptr = shmat(shmid, NULL, 0);     /* attach segment */
    if ((int)shmptr == -1) {
        perror("Can't attach shared memory");
        exit(1);
    }
    blockptr = (shm_block *)shmptr;
    while (1) {
        request = 0;
        printf("Request # (0 to quit): ");
        scanf("%d", &request);          /* get request # from user */
        if (request == 0) {     /* exit requested */
            shmdt(shmid);
            exit(0);
        }
        blockptr->request = request;    /* place request */
        blockptr->reply = 0;            /* clear reply */
        /* check for response */
        for (trycount = 0; trycount < 10; trycount++) {
            if (blockptr->reply != 0) { /* reply waiting */
                printf("Server reply (%d): %s\n", blockptr->reply,
                    blockptr->data);
                /* clear after processing so server won't try to
                    respond again */
                blockptr->request = blockptr->reply = 0;
                trycount = 12;  /* flag success */
                continue;
            }
            sleep(1);
        }
        if (trycount != 13)     /* timed out waiting for server */
```

```
        printf("Server didn't respond\n");
    }
}
```

While these programs are a fair example of how to make a connection and pass data through shared memory, the way they use that connection leaves a lot to be desired. What remains to be done has nothing to do with shared memory per se, so you need some background so that you can come up with your own solutions.

A UNIX server program that uses shared memory is not limited to serving a single client. The example, however, falls apart once a second client is brought on-line. Why? The request block has room for only one request at a time, and has no mechanism for arbitrating requests from multiple clients. The client and server programs both lack code that ensures that client requests do not overlap.

How can a server make sure this overlap doesn't take place? You could use messages or semaphores to control access to the shared memory segment. Instead, let's consider a solution that sticks with shared memory. You'll note that the request block structure has room for a process ID. This could be the basis of a form of arbitration. A client desiring a connection places its PID in the shared memory segment, along with its request. Another client can examine this integer before placing a connect request. If blockptr->pid is non-zero, the client will know the server is busy, and it will wait until this integer comes up zero, that is, when it is reset by the server after filling the active client's request.

It is still possible for two or more clients to read the PID as zero at roughly the same time, and all rush to put in their requests. These requests would over-write each other; only the last would be heard. One solution is to let it happen. The clients need only check the PID value after placing the request to make sure they really got the connection they expected. If the PID in the shared memory segment doesn't match the client's PID, obtained through the getpid system call, it will know that another client got in first. The jilted client will then return to its wait/request loop.

For this scheme to work, the server would operate in a *connectionless* mode. Sharing a single memory segment between a server and multiple clients requires that the server dispense with requests as rapidly as possible; there is no way to know how many clients are waiting for the server to reset the PID and give them a chance to put in a request. A connectionless link to a server means that each request is a distinct transaction. A client with several requests must place each one individually, waiting for the server to become available again before placing the next request. In essence, the client is making a short connection to the server only long enough to get its request handled.

The shmexam.h file includes the constants needed to handle another style of communication, the opposite of connectionless mode. Here, the shared request block is not to be used for database requests at all. Instead, it is reserved for clients requesting sustained connections to the server. The server responds with a REQUEST_ACCEPTED or REQUEST_REFUSED. An accepted connection request draws a response from the server that includes the segment ID of a new shared memory segment, allocated by the server exclusively for the requesting client. The client then has its own data channel to the server. Requests placed there cannot be overwritten by other clients. The server needs to make a round-robin polling of each connected client's request block, responding and moving on. When finished, the client places a DISCONNECT_REQUEST in its private request block. The server shuts down the private channel, deallocating the shared memory.

A connection-based client/server application with private data channels is the easiest to use. There is no worry about concurrency control, or that another client may slide in under the doorway when the server isn't looking.

All this is fine for processes running on a single machine, but there is often a need to apply similar principles to processes running on *different* machines. That is where networking comes in, and that's the subject of the next chapter.

The best exercise of what you've learned in this chapter might be to finish the client/server program, making it perform some real disk I/O, and patching it to handle multiple client connections. Once you've done this, tie the database client code to the card file example in Chapter 3. You'll note that the size of the data block is more or less right for the amount of data in the card. Stick with fixed-length record files for now.

Chapter 5

Network Inter-Process Communications

The material in this chapter requires that TCP/IP services be available and operating on at least one system. Although the examples will best illustrate network IPC when connecting two separate systems, everything will work just as well when both client and server programs run on the same machine.

This chapter also requires the programming header files and libraries that are needed to tap C programs into TCP/IP networking services. These tools are part of the SCO Open Desktop development set, and are also available for other versions of PC UNIX, including System V, Release 4.

The last chapter's discussions of pipes and shared memory illustrated two methods for passing data between disjoint processes. These methods work very well for connecting clients to servers, but they fall far short of being complete solutions. The main problem is that pipes and shared memory work only when both processes reside on the same system.

One of the most compelling reasons to split an application into client and server modules is to take advantage of pools of greater computing power, resource availability, or some combination of these. In a small network, it makes sense to place the database server on the machine with the fastest, highest-capacity disk drives. Likewise, a demanding calculation might be handled in much less time by a system other than the one on your desk.

Obviously, it *is* possible to connect two processes across a network link, otherwise, this chapter would have no reason to exist. Beyond the mere fact that it can be done lie a number of problems that need to be solved. We'll examine some of those problems, and then use examples to show how to handle them. By chapter's end, you will understand how to use TCP/IP networking services to connect C programs on different machines.

The Networking Dilemma

Making a connection with a pipe is easy; the child simply inherits the connection from its parent. Communication between two processes on the same machine are bolstered by signals, and the channel and its components can be easily managed from a single point of control.

Once a network enters the picture, everything changes. Let's deal with the theoretical case that we wish to connect two processes, client and server. To start with, let's think about some of the other considerations.

- **Client and server processes must be able to run anywhere.** There should be no limitations on the placement of the client and server processes, other than those imposed by the user's network access permissions. Both programs should also be able to run on the *same* system.

- **The client must know how to find the server.** The user can be reasonably expected to provide the name of the system on which the server resides (the *server host*). With that knowledge, the client should be able to locate and connect to the server process.

- **The server process should support multiple clients from different locations.** Users should not have to concern themselves with whether or not a server can handle their connection requests. Requests should be denied only when system resources demand it.

- **Data integrity must be ensured on both sides of the link.** Under no circumstances should inaccurate data be allowed to pass through a network connection. If a reliable link is not guaranteed by the system, the programs themselves must check the data.

- **Data about the condition of the server process and the network connection should be available through the network.** Lots of things can go wrong with a network connection. Users (or administrators, if you wish to restrict access) should be able to query the server process for data about server status, connection attempts, traffic counts and error summaries. Even if the server is not accepting requests, it should respond to queries so that clients will not attempt to connect in vain.

■ **Client and server processes must be prepared to lose their connections at any moment.** When you multiply the number of machines involved in a task, you increase the chances that completion will be interrupted by equipment or software failure. Network programs must be prepared to close their files and exit gracefully if the connection should be lost at any time.

■ **A client program should place an appropriate level of demand on its host system, and defer the rest to the server.** Consider your reasons for splitting your application between client and server. If conserving client system resources is among your objectives, take care not to allow the client to become too large and demanding.

■ **Never assume that the client and server are running on the same type of system.** You may be working exclusively with PC systems now, but in the future, your programs may need to run on a RISC or other type of system.

You can see already that working with network IPC is much more demanding than those methods discussed in Chapter 4. Why is there so much to consider? Think about it: The server can be *anywhere*. Networks exist that bridge systems halfway around the world. The connection must, to the extent possible, monitor and take care of itself. Once intervention is required, the cost can be much more than mere inconvenience.

Building intelligence into your network applications does more than save the user some time and aggravation. You must not assume that users of your software even understand how a network operates. How much do *you* need to understand about TCP/IP to write applications that use it? Luckily, very little, except that it must be running. The assumption throughout this chapter is that either you understand how to start and use TCP/IP, or you have access to someone who does.

Let's look at some of the basic techniques of network IPC.

Network IPC Basics

As you start to dig into network IPC, you'll begin to realize that only a little of what you learned in Chapter 4 applies here. There is no solution as elegant and accessible as shared memory when it comes to connecting disjoint systems.

Briefly stated, a connected-mode session between a client and a server starts with the client requesting a connection to the server. In the case of shared memory, connected-mode sessions are managed entirely by the applications on either end of the connection; there is no protocol built into the shared memory mechanism.

With network connections, a protocol does exist. This protocol imposes a certain structure on network programs, and helps ensure that they will be portable across different kinds of systems. The application-level protocol, as defined by the functions and structures which support TCP/IP, is well-organized and relatively easy to use. That is, once you know the basics.

PC UNIX systems, including Open Desktop and System V, Release 4, provide two ways to set up communications via TCP/IP: AT&T's Transport Layer Interface (TLI), and the Berkeley socket mechanism. Of the two, Berkeley sockets are more widely supported, appearing on both BSD and System V UNIX systems. TLI is less likely to be found on BSD systems. Berkeley sockets are also a bit easier to understand and use. Before you can get started with sockets, you need to know a little about TCP/IP.

Each machine on a network is tagged with a name for convenience, but internally, TCP/IP uses a unique numeric value (host ID) to identify each system. These values are assigned by the system administrator, although some machines with connections to wide-area networks may have host numbers assigned to them by some governing body. Likewise, each service offered by a TCP/IP server has a unique number, or port, associated with it.

From now on, "server" will refer to the server process, and "server host" to the system on which that process runs. Like most client/server relationships, it is the server that decides to make a particular service available. It needs to "advertise" that service somehow. TCP/IP uses a means similar to the shared memory key discussed earlier, a widely-known numeric value that is unique to that service, at least within the bounds of the network. That numeric value is the aforementioned port, and, as with the shared memory key, a client that desires a connection needs to know that port number.

That would be enough if we were sure the client and server were running on the same system, but that is rarely the case with TCP/IP. Therefore, in addition to the port, we need to know the *Internet address* of the host running the server process.

A moment's digression: An Internet address is a four-byte numeric, often expressed in "dotted decimal" notation. For example, "192.1.1.18" is a legal address. Since these addresses are difficult to remember, TCP/IP has a built-in method for translating arbitrary alphanumeric names to Internet addresses. On small networks, this translation is performed by reading the contents of the file /etc/hosts. Larger networks may have TCP/IP server processes called name servers to handle the translation. Either way, all you need to know is either the host name or the Internet address of any machine you wish to connect to. Whether or not your network uses /etc/hosts or a name server, you use the same functions in your network programs to translate names to addresses and vice versa.

As mentioned earlier, TCP/IP provides a protocol for negotiating connections between clients and servers. A client who wishes to connect needs to know not only the host name or address and port number, but also the type of connection. There are two important types of client/server channels in TCP/IP, UDP (User Datagram Protocol) and TCP (Transmission Control Protocol). UDP channels are usually connectionless, and always unreliable. That means that the protocol does not verify the integrity of the data, or even that it arrived at all. The connectionless aspect of UDP channels makes them best suited for one-shot messages (hence the term, "datagram") for which opening and shutting down a connection would be a waste of time.

Because of the unreliable nature of UDP (that's a feature, not a flaw), we won't discuss it here. Nearly all of the concepts and code you will learn in this chapter can be applied to UDP channels as well. But the TCP channel is a connected, reliable one, and that is just what we need for an interactive client/server application.

Once opened, a TCP channel behaves a lot like a pipe. In this case, one file (or, more accurately, socket) handle is used for both reading and writing. Similarly, read() and write() calls can be used to transfer data. The TCP ensures that transmitted data arrives, and that received data is accurate. It automatically retransmits erroneous packets, weeds out duplicates, and makes sure packets are received in the order sent. These are things you probably expect, but they are not part of UDP.

One thing you won't get from TCP is a guaranteed preservation of record boundaries. If you send 2,048 bytes, the receiver might get it all with one read(). Then again, it could require any number of consecutive reads. TCP makes sure you get it all, unless some horrible tragedy befalls the network, but it may take several read() calls to get it. Luckily, read() returns the number of bytes read, and you can loop until you read all the data you expected. Similarly, it can take several write() calls to send a single block of data.

Losing record boundaries makes things only a little more complicated. To use TCP effectively, you need to know how many bytes are expected, so, in addition to TCP, you need to invent a protocol of your own which encapsulates your data in a message block. At the very least, this block should contain a data length value and, of course, the data itself. Once you get used to the idea of using a message block structure instead of simply squirting bytes across a channel, you may begin to think of some other things that might go well in such a block. For this chapter's first example, we will use a general-purpose message block structure, a two-byte opcode (command code), followed by a two-byte data block length, followed by the data block. We will be constructing a pair of support functions which pass this block-encoded data back and forth. The function syntax looks like this:

```
int     socket_handle;
ushort  opcode, block_length;
char    *buffer;

block_length = read_blk(socket_handle, &opcode, buffer);
write_blk(socket_handle, opcode, block_length, buffer);
```

Even though the data buffer is cast as a character pointer, it is not necessarily a null-terminated string. Binary data can be transmitted as well as alphanumeric, but sometimes there is a trick to it.

If you want to send a single byte, or a stream of single bytes, across a socket connection, no problem. The catch comes when you want to send a multi-byte numeric value, like an int. Since the programs you're running might be on different kinds of machines, numeric representations may differ. With a four-byte integer (the int data type for most systems), one system may put the least significant byte first, while another may start with the most significant byte. Fortunately, you don't have to keep this straight. The TCP/IP services provide a number of functions for converting multi-byte numeric values to and from the *network byte order* (see Table 5-1). This network byte order is the same for all implementations of TCP/IP, regardless of the hardware. This ensures that dissimilar systems can exchange multi-byte integer data without worrying about getting the bytes reversed. In addition to protecting the byte order of transmitted data, these functions are used to translate certain values, such as network addresses provided by

TCP/IP library functions. Unless you intend to display them, addresses usually remain in network byte order. Typically, all you do with them is copy them from one structure to another; all of the socket functions expect their multi-byte integers in network byte order.

Table 5-1: Byte-order Functions

Function	Description
htonl(long)	Translate long int from host to network byte order
ntohl(long)	Translate long int from network to host byte order
htons(short)	Translate short int from host to network byte order
ntohs(short)	Translate short int from network to host byte order

Getting Connected: How Tough Can It Be?

It is the nature of client/server-based services for the server to get things going first. In the case of TCP sockets, there is a simple sequence associated with putting a service on the air. Table 5-2 on the next page shows a simplified view of the process. Actually, the code snippets in the figure were taken directly from our first example. You will see that not much more code is required to support a very basic server.

A great deal of flexibility is built into the Berkeley socket mechanism for handing other types of protocols, and even handling networks other than TCP/IP. Very few socket library implementations make use of these extensions to support alternate networks, but these extensions do make things a little more difficult. The socket() call wants to be told that it is working on a TCP/IP network through the AF_INET parameter. When you're dealing with representations of Internet addresses in structures, you often need to provide the length of that address in bytes. The address length might be different if you were using some networking scheme other than TCP/IP. Other seldom-used extensions, such as the capacity for a single host to have multiple network addresses, put a few minor kinks in the road to producing a network application.

There isn't anything inherently difficult about network programming, as long as you're willing to take a few things on faith. You see, even with all the flexibility built into the socket library, there are certain predictable steps that every network application must go through. It is perfectly safe to make use of these network services in your programs without having an intimate understanding of the underlying layers. There is no problem with just copying the example code from this book and using it; every network program you write will necessarily follow the same path up to a point.

Table 5-2:   Steps for Network Programming

Select Port/Listening Address
```
#define PORT (short) 13760
server_sockaddr.sin_port =
htons (PORT) ;
server_sockaddr.sin_addr.s_addr =
htonl (INADDR_ANY) ;
```
Step 1: The server establishes a "widely-known" port number to which clients can connect. It then specifies which Internet addresses may request a connection (in this case, any client may connect).

Open Socket
```
server_socket = socket(AF_INET,
SOCK_STREAM, 0) ;
```
Step 2: An Internet TCP socket is opened. This required step only prepares the necessary resources.

Bind Socket to Port/Address
```
bind(server_socket, &server_sockaddr,
sizeof(server_sockaddr)) ;
```
Step 3: The socket is identified with the port number and acceptable client addresses prepared in Step 1.

Create Queue for Incoming Connections
```
listen(server_socket, 5) ;
```
Step 4: A queue for backlogged client connect requests is established.

Wait for Connection
```
client_socket = accept(server_socket,
&client_sockaddr, &addr_len) ;
```
Step 5: This calls blocks until a client requests a connection to this server's port. This call is repeated until the server quits. The client_socket handle is a new socket created by the accept call, allowing the server to continue listening to the original socket for new connection requests.

The first thing you will do if you are tackling this alone is to create a set of encapsulating functions to take the drudgery out of basic tasks like connecting to a server, and exchanging length-encoded data. Lucky for you, what follows is just such a library. Get this code into your system as tcpcalls.c. This code will not compile or execute on its own—it is a support library for the first sample client and server programs we will be creating shortly. The library includes two routines, create_service() and connect_to_server, that can be used in all sorts of

network applications. First, here's tcpcalls.c. It is followed by two programs, a
very simple client and a server.

```
/* tcpcalls.c: shared TCP/IP calls; used in examples in chapter 5 */
/* tabs in this file are four spaces apart */

#include <sys/types.h>
#include <sys/socket.h>
#include <netinet/in.h>
#include <netdb.h>
#include <stdio.h>


/* create a new TCP service, return socket handle for listening port */
int create_service(port)
ushort  port;
{
    struct sockaddr_in  server_sockaddr;
    int                 server_socket;

    bzero(&server_sockaddr, sizeof(server_sockaddr));
    /* convert port number to network byte order */
    server_sockaddr.sin_port = htons(port);
    server_sockaddr.sin_family = AF_INET;   /* always */
    /* allow connections from all clients */
    server_sockaddr.sin_addr.s_addr = htonl(INADDR_ANY);
    /* create TCP socket */
    server_socket = socket(AF_INET, SOCK_STREAM, 0);
    if (server_socket < 0) {    /* socket call failed */
        perror("socket");
        return(-1);
    }
    /* bind socket to port and client address range */
    if (bind(server_socket, &server_sockaddr,
        sizeof(server_sockaddr)) < 0) {
        perror("bind");
        return(-1);
    }
    /* set up a queue for up to 5 connection requests */
    listen(server_socket, 5);
    /* kick back with socket handle for listening */
    return(server_socket);
}

/* open a connection to a server socket */
/* "name" can be either a host name or a character string representing
    an Internet address (like "192.1.1.8"). If "name" is either NULL
```

```
      or an empty string, a connection to the current host is
      attempted. */
int connect_to_server(name, port)
char    *name;
ushort  port;
{
      struct sockaddr_in   server_sockaddr;
      struct hostent       *server_hostent;
      int                  toserver_socket, i;
      char                 str[255];
      ushort               opcode;
      unsigned long        hostaddr;
      char                 *server_name[255];

      if ((name == NULL) || (*name == 0)) {
          /* no host name provided */
          strcpy(server_name, "localhost");   /* use this machine */
      } else strcpy(server_name, name);   /* use hostname provided */

      /* null out server address structure */
      bzero(&server_sockaddr, sizeof(server_sockaddr));

      /* translate host name given on command line to Internet address */
      /* allow Internet address as well */
      hostaddr = inet_addr(server_name);  /* Is it an address? */
      if ((long)hostaddr != (long)-1) {   /* we've got an address */
          bcopy(&hostaddr, &server_sockaddr.sin_addr,
              sizeof(hostaddr));  /* copy address to sockaddr struct */
      } else {    /* must be a host name */

          /* ask host database/name server for host entry */
          server_hostent = gethostbyname(server_name);
          if (server_hostent == NULL) {
              fprintf(stderr, "Can't locate host \"%s\"\n", server_name);
              return(-1);
          }
          /* copy address from host entry to socket struct */
          bcopy(server_hostent->h_addr,
              &server_sockaddr.sin_addr,
              server_hostent->h_length);
      }

#ifndef QUIET
      /* let the developer know the address translation worked */
      printf("trying to connect to %s\n",
          inet_ntoa(server_sockaddr.sin_addr));
#endif
      server_sockaddr.sin_family = AF_INET;   /* always */
```

```
    server_sockaddr.sin_port = htons(port);

    /* create a raw socket */
    if ((toserver_socket = socket(AF_INET, SOCK_STREAM, 0)) < 0) {
        perror("socket()");
        return(-1);
    }

    /* use that socket to request a connection to a server */
    /* (server must be running for this call to succeed--it won't
        wait for a server to come on-line) */
    if (connect(toserver_socket, &server_sockaddr,
        sizeof(server_sockaddr)) < 0) {
        perror("connect()");
        return(-1);
    }
    /* connection is made. The returned handle can now be used with
        ordinary I/O calls to transfer data. */
    return(toserver_socket);
}

/* read 2-byte integer from socket, convert to host byte order */
int read_short(sock, num)
int     sock;
ushort  *num;
{
    char    tmp[2];
    int     result;

    *num = (short)0;
    /* try to grab the 2 bytes in one read. There's a slim
        chance they'll be split */
    result = read(sock, tmp, 2);
    if (result <= 0) {   /* trouble--either error or EOF */
        if (result < 0) perror("read_short");
        return(result);
    }
    if (result == 1) {   /* one byte was read--get the rest */
        result = read(sock, tmp + 1, 1);
        if (result <= 0) {
            if (result < 0) perror("read_short");
            return(result);
        }
    }

    /* assume we now have two bytes in tmp--convert them */
    *num = ntohs(*(ushort *)tmp);
    return(result);
```

```
}


/* write 2-byte integer to socket in network byte order */
int write_short(sock, num)
int     sock;
ushort  num;
{
    char    tmp[2];
    int     result;

    *(short *)tmp = htons(num);
    /* attempt the write in one swat. Again, could be split for some
        reason */
    result = write(sock, tmp, 2);
    if (result <= 0) {  /* trouble--either error or EOF */
        if (result < 0) perror("write_short");
        return(result);
        }
    if (result == 1) {  /* write the second byte */
        result = write(sock, tmp + 1, 1);
        if (result <= 0) {
            if (result < 0) perror("write_short");
            return(result);
            }
        }
    return(result);
}

/* read length-encoded message from a socket;
    first two bytes are opcode and block length, followed by data */
int read_blk(sock, opcode, str)
int     sock;
ushort  *opcode;
char    *str;
{
    char    *ptr = str; /* set to beginning of string */
    int     result;
    ushort  block_len, b;

    /* try to grab 2-byte opcode and block length */
    if ((result = read_short(sock, opcode)) <= 0)
        return(result);     /* read failed */
    if ((result = read_short(sock, &block_len)) <= 0)
        return(result);
    b = block_len;  /* hold onto this for later */

    /* loop on read until entire block is read in */
```

```
        while (block_len > 0) {
            result = read(sock, ptr, block_len);
            if (result <= 0) {
                if (result < 0) perror("socket read");
                return(result);
                }
            block_len -= result;
            ptr += result;
            }
        return(b);  /* so caller knows length of block */
}

/* write length-encoded block to socket */
int write_blk(sock, opcode, block_len, str)
int     sock, block_len;
ushort  opcode;
char    *str;
{
    char    *ptr = str;
    int     result;

    /* write opcode and block length */
    if ((result = write_short(sock, opcode)) <= 0)
        return(result);
    if ((result = write_short(sock, block_len)) <= 0)
        return(result);

    /* loop until entire block is written */
    while (block_len > 0) {
        result = write(sock, ptr, block_len);
        if (result <= 0) {
            if (result < 0) perror("socket write");
            return(result);
            }
        block_len -= result;
        ptr += result;
        }
    return(1);
}
```

Now for the server module. Like the client which follows it, this *is* an executable program. Here are the parameters for tcpserv's makefile:

```
PROGNAME=       tcpserv
OBJS=           tcpserv.o tcpcalls.o
LIBS=           -lsocket
```

NOTE: *The name of the socket library may vary depending on your operating system; the above LIBS setting will work for SCO UNIX/Open Desktop systems. Interactive UNIX (System V, release 3.2) users should substitute -linet. If neither of these settings work on your system, consult your Network Programmer's Guide.*

```c
/* tcpserv.c: TCP server process example for chapter 5 */
/* tabs in this example are four spaces apart */

#include <sys/types.h>
#include <sys/socket.h>
#include <netinet/in.h>
#include <netdb.h>
#include <stdio.h>

#define PORT (short)13760

main(argc, argv)
int     argc;
char    **argv;
{
    struct sockaddr_in  server_sockaddr, client_sockaddr;
    int                 server_socket, client_socket, addr_len;
    int                 pid, i;
    char                str[255];
    ushort              opcode;

    /* create new socket and initialize TCP service on selected port */
    server_socket = create_service(PORT);
    if (server_socket < 0) {
        fprintf(stderr, "Can't create service\n");
        exit(1);
    }

    addr_len = sizeof(client_sockaddr);
    /* loop looking for client connection requests */
    while (1) {
        /* the following call blocks until a client wants to connect */
        client_socket = accept(server_socket, &client_sockaddr,
            &addr_len);

        /* announce the connection */
        printf("connection request from %s\n",
            inet_ntoa(client_sockaddr.sin_addr.s_addr));
```

```
    /* we now have two sockets: server_socket, which is bound to a
        well-known port for listening, and client_socket, which is
        attached to our recently-connected client.

        We now fork so that a child process can handle the client's
        processing, and the parent can return to listening on the
        well-known port for other client requests */
    pid = fork();
    if (pid < 0) {  /* fork failed */
        perror("fork");
        exit(1);
        }

    /* child--do the work for the client */
    if (pid == 0) {
        close(server_socket);   /* we don't need this socket */

        /* for this simple server, we just bring in short integers.
            Unless it's our reserved opcode, we just display it. */
        while (read_short(client_socket, &opcode) > 0) {
            printf("Message received: %d\n", opcode);
            if (opcode == 888) {     /* block follows */
                read_blk(client_socket, &opcode, str);
                printf("Opcode 888 block: Opcode=%d, str='%s'\n",
                    opcode, str);
                write_short(client_socket, 7171);
                }
            }
        printf("Connection closed.\n");
        shutdown(client_socket, 2);
        close(client_socket);
        exit(0);
        }
    close(client_socket);
    }
}
```

Here's the client (modify the makefile boilerplate with these settings for tcpcl):

```
PROGNAME=       tcpcli
OBJS=           tcpcli.o tcpcalls.o
LIBS=           -lsocket


/* tcpcli.c: TCP client process example for chapter 5 */
/* tabs in this example are four spaces apart */

#include <sys/types.h>
```

```c
#include <sys/socket.h>
#include <netinet/in.h>
#include <netdb.h>
#include <stdio.h>

#define PORT 13760

main(argc, argv)
int     argc;
char    **argv;
{
    int     toserver_socket, i;
    ushort  opcode;
    char    str[80];

    /* try to connect to a server, either by the name/address on the
        command line, or to the default (the current host) */
    toserver_socket =
        connect_to_server(argc > 1 ? argv[1] : "\0", PORT);
    if (toserver_socket < 0)
        exit(1);

    /* ship some data to test our connection */
    printf("Press Return: ");
    gets(str);
    for (i = 0; i < 5; i++) {
        opcode = 256 * i * 10;
        printf("Sending: %d\n", opcode);
        write_short(toserver_socket, opcode);
    }
    printf("Sending block 1\n");
    write_short(toserver_socket, 888);  /* code for block */
    strcpy(str, "Now is the time\nfor all good persons\n");
    write_blk(toserver_socket, 888, strlen(str) + 1, str);
    printf("Sending block 2\n");
    write_short(toserver_socket, 888);  /* code for block */
    strcpy(str, "to come to the aid\nof network programming\n");
    write_blk(toserver_socket, 888, strlen(str) + 1, str);

    /* grab one short integer from the server */
    read_short(toserver_socket, &opcode);
    printf("Received: %d\n", opcode);
    printf("Press Return: ");
    gets(str);

    /* close up and go. Server should notice the loss of the
        connection. */
```

```
    shutdown(toserver_socket, 2);
    close(toserver_socket);
}
```

You can see how simple the client and server programs become once the support functions are defined. That is particularly true of the client, in which all the unpleasantness of connecting to a server is fully encapsulated in one function call. That function, connect_to_server, is all any networking client needs to connect to any TCP service.

Running these sample programs is simple. For best effect, they should be run either on two different systems, or at least from two different windows so that the output from each can be seen. tcpserv takes no arguments, and runs until an interrupt or signal terminates it. tcpcli takes an optional argument of the server host's alphanumeric name or dotted-decimal address. If you leave the argument out, the client connects to the server through a special address called localhost. This always connects to the current system, and is usually implemented in a way that bypasses the network hardware. You should use localhost when the client and server reside on the same system.

As simple as it is, the server in the example above illustrates some key advantages to TCP connections. First, you'll note that when a client connection request comes in, the server spawns a child process that communicates with the client through a new socket. This leaves the original socket, the one bound to the well-known port, free to accept more connection requests. No client will have to wait for a connection longer than the time it takes to perform a fork call, and that's only an instant on most systems. The request queue set up with listen() (see create_service() in tcpcalls.c) lets as many as five clients stand in line. It is extremely unlikely that a backlog will develop, given the way this server handles requests. Incidentally, passing a higher number to the listen() call might make you feel better, but it has no effect: Current implementations of TCP/IP limit the backlog queue to a maximum of five entries.

The other point made by our simple client/server program is that they are interactive. The server does a looping read, looking for numeric opcodes. In this example, the server prints the code, except for the single opcode "888". This code specifies that a string, embedded in a length-encoded block, follows. This simple, fast, method allows the client to submit requests to the server in any order. When requests are generated as a result of user interaction, you need the ability to pass any request to the server at any time. A server that served some useful purpose has a number of opcodes that are understandable to both the client and server. This method was alluded to in Chapter 4's shared memory example.

A Real Server

Here's where things get interesting. You recall Chapter 3's card file program, and the warning at the end of the chapter that the code used there would be revisited later. It's later.

Our goal, in case you haven't guessed, is to convert the card file program into a client/server application. All reads and writes to the database file will be done exclusively through the server. We'll use the opcode method described earlier to pass requests and responses back and forth.

The eticards application is contained in a single file. Copy eticards.c to a new file called netcards.c. We will change the I/O functions in netcards.c so that instead of working directly with a disk file, they'll work with a remote server. By maintaining the original names for the I/O calls, and by keeping the same return code strategy, we should be able to surgically replace the disk functions with network ones.

We will also need to create a database server that deals with files exactly the same way eticards did. Extract the open_db, read_rec and write_rec functions from eticards.c and place them in a file called dbdisk.c. This will be our server's set of database disk I/O calls. The read_rec and write_rec calls refer to a dbrec structure to obtain the length of each data record on disk. To make our server more versatile, we'll bring the record length in from the client. This requires an additional argument to the write_rec and read_rec functions. dbdisk.c, after modification, should look like this:

```
/* dbdisk.c: disk I/O functions for chapter 5's card file server */
/* tabs are, well, you know */

#include <fcntl.h>
#include <stdio.h>

/* open a database (close current one if open), return handle to it */
int open_db(filename)
char    *filename;
{
    static int  dbfd = -1;  /* remember whether db is open */

    if (dbfd >= 0) {    /* database is currently open--close first */
        close(dbfd);
```

```
            dbfd = -1;
            }
    return(dbfd = open(filename, O_RDWR));
}


/* read a record from the database */
int read_rec(fd, buf, recnum, reclen)
int     fd, recnum;
short   reclen;
char    *buf;
{
    long    result, pos;

    pos = (long)((recnum - 1) * reclen);
    /* seek to record position */
    if (recnum != 0) {
        if ((result = lseek(fd, (long)pos, SEEK_SET)) < OL) {
            return((int)result);
        }
    } else {
        if ((result = lseek(fd, (long)(-reclen),
            SEEK_END)) < OL) {
            return((int)result);
        }
    }
    pos = result;   /* save byte position to report on return */
    /* read record at that position */
    if (result = (long)read(fd, buf, reclen) <= 0)
        return(-1); /* bad read */
    return((int)pos);
}


/* write record to database. if recnum == 0, append to end of file */
int write_rec(fd, buf, recnum, reclen)
int     fd, recnum;
short   reclen;
char    *buf;
{
    long    result, pos;

    if (recnum != 0) {
        if ((result = lseek(fd, (long)(--recnum * reclen),
            SEEK_SET)) < 0)
            return((int)result);
    } else {
        if ((result = lseek(fd, OL, SEEK_END)) < 0)
            return((int)result);
    }
```

```
    pos = result;
    if (write(fd, buf, reclen) <= 0)
        return(-1);
    return((int)pos);
}
```

That takes care of the disk I/O, so let's move on to the network link. The client and server need to be agreed on a set of opcodes for requests and responses. In this case, we need only opcodes that represent the basic file operations: open, read and write. For responses, we'll pass the return codes from the disk I/O functions.

First, we need a set of shared definitions for the server's listening port and the I/O opcodes:

```
/* netcards.h: shared definitions for network card database */

/* the listening port address */
#define PORT 13901

/* I/O opcodes */
#define CARD_OPEN 1
#define CARD_READ 2
#define CARD_WRITE 3

#include <sys/types.h>
```

Here's the server:

```
PROGNAME=       cardserv
OBJS=           cardserv.o dbdisk.o tcpcalls.o
LIBS=           -lsocket

/* cardserv.c: card file database server for chapter 5 */
/* tabs in this example are four spaces apart */

#include "netcards.h"
#include <sys/types.h>
#include <sys/socket.h>
#include <netinet/in.h>
#include <netdb.h>
#include <stdio.h>

main(argc, argv)
int     argc;
```

```
char     **argv;
{
    struct sockaddr_in   server_sockaddr, client_sockaddr;
    int                  server_socket, client_socket, addr_len;
    int                  pid, i, dbfd, reclen, connected;
    char                 buf[4096];
    ushort               opcode;

    /* create new socket and initialize TCP service on selected port */
    server_socket = create_service(PORT);
    if (server_socket < 0) {
        fprintf(stderr, "Can't create card service\n");
        exit(1);
    }

    addr_len = sizeof(client_sockaddr);
    /* loop looking for client connection requests */
    while (1) {
        /* the following call blocks until a client wants to connect */
        client_socket = accept(server_socket, &client_sockaddr,
            &addr_len);

        /* announce the connection */
        printf("connection request from %s\n",
            inet_ntoa(client_sockaddr.sin_addr.s_addr));

        /* we now have two sockets: server_socket, which is bound to a
            well-known port for listening, and client_socket, which is
            attached to our recently-connected client.

            We now fork so that a child process can handle the client's
            processing, and the parent can return to listening on the
            well-known port for other client requests */
        pid = fork();
        if (pid < 0) {   /* fork failed */
            perror("fork");
            exit(1);
            }

        /* child--do the work for the client */
        if (pid == 0) {
            close(server_socket);   /* we don't need this socket */
            connected = 1;          /* active connection flag */

            /* wait for opcode-encoded request from client */
            while (read_short(client_socket, &opcode) > 0) {
                switch (opcode) {
                    case CARD_OPEN:       /* open database */
```

```
                    /* record length passed first */
                    read_short(client_socket, &opcode);
                    reclen = (int)opcode;
                    fprintf(stderr, "reclen=%d\n", reclen);
                    /* database name passed in buf */
                    read_blk(client_socket, &opcode, buf);
                    fprintf(stderr, "open request for %s\n", buf);
                    dbfd = open_db(buf);
                    if (dbfd < 0)
                        opcode = 0;
                    else
                        opcode = 1;
                    fprintf(stderr, "returning with %d\n",
                        (int)opcode);
                    /* send back return code */
                    write_short(client_socket, opcode);
                    break;

                case CARD_READ:      /* read card record */
                    fprintf(stderr, "Read request\n");
                    /* get record number */
                    read_short(client_socket, &opcode);
                    fprintf(stderr, "rec num %d\n", (int)opcode);
                    /* read record from database */
                    i = read_rec(dbfd, buf, (int)opcode,
                        reclen);
                    /* translate byte position to record # */
                    if (i > 0)
                        opcode = (short)(i / reclen);
                    else opcode = 0;
                    /* pass back rec & return code */
                    write_blk(client_socket, opcode, reclen, buf);
                    break;

                case CARD_WRITE:     /* write card record */
                    /* get record from client--opcode is rec # */
                    read_blk(client_socket, &opcode, buf);
                    /* write to database */
                    fprintf(stderr, "Writing record %d\n",
                        (int)opcode);
                    i = (short)write_rec(dbfd, buf, (int)opcode,
                        reclen);
                    /* pass back return code */
                    if (i > 0)
                        opcode = (short)(i / reclen);
                    else opcode = 0;
                    write_short(client_socket, opcode);
                    break;
```

```
                default:
                    break;
            }
        }
        if (dbfd >= 0) close(dbfd);
        printf("Connection closed.\n");
        shutdown(client_socket, 2);
        close(client_socket);
        exit(0);
    }
    close(client_socket);
}
}
```

As for the client, only the disk I/O functions need to be replaced. A new makefile should be created with the following parameters:

```
PROGNAME=        netcards
OBJS=            netcards.o show_error.o tcpcalls.o
LIBS=            -lform -lmenu -lcurses -lsocket
```

The modified portions of netcards.c follow:

```
/* netcards.c: Card file application using ETI and TCP/IP */
/* for chapter 5 */
/* tabs in this file are four spaces apart */

#include "netcards.h"

/* globals */
int      server_socket = -1;      /* flag for no connection */

/* ask the server to open a database for us */
int open_db(filename)
char     *filename;
{
    ushort  opcode;

    if (server_socket < 0) {      /* we're not connected yet */
        /* connect to localhost */
        server_socket = connect_to_server("localhost", PORT);
        if (server_socket < 0)
            return(-1);
    }
    write_short(server_socket, CARD_OPEN);  /* request opcode */
```

```
        write_short(server_socket, (short)sizeof(dbrec));   /* rec len */
        /* send filename to server */
        write_blk(server_socket, opcode, strlen(filename) + 1, filename);
        read_short(server_socket, &opcode); /* get return code */
        if (opcode == 0)
            return(-1);
        else return(0);
}

/* read a record from the database */
int read_rec(fd, buf, recnum)
int      fd, recnum;
char     *buf;
{
    ushort  opcode;

    write_short(server_socket, CARD_READ);  /* read request */
    write_short(server_socket, (short)recnum);  /* pass rec # */
    read_blk(server_socket, &opcode, buf);  /* fetch data */
    if (opcode > 0)
        return((int)(opcode * sizeof(dbrec)));
    else return(-1);

}

/* write record to database. if recnum == 0, append to end of file */
int write_rec(fd, buf, recnum)
int      fd, recnum;
char     *buf;
{
    ushort  opcode;

    write_short(server_socket, CARD_WRITE); /* db write request */
    /* send record with record # as opcode */
    write_blk(server_socket, (short)recnum, sizeof(dbrec), buf);
    read_short(server_socket, &opcode); /* return value */

    /* pass back byte position or error */
    if (opcode > 0)
        return((int)(opcode * sizeof(dbrec)));
    else return(-1);
}
```

What's Wrong With This Picture?

Assuming you had no trouble getting this example to compile and run on your
system, there are a lot of things left to be done. With space and time for this

chapter running out, we'll discuss some of the remaining tasks in theory. The implementation will be up to you.

This chapter opened with a number of requirements that well-behaved client/server applications should fulfill. The card file application, surprisingly, meets most of them. "Provides a service people might actually want to use" was not on the list. One of the more interesting projects to take on that is related to this topic is the addition of statistics gathering and reporting. The server, and the children it spawns to handle connected clients, should keep tabs on the addresses of connected clients, and on the traffic each client generates. This information is invaluable for debugging client/server applications, and it is also helpful when tracking down network problems. A special client program should be written that asks the server to cough up these statistics, but far more intriguing than this is the issue of communication between the server and its child processes.

Think about the problem for a moment. The original server process can only generate *some* of the needed statistics on its own. Traffic (byte counts for read and write, number of requests, etc.) statistics must be kept by the children spawned the original server. How do the children get these statistics to the original server process? How often should this transfer take place? You might find the methods you learned in Chapter 4 to be helpful.

While working on this example, you may come across a thing or two in the file I/O code that doesn't work quite right.

The current version of the server program has no way to exit cleanly. It has to be interrupted. You might work up a special opcode that shuts down the server, or at least create a signal handler that closes the socket before quitting. As it is now, it can take the TCP/IP services up to several minutes to figure out that the server has exited.

Finally, a subtle point: To avoid reprinting the entire do_cards function, a way wasn't added to specify the server host name on the command line. Because of this, the client and server must be run on the same system. This obviously should be changed.

With what you now understand about connecting applications across a network link, use your imagination to come up with some ideas of your own, perhaps a simple way of using a printer on another machine, or transferring electronic mail. Put your knowledge to good use.

## Chapter 6

Advanced Network Programming

In the previous chapter, you learned how to use TCP/IP services to connect programs that could be running on separate machines. While the methods described there were complete enough to meet most network application requirements, there are some additional services that can make network programs easier to write and use.

Patching Into inetd

NOTE: *Some of the procedures in this section require root (or superuser) privileges. Because these procedures call for changes to sensitive files (a botched edit could effectively isolate your system from the rest of the network), proceed only after you have made safe copies of the affected files. If you do not have root access permission on your system, don't fret; the material in this section can be well understood without working through the examples.*

Imagine that, armed with the knowledge you gained in the previous chapter, you were suddenly consumed by a passion to create networked applications. You'd churn out server after server to provide services ranging from necessary to obscure. You would gleefully place each server on-line, one after another. Pretty soon, your system's process list would be crowded with servers, each one waiting for a connection, each one forking still another copy of itself when a connection was made.

That's a fair picture of how TCP/IP network hosts looked before there was a way to get a handle on it. It used to be that, for every network service you chose to make available, a server process had to be running. There is a better way. Assuming that your system is running TCP/IP, grab a check of your process list (with ps). Unless someone is actively using rlogin, telnet or ftp, you'll notice that there are no processes running which make these services available. As soon as someone uses rlogin to access your system, however, an rlogind program appears in the process list to service that connection. Where does it come from?

Most of the standard TCP/IP services don't run processes that sit and wait for connections. Instead, they delegate that responsibility to a sort of super server called inetd. It's inetd's job to wait for connections, then call up the appropriate server program when a connection comes through. inetd, through configuration files, keeps track of the name, port number, connection type (UDP or TCP), program name, and command-line arguments associated with each service. It binds sockets to all of the registered services' port numbers, and listens for connections. When a connection is requested, inetd accepts it and spawns the server program (with the configured arguments) with its standard input and output attached to the new socket.

There are several advantages to this approach, some obvious, others not. The obvious plus is that inetd passes the socket as standard I/O file handles. Because of this, it's possible to create simple server processes that never make any socket-related calls. From the moment the server is called by inetd, all it needs to converse with the client are ordinary I/O calls. Many servers want to know more about the program on the other end of the wire. The TCP/IP function call getpeername queries an existing socket (such as the one passed by inetd), and gathers information about the other host.

The not-so-obvious benefit to inetd is in its configuration files. These files map service names to port numbers, and the TCP/IP library includes functions that query these files. So your program, instead of having to somehow know that it uses port number 13760, can find its port number by calling getservbyname(). Both your client and the server should "find themselves" in this manner; you can change the port address of both programs by making a change to a single configuration file (no recompiling).

There is a small catch: The inetd configuration files must have identical entries for all shared services across all machines. You see, getservbyname() and the other calls that depend on inetd's database only read the files installed on the *current* system. It's not smart enough to reach across the network to consult a central configuration server. This means that each time you change one of the inetd files, you must distribute those changes to all of the affected machines on your network. If you're sure a certain machine will never use a certain service, it need not be registered.

NOTE: *Sun's Network Information Service (NIS, previously referred to as "Yellow Pages") distributes key configuration files among hosts on a network. NIS is not currently a default part of Open Desktop and other popular PC UNIX systems, but it is available.*

There are two parts to registering a service with inetd. First, the service name is associated with its port ID in /etc/services. This file is what getservbyname() consults, and it can be used even by services that *don't* rely on inetd. Entries in /etc/services are brief and easy. List yours. It should include these entries:

```
ftp         21/tcp
telnet      23/tcp
login       513/tcp
```

The corresponding entries in your /etc/services file most likely match those shown above, because certain key TCP/IP services are given reserved port numbers. These port numbers are expected to be the same for all systems supporting TCP/IP. If these numbers don't match your system, don't change them. Your system administrator may have (possibly warped) reasons of his or her own for changing the port assignments. If one or more of these entries doesn't appear, it's more likely that the administrator disabled the service in the interest of security.

Adding your own entry to /etc/services is straightforward (it's safe to add this now if you like):

```
cardfile    13901/tcp
```

The alternative to tcp for socket type is udp. Again, because of their unreliable nature, UDP sockets will be left out of this discussion. The entry above is a preparation for a coming example. We'll build a slightly modified version of last chapter's card database server, then register it with inetd.

The second configuration file associated with inetd is /etc/inetd.conf. This file is more complex, with each entry formatted thus:

```
name type protocol wait login program arg0 ... arg4
```

The name identifies the service, and must be the same name used in /etc/services. There's no requirement for the name of the service to match the program name, however. type is either stream or dgram, typically corresponding to TCP and UDP sockets, respectively. Sticking with TCP sockets as we are, the type entry will be stream. Similarly, protocol will be tcp.

The wait flag is set to either wait or nowait, depending on how the server chooses to handle new connections. The vast majority of servers use nowait. With this, inetd listens for a connection on the registered port, creates a new socket (with accept()) when a connection comes in, and passes that socket to the server process. inetd then continues to watch the registered port for more connections. In wait mode, inetd gives up control of the registered port to the server process after the first connection is made. At that point, inetd stops listening to the registered port; the server process is responsible for handling new connections. When the server exits (presumably after the last connection has been closed), inetd resumes listening to the registered port.

Of the two, nowait mode is the most frequently used. It's more convenient to have inetd wait for connections.

The login part of the entry identifies the user ID under which the server will run. Because inetd runs as root, it can use setuid() after the fork() (and before the exec() of the server program) to have the server run as any user you choose. This is mostly an aid to security; the server process will only be able to access those files for which the specified user has permission.

The program and arg0 ... arg4 define the server program's location on disk, and the arguments to be passed to it through exec(). The program entry should always be a complete path name, starting with the root directory. Remember, too, that argument 0 of a program is always the name of the program itself. inetd limits the number of arguments to 5 (actually, 4, considering the first argument is "wasted").

The /etc/inetd.conf file on your system should include these entries (subject to the considerations in the above note):

```
ftp     stream  tcp     nowait  root    /etc/ftpd       ftpd
login   stream  tcp     nowait  root    /etc/rlogind    rlogind
```

When the time comes to add our card file server to this file, the entry will be something like this (don't add it now):

```
netcards stream tcp nowait username /usr/local/bin/cardserv cardserv
```

Once an entry has been added to inetd.conf, the inetd program notices the change and starts waiting on that port. We won't add our entry to this file until we have a server. Also, you probably figured out that username and /usr/local/bin/cardfile should be replaced with the user name and server program path you deem appropriate.

The changes we need to make to cardserv.c are trivial, and mostly amount to the deletion of those lines that handled waiting for connections and dispatched child processes to serve them. There's also no longer any need for the hard-coded port number in netcards.h. Here's how cardserv.c looks after being modified for inetd operation:

```
/* cardserv.c: card file database server for chapter 5 */
/* modified for inetd operation as detailed in chapter 6 */
/* tabs in this example are four spaces apart */

#include "netcards.h"
#include <sys/types.h>
#include <sys/socket.h>
#include <netinet/in.h>
#include <netdb.h>
#include <stdio.h>

main(argc, argv)
int     argc;
char    **argv;
{
    struct sockaddr_in  client_sockaddr;
    int                 client_socket, addr_len;
    int                 i, dbfd, reclen;
    char                buf[4096];
    ushort              opcode;

    /* socket handle passed to us as stdin/stdout */
    client_socket = 0;  /* attach to stdin */
    addr_len = sizeof(client_sockaddr);
    /* get address of connected client in case we need it */
    i = getpeername(client_socket, &client_sockaddr, &addr_len);
    /* if this call failed, we don't have a valid socket */
    if (i < 0) {
        perror("getpeername");
        exit(1);
    }

    /* wait for opcode-encoded request from client */
    while (read_short(client_socket, &opcode) > 0) {
```

```
    switch (opcode) {
        case CARD_OPEN:        /* open database */
            /* record length passed first */
            read_short(client_socket, &opcode);
            reclen = (int)opcode;
            /* database name passed in buf */
            read_blk(client_socket, &opcode, buf);
            dbfd = open_db(buf);
            if (dbfd < 0)
                opcode = 0;
            else
                opcode = 1;
            /* send back return code */
            write_short(client_socket, opcode);
            break;

        case CARD_READ:        /* read card record */
            /* get record number */
            read_short(client_socket, &opcode);
            /* read record from database */
            i = read_rec(dbfd, buf, (int)opcode,
                reclen);
            /* translate byte position to record # */
            if (i > 0)
                opcode = (short)(i / reclen);
            else opcode = 0;
            /* pass back rec & return code */
            write_blk(client_socket, opcode, reclen, buf);
            break;

        case CARD_WRITE:       /* write card record */
            /* get record from client--opcode is rec # */
            read_blk(client_socket, &opcode, buf);
            /* write to database */
            i = (short)write_rec(dbfd, buf, (int)opcode,
                reclen);
            /* pass back return code */
            if (i > 0)
                opcode = (short)(i / reclen);
            else opcode = 0;
            write_short(client_socket, opcode);
            break;

        default:
            break;
    }
}
if (dbfd >= 0) close(dbfd);
```

```
printf("Connection closed.\n");
shutdown(client_socket, 2);
close(client_socket);
exit(0);
}
```

Except for the getpeername call, there's very little about the new server that suggests it is a network application. It's much simpler than our previous version. In addition to removing the code that waited for and handled new connections, it was also necessary to remove the fprintf() statements. When inetd spawns a server process, it doesn't make arrangements for console output. Because there is no open file associated with stderr, any attempt to output to it will cause the server to fail. What's more, since stdin and stdout are attached to the socket (with a client listening on the other end), printf() and similar calls would wind up shooting their output through the socket.

The getpeername call fills a sockaddr_in structure (see the file /usr/include/sys/netinet/in.h (/usr/include/netinet/in.h on some systems) for the contents) with the address of the connected host. This provides exactly the same information as the accept call in the previous version of the server. We don't fprintf() it to stderr any more, of course, because we have no console connection. The getpeername call was included in case you wanted to do something else with the address.

There are only a couple of minor changes needed to the client side programs. tcpcalls.c should be changed to look up the service name instead of using a hard-coded port address. netcards.c has to be changed, too, to pass a service name instead of a port number as an argument to tcpcalls.c's connect_to_server(). Here is that function, modified to connect to an /etc/services-registered service:

```
/* open a connection to a server socket */
/* "hostname" can be either a host name or a character string
   representing an Internet address (like "192.1.1.8"). If "hostname"
   is either NULL or an empty string, a connection to the current
   host is attempted. "servname" can be either an ASCII service name
   from /etc/services, or an ASCII-encoded TCP port number. */

int connect_to_server(hostname, servname)
char    *hostname, *servname;
{
  struct sockaddr_in   server_sockaddr;
  struct hostent       *server_hostent;
  struct servent       *server_servent;
```

```
int              toserver_socket, i;
char             str[255];
ushort           opcode;
ushort           port;
unsigned long    hostaddr;
char             *server_name[255];

if ((hostname == NULL) || (*hostname == 0)) {
    /* no host name provided */
    strcpy(server_name, "localhost");    /* use this machine */
} else strcpy(server_name, hostname);    /* use hostname provided */

/* null out server address structure */
bzero(&server_sockaddr, sizeof(server_sockaddr));

/* translate host name given on command line to Internet address */
/* allow Internet address as well */
hostaddr = inet_addr(server_name);   /* try it as an address*/
if ((long)hostaddr != (long)-1) {    /* we've got an address */
    bcopy(&hostaddr, &server_sockaddr.sin_addr,
        sizeof(hostaddr));   /* copy address to sockaddr struct */
} else {     /* must be a host name */

    /* ask host database/name server for host entry */
    server_hostent = gethostbyname(server_name);
    if (server_hostent == NULL) {
        fprintf(stderr, "Can't locate host \"%s\"\n", server_name);
        return(-1);
    }
    /* copy address from host entry to socket struct */
    bcopy(server_hostent->h_addr,
        &server_sockaddr.sin_addr,
        server_hostent->h_length);
}

/* try to translate service name to port number */
if((port = (ushort)atoi(servname)) <= 0) {   /* probably a name */
    /* look up service in /etc/services */
    if ((server_servent =
        getservbyname(servname, "tcp")) == NULL) {
        /* it's not there */
        fprintf(stderr, "Can't locate service \"%s\"\n", servname);
        return(-1);
    }
    port = ntohs((ushort)server_servent->s_port);
    fprintf(stderr, "port is %d\n", port);
}
```

```
#ifndef QUIET
  /* let the developer know the address translation worked */
  printf("trying to connect to %s\n",
      inet_ntoa(server_sockaddr.sin_addr));
#endif
  server_sockaddr.sin_family = AF_INET;    /* always */
  server_sockaddr.sin_port = htons(port);

  /* create a raw socket */
  if ((toserver_socket = socket(AF_INET, SOCK_STREAM, 0)) < 0) {
      perror("socket()");
      return(-1);
  }

  /* use that socket to request a connection to a server */
  /* (server must be running for this call to succeed--it won't
      wait for a server to come on-line) */
  if (connect(toserver_socket, &server_sockaddr,
      sizeof(server_sockaddr)) < 0) {
      perror("connect()");
      return(-1);
  }
  /* connection is made. The returned handle can now be used with
      ordinary I/O calls to transfer data. */
  return(toserver_socket);
}
```

Only one line in netcards.c needs changing:

```
server_socket = connect_to_server("localhost", "netcards");
```

With these changes in place, you can modify (if you have permission) the /etc/services and /etc/inetd.conf files to add the card database server. In a minute or so, inetd should notice the changes and start waiting on the registered port. After that, the netcards program should behave exactly as before.

Any server application you write which will see use by more than one or two machines should be configured for launching by inetd.

XDR and RPC

As you learned in an earlier chapter, shared memory is a marvelous way to share data between processes on the same machine. It looks just like regular memory and, after some initial wrangling, it is incredibly easy to work with. Often, the best way to simplify some complex task is to wrap it in a simpler mechanism.

With the convenience routines presented in the previous chapter, communicating between two processes on different systems is made easier. But if you think of the role of the server in a client/server relationship (as illustrated by the example in Chapter 5), there should be an easier way. When we set about changing the eticards application, we replaced the original function calls that read and wrote database records with calls that shot the request across a network channel and waited for a response. Wouldn't it be simpler if we could make a traditional function call in the client that executed in the server?

Such a mechanism exists as the Remote Procedure Call (RPC). The server application maintains a group of functions (called programs), identified by number, each of which can perform several procedures that are also identified by numbers. Each program is tagged with a version number, permitting a server to provide compatibility with obsolete services. The client requests execution through a program/version/procedure triplet, and passes arguments to be used by the procedure. The server executes the requested procedure, and passes back a result (which can be nearly any data type). From the client side, all of this is handled with a single function call. What's more, by using UDP sockets, RPC handles making the connection and passing and verification of data; the client can use RPCs while remaining oblivious to the complexities of networking. Things are equally uncomplicated for the server.

You might have noticed the bit above about "nearly any data type," and paused for a moment to consider the familiar bugaboo of byte-ordering. How can you pass data between procedures on different machines without worrying about byte order? The answer, of course, is that you can't. You *must* worry about byte order, and RPCs are no exception. Fortunately, a companion to the RPC is XDR, eXternal Data Representation. Like the TCP calls that translate integers to and from a network-uniform byte order, XDR lets you maintain the integrity of arbitrary data types across network links. The difference is that XDR is much more robust. Signed and unsigned short and long integers, floating-point numbers, byte arrays, null-terminated strings, and even structures can be passed through the XDR mechanism. Complex collections of data can be represented though combinations of primitive data types.

Because they are so capable, the documentation for RPC and XDR together are almost impassibly dense. We simplify things here by foregoing coverage of the most complex and obscure features of RPC and XDR, focusing instead on those portions of it that you are most likely to use. As always, if you feel the need to know more, dig into your documentation after this chapter's end.

A Simple RPC Application

The simplest form of RPC is one which takes in only one argument and passes back a single return value. In our case, we'll pass an integer argument to a server and bring back a null-terminated string. This might be applied to reading a numerically-indexed string from a message file. To keep the next few examples short, they will perform no useful functions other than to illustrate the principle being discussed.

Since we're passing an integer as an argument, we should use XDR to encode and decode it. In XDR, this is referred to as *serialization* and *deserialization*. The null-terminated string returned by the server must also pass through XDR as well, for reasons that will be explained shortly.

The highest level of RPC reduces both client and server involvement to a set of three function calls: callrpc, registerrpc and svc_run. These three calls are undoubtedly the easiest way to connect client and server applications.

High-level RPC works on an event-driven model. The server makes the necessary preparations to put a service on-line, then calls the registerrpc function to register the service. It then calls svc_run(), which never returns. svc_run() dispatches client requests to the appropriate functions in the server, handling the serialization and deserialization of data through user-specified XDR filters.

Registering a service requires that it be assigned a unique program number. This is generally represented as a 32-bit hex number. Large blocks of program numbers are reserved for current and future use, leaving you with two ranges of program numbers to use in your applications: 20000000-3fffffff and 40000000-5fffffff. The latter range is intended to be used by transient services, as opposed to services that remain available for an indefinite period of time.

The callrpc function has the following syntax:

```
int callrpc(hostname, prog_num, ver_num, proc_num, to_xdr_func,
to_data, from_xdr_func, from_data)
```

The hostname argument contains a string pointing to the name (or network number) of the remote host, prog_num, ver_num and proc_num are long (32-bit) integers identifying the program, version, and procedure numbers. All three must exactly match those used by the server to register the service. to_xdr_func and to_data represent the XDR filter used to serialize the argument(s) being passed *to* the server, and the data itself (respectively). Likewise, from_xdr_func and from_data point to the XDR *de*serialization function, and the repository for data being returned from the server. XDR data arguments are *always* pointers. For the simplest transactions (like ours), the XDR function arguments are taken from the list of predefined XDR filters. There are others; this list includes the most common ones:

Table 6-1: XDR Function Arguments

Function	C type	Description
xdr_char	char	single character
xdr_u_short	unsigned short	unsigned short integer
xdr_short	short	short integer
xdr_u_int	unsigned	unsigned integer
xdr_int	int	integer
xdr_u_long	unsigned long	unsigned long integer
xdr_long	long	long integer
xdr_float	float	floating point
xdr_double	double	double-precision floating point
xdr_void	void	encodes no argument/return value
xdr_string	char *	null-terminated string
xdr_bytes	char *	variable-length byte array

By convention (not enforced by the RPC mechanism), both version and procedure numbers start at 1. Program numbers should be defined within an accepted range.

The server's most complicated call is to registerrpc(). It has the following syntax:

```
int registerrpc(prog_num, ver_num, proc_num, func, from_xdr_func,
  to_xdr_func);
```

There shouldn't be any serious surprises here, except that there's no room on this line for the names of the variables used to store the incoming and outgoing data; XDR takes care of that. More detail after the first example.

For our first example, we'll stick with a program number that is hard-coded into both the client and the server. The /etc/rpc file permits an /etc/services-like mapping of RPC program numbers to program RPC service names. The getrpcbyname function, given an RPC program name, fills an rpcent structure with data including the program number. See the getrpcent reference manual page for more information. We will proceed here without registering our service in /etc/rpc.

Both the client and server are dependent on the following header file:

```
/* rpccli1.h */
/* header file for rpccli1/rpcsrv1, RPC/XDR examples for chapter 6 */

#define MESSAGE_PROGRAM        (long)0x20013760
#define MESSAGE_VERSION        (long)1
#define MESSAGE_PROCEDURE      (long)1
#define MESSAGE_QUIT_PROC      (long)2
```

Next is the client portion. Use the following parameters in your boilerplate makefile:

```
PROGNAME=    rpccli1
OBJS=        rpccli1.o
LIBS=        -lrpc -lsocket

/* rpccli1.c: client program using high-level RPC calls */
/* tabs in this example are four spaces apart */

#include <stdio.h>
#include <rpc/rpc.h>
#include "rpccli1.h"

main(argc, argv)
int      argc;
char     **argv;
{
 char     str[80], *strptr = str;
 int      message_number, result;

 setbuf(stdout, NULL);    /* output is not buffered */
 if (argc != 2) {
     fprintf(stderr, "usage: %s hostname\n", argv[0]);
     exit(1);
 }

 while (1) {
     /* get an integer from the user */
     printf("Message number (0 to terminate): ");
     if (scanf("%d", &message_number) != 1) {
         fprintf(stderr, "Integer input required\n");
         exit(1);
     }
```

```
    if (message_number == 0) {  /* quit--dump server first */
        result = callrpc(argv[1], MESSAGE_PROGRAM, MESSAGE_VERSION,
            MESSAGE_QUIT_PROC, xdr_void, 0, xdr_void, 0);

        if (result != 0) {  /* error occurred */
            /* extract error ID and print associated string */
            printf("callrpc() failed: %s\n", clnt_sperrno(
                (enum clnt_stat)result));
            exit(1);
        }
        exit(0);
    }

    /* call the server */
    result = callrpc(argv[1], MESSAGE_PROGRAM, MESSAGE_VERSION,
        MESSAGE_PROCEDURE, xdr_int, &message_number,
        xdr_wrapstring, &strptr);
    /* check for failure */
    if (result != 0) {  /* error occurred */
        /* extract error ID and print associated string */
        printf("callrpc() failed: %s\n", clnt_sperrno(
            (enum clnt_stat)result));
        exit(1);
    }
    printf("Server returned: %s", str);
  }
}
```

Now for the server. Here are the makefile parameters:

```
PROGNAME=       rpcsrv1
OBJS=           rpcsrv1.o
LIBS=           -lrpc -lsocket

/* rpcsrv1.c: RPC server example for chapter 6 */
/* tabs in this example are four spaces apart */

#include <stdio.h>
#include <rpc/rpc.h>
#include "rpccli1.h"

/* define a function to be called when client asks for procedure #1 */
char **message_proc_1(message_number)
int     *message_number;
{
```

```
static char      message[80];    /* used in place, static req'd */
static char      *msgptr = message;  /* must pass pointer
     to pointer */

/* put integer argument in string and return */
sprintf(message, "Integer %d was passed to server.\n",
    *message_number);
printf("Server got a %d\n", *message_number);
return(&msgptr);
}

/* this function causes the server to exit. Server can't exit from
 within this function--it must return so client will unblock.
 alarm function sets up SIGALRM signal after 5 second delay. Default
 action is termination. */
void message_proc_2()
{
fprintf(stderr, "Server exit requested\n");
alarm(5);
return;
}

main()
{
 int      result;

/* attempt to register message service (procedure #1) */
result = registerrpc(MESSAGE_PROGRAM, MESSAGE_VERSION,
    MESSAGE_PROCEDURE, message_proc_1, xdr_int, xdr_wrapstring);
if (result != 0) {  /* failed, no error code */
    fprintf(stderr, "registerrpc: Cannot register msg service\n");
    exit(1);
}

/* register quit service (procedure #2) */
result = registerrpc(MESSAGE_PROGRAM, MESSAGE_VERSION,
    MESSAGE_QUIT_PROC, message_proc_2, xdr_void, xdr_void);
if (result != 0) {  /* failed, no error code */
    fprintf(stderr, "registerrpc: Cannot register quit service\n");
    exit(1);
}
svc_run();  /* wait for and process client requests */
}
```

To run the above example, first launch the rpcsrv1 program in the background:

```
$ rpcsrv1 &
```

Then run rpccli1. You will be prompted for an integer message number. Respond with a valid integer. That integer will be passed to the server, which will send back a formatted string containing the integer you entered. The client then displays that string, and asks for another number. Enter "0", and the client will exit after messaging the server to do the same. In five seconds or so, you should see a message on your terminal resembling this:

```
rpcsrv1: Alarm call
```

This signals the termination of the server program.

There are some peculiarities in the above code that need explaining. First, you'll notice that xdr_string was *not* specified as the XDR filter for our string return value. The XDR filters are functions (xdr_string is a function pointer), and nearly all of them take two arguments: the XDR stream handle, and a pointer to the data. In the case of xdr_string, a third argument, representing the maximum length of the string, is also required. Unfortunately, the high-level convenience routines always call the XDR filters with two arguments. rpcsvr1.c uses the xdr_wrapstring filter because it accepts two arguments, passing them to xdr_string() with a third argument equal to the largest possible integer. That's plenty of room. To use xdr_string() with a third argument that truly represents the amount of string space allocated, you'll have to resort to lower-level routines or write your own XDR filter.

These high-level RPC routines use UDP sockets to transfer data, and that imposes certain restrictions. UDP is a connectionless protocol, so these routines do not support protocol-maintained connected sessions. Since the connection has to be made and broken for each remote call, there is a fair amount of overhead. You certainly wouldn't want to use these RPC routines to send the contents of a file to another machine one byte at a time. Keep the overhead in mind, and write your procedures to transfer as much data as possible (within the 8K UDP-imposed limit) with a single call. Also try to keep the call frequency as low as possible; combine multiple functions into one when you can.

To illustrate the capacity of a server to register more than one function, there is a MESSAGE_QUIT_PROC procedure in rpcsrv1.c. When the user enters a value of "0" in rpccli1, a remote call is made (notice that xdr_void is used to specify no arguments and no return value) to rpcsvr1's MESSAGE_QUIT_PROC procedure. As noted in the comments, the server can't exit within the procedure. The client's callrpc() blocks until a response is received from the server. If the called procedure exits before returning, no response is ever sent. The client times out after a while, but it should be free to exit. Instead, the server's MESSAGE_QUIT_PROC function (message_proc_2()) makes a call to the alarm system call without first setting up a SIGALRM interrupt handler. The result, five seconds or so after the alarm call, is termination of the server.

A bit of strangeness evident here is the way XDR handles strings. For the integer conversion, we simply pass a pointer to an integer. It would seem correct, then, to pass a character pointer for a string conversion. Not so—XDR is looking for a pointer *to the pointer*. That's why it was necessary in message_proc_1() in rpcsrv1.c to declare a superfluous string pointer, msgptr. The message_proc_1 routine then returns a pointer to *that* pointer: a pointer to a pointer to a character (char **). The code in rpccli1.c that deals with the string suffers a similar crookedness. Don't deviate from this, and remember that if you have declared char str[80], you can't shortcut XDR's requirement with &str. Also, take care to initialize your string pointer to point to the original string. Otherwise, XDR will attempt to store its data in whatever memory that pointer points to. It's confusing, but this is one of those quirks you just have to memorize, and then move on.

If you're still a little in the dark about exactly what's happening in this example, here's a travelogue: Our server provides one version of one program, with two procedures. The server first uses registerrpc to register these procedures. The procedures are numbered according to #defines in rpccli1.h. First, there's MESSAGE_PROCEDURE, the main routine called by the client to turn an integer argument into a formatted string. A client request to execute MESSAGE_PROCEDURE results in a server call to message_proc_1() (the procedure's function name is arbitrary). This function is called with the argument type specified in the fifth argument of registerrpc(), in this case, an integer. To pass this argument to message_proc_1(), rpcsrv1 specifies the name of the XDR filter function matching the type of the data to be passed: xdr_int. When a client calls MESSAGE_PROCEDURE, the integer passed with the call is automatically handed down to message_proc_1() as an ordinary function argument, a *pointer* to an integer. When message_proc_1 returns, it passes back a value compatible with the xdr_wrapstring (actually, xdr_string) filter, effectively passing a null-terminated string back to the client. There is no need in the registerrpc call to specify the location of the data coming in or out of each server function. RPC already has the incoming data buffered, but the outgoing buffer must be provided by the server function. message_proc_1() provides this buffer in the form of a static character array, but it could just as well have been provided with a block of malloc()ed storage. The key here is that the storage is used in place by the XDR filters, and subsequently by the low-level routines that pass that data back to the client. Don't return a pointer to an automatic variable. This will be a pointer to data that will disappear when the function exits.

With the program, version, and two procedures registered by the server, the client only needs to use callrpc() to contact the server. Data being passed to and returned from the server must be specified in the callrpc() argument list because callrpc() results in a direct call to the server without going through an intervening user-defined function. The integer is passed via a pointer (&message_number), and the string, as explained above, is a pointer to a pointer to a character. A successful call to the server deposits the returned string in the memory pointed to by str, with the needed indirection provided by the string pointer strptr. In the case of the client, you must make sure that the storage pointed to has been allocated, and that it is of sufficient size to handle the incoming data.

There's a lot going on for the handful of RPC-related function calls involved. Don't be discouraged if you're still a little confused. We're moving on from here, but please try your best to understand how this first example works before you venture into the next section.

Custom XDR Filters

The function associated with every remote procedure is allowed exactly one incoming argument and one return value. This corresponds to a pair, and only a pair, of XDR routines to handle the incoming and outgoing data. If you need to pass more than one argument, or return more than a single value, it is obvious that the built-in XDR primitive filters won't work. You could pass everything in strings and decipher them yourself, but there is a better way: custom XDR filters.

Most custom XDR filters are actually wrappers, filters that call the built-in primitive filters in a certain order to build a data stream. For instance, if you wanted to pass the following structure

```
struct appointment {
  long    date;
  int     id;
  char    *description;
};
```

you'd call the xdr_long, xdr_int and xdr_string functions from within your custom filter. As long as you used the same filter on both sides of the connection, your data would be packed and unpacked exactly as you specified. You would have the convenience of dealing with a single structure pointer on both the client and server sides, and the versatility of being free to change that structure as required.

A single XDR routine is used for both encoding and decoding. You don't normally need to worry which operation is being performed—XDR handles that ingeniously. XDR data conversions are performed on a data stream. Data being prepared for transmission is taken from its native form (C data structures), converted, and appended to the stream. Received data is read from the stream, converted, and turned back into C data structures. This stream normally resides in memory, but XDR also works with file-based data streams. The ability to store XDR-encoded data in files, while not specifically covered here, provides the developer with one means of formatting data files to be readable regardless of hardware type.

The RPC Card Database

For the final example in this chapter, let's rework the card file database yet again, this time to do its network I/O through remote procedure calls. The client's behavior will remain the same, but we'll add a special RPC procedure to the server that returns simple I/O statistics.

Because there is only one server program (which never spawns itself), requests coming into this RPC server, as with the previous RPC example, are handled serially. This is an advantage *and* a disadvantage. The disadvantage is that an open() and close() must be done for each request, unless the server chooses to maintain a connection of some sort. A completely connectionless service is one in which the server maintains no information between calls. Therefore, each call must carry with it all of the data needed to fulfill the request. Instead of sending the server an "open database" request first with the database name, our connectionless client will (necessarily) include the database name and absolute record number with each read and write request. That's where our custom XDR filters come in. First, we need some constants and a couple of structure definitions:

```
/* rpccards.h: shared definitions for RPC card database */

#define CARDPROGRAM (long)0x20013760
#define CARDVERSION (long)1
#define CARDREAD    1
```

```
#define CARDWRITE   2
#define CARDSTAT    3
#define DBRECLEN    205

struct rec {
  char     *dbname;     /* name of database file to use */
  int      recnum;      /* record number for this request */
                        /* also used for return code */
  char     *data;       /* database data */
};

struct stat {
  unsigned long        chars_read, chars_written;
};
```

Those structures are used to pass data between the client and server. Remember, you're limited to one argument and one return value for any remote call. These structures show the most common way to get around this limitation. Let's move on to the custom XDR filters and client-side RPC routines:

```
/* XDR filters and RPC I/O routines for chapter 6 RPC example */
/* tabs are four spaces apart */

/* matches structures in header file */
#include "rpccards.h"
#include <rpc/rpc.h>

/* filter for "rec" structure, used to pass database record data
   back and forth */
xdr_rec(xdr_stream, recp)
XDR         *xdr_stream;
struct rec  *recp;
{
  static int       reclen = DBRECLEN;

  /* convert dbname */
  if (!xdr_string(xdr_stream, &recp->dbname, 1024))
      return(0);
  /* convert recnum */
  if (!xdr_int(xdr_stream, &recp->recnum))
      return(0);
  /* convert data */
  if (!xdr_bytes(xdr_stream, &recp->data, &reclen, DBRECLEN))
      return(0);

  /* if we made it this far, everything's OK */
```

```
 return(1);
}

xdr_status(xdr_stream, statp)
XDR          *xdr_stream;
struct stat *statp;
{
 /* convert chars_read */
 if (!xdr_u_long(xdr_stream, &statp->chars_read))
     return(0);
 /* convert chars_written */
 if (!xdr_u_long(xdr_stream, &statp->chars_written))
     return(0);

 return(1);
}

/* send a read request to the server */
int read_call(fname, buf, recnum)
char     *fname, *buf;
int      recnum;
{
 static struct rec    outgoing;
 static struct rec    incoming;
 char                 fname1[255];
 int                  result;

 /* build outgoing argument list */
 strcpy(fname1, fname);  /* don't clobber global filename */
 outgoing.dbname = fname1;
 outgoing.data = buf;
 outgoing.recnum = recnum;

 /* prepare storage for return */
 incoming.data = buf;
 incoming.dbname = fname1;
 incoming.recnum = 0;

 /* make the call */
 /* (currently limited to "localhost"--find a way to add support for
     user-specified server host) */
 result = callrpc("localhost", CARDPROGRAM, CARDVERSION, CARDREAD,
     xdr_rec, &outgoing, xdr_rec, &incoming);
 if (result != 0)
     return(-1);
 return(incoming.recnum);     /* pass back file position */
}
```

```
/* send a write request to the server */
int write_call(fname, buf, recnum)
char    *fname, *buf;
int     recnum;
{
 static struct rec   outgoing;
 static struct rec   incoming;
 char                fname1[255];
 int                 result;

 /* build outgoing argument list */
 strcpy(fname1, fname);  /* don't clobber global filename */
 outgoing.dbname = fname1;
 outgoing.data = buf;
 outgoing.recnum = recnum;

 /* prepare storage for return */
 incoming.data = buf;
 incoming.dbname = fname1;
 incoming.recnum = 0;

 /* make the call */
 /* (currently limited to "localhost"--find a way to add support for
     user-specified server host) */
 result = callrpc("localhost", CARDPROGRAM, CARDVERSION, CARDWRITE,
     xdr_rec, &outgoing, xdr_rec, &incoming);
 if (result != 0)
     return(-1);
 return(incoming.recnum);     /* pass back file position */
}
```

There is nothing very mysterious about the workings of XDR filters. It's really just a matter of climbing through a data structure, one member at a time, and calling the primitive (or user-created, if you like) XDR filter that matches the member's data type. The stream (pointed to by xdr_stream in the file above) is created before the filters are called, and managed after the filters exit. Those filters are the most complicated thing about passing arbitrary data through an RPC channel. Well, almost . . .

Even for an experienced programmer, it's easy to lose track of the pointer manipulations that go on. Even though XDR works exclusively with pointers, you must always be sure that the pointers you are providing always point to allocated storage. This can be easily forgotten, especially since many C functions that call for pointers do their own allocation (like fopen() which returns a FILE pointer). There is a way to get some XDR routines to allocate their own storage, but you must remember to free it, and it adds complexity to what is, once understood, a very simple mechanism. Just remember: XDR-manipulated data is *always* dealt with through pointers. Make sure all your pointers are valid, and you'll be safe.

rpcxdr.c is also the repository for the callrpc calls that communicate with the server. The read_call and write_call functions are called by the main client program, rpccards.c (below).

Another supporting file is the dbdisk.c we used before. There must be a database open and close for every I/O call, and the arguments to the read_rec and write_rec functions must now include the name of the database file. The file is short enough to reprint here in its entirety:

```
/* dbdisk.c: disk I/O functions for chapter 5's card file server */
/* modified for use with last RPC example in chapter 6 */
/* tabs are, well, you know */

#include <fcntl.h>
#include <stdio.h>

/* read a record from the database */
int read_rec(fname, buf, recnum, reclen)
char    *fname;
int     recnum;
short   reclen;
char    *buf;
{
  long     result, pos;
  int      fd;

  fd = open(fname, O_RDONLY);
  if (fd < 0)
      return(-1);
  pos = (long)((recnum - 1) * reclen);
  /* seek to record position */
  if (recnum != 0) {
      if ((result = lseek(fd, (long)pos, SEEK_SET)) < OL) {
          close(fd);
          return((int)result);
      }
  } else {
      if ((result = lseek(fd, (long)(-reclen),
          SEEK_END)) < OL) {
          close(fd);
          return((int)result);
```

```
    }
}
pos = result;    /* save byte position to report on return */
/* read record at that position */
if (result = (long)read(fd, buf, reclen) <= 0) {
    close(fd);
    return(-1); /* bad read */
}
close(fd);
return((int)pos);
}

/* write record to database. if recnum == 0, append to end of file */
int write_rec(fname, buf, recnum, reclen)
char    *fname;
int     recnum;
short   reclen;
char    *buf;
{
long    result, pos;
int     fd;

fd = open(fname, O_RDWR);
if (recnum != 0) {
    if ((result = lseek(fd, (long)(&recnum * reclen),
        SEEK_SET)) < 0) {
        close(fd);
        return((int)result);
    }
} else {
    if ((result = lseek(fd, 0L, SEEK_END)) < 0) {
        close(fd);
        return((int)result);
    }
}
pos = result;
if (write(fd, buf, reclen) <= 0) {
    close(fd);
    return(-1);
}
close(fd);
return((int)pos);
}
```

Now for the server module. Here are the makefile parameters:

```
PROGNAME=      rpcserv
OBJS=          rpcserv.o dbdisk.o rpcxdr.o
LIBS=          -lrpc -lsocket
```

```
* rpcserv.c: card file database server for chapter 5 */
/* modified for RPC operation as detailed in chapter 6 */
/* tabs in this example are four spaces apart */

#include "rpccards.h"
#include <rpc/rpc.h>
#include <stdio.h>


/* globals to carry character counts */
unsigned long chars_read = 0, chars_written = 0;

/* read record from database */
struct rec *readfunc(recp)
struct rec *recp;
{
 static struct rec   myrec, *myrecp = &myrec;
 static char       response[DBRECLEN], junk[1];
 int result;

 *junk = 0;   /* null out a unimportant string */
 result = read_rec(recp->dbname, response,
     recp->recnum, DBRECLEN);
 myrecp->recnum = result;    /* return position in file
                                 or error (-1) */
 myrecp->data = response;
 myrecp->dbname = junk;
 /* update character count */
 if (myrecp >= 0) chars_read += (unsigned long)DBRECLEN;
 return(myrecp);
}

/* write record to database */
struct rec *writefunc(recp)
struct rec *recp;
{
 static struct rec   myrec, *myrecp = &myrec;
 static char       junk[1];
 int result;

 result = write_rec(recp->dbname, recp->data, recp->recnum,
     DBRECLEN);
 myrecp->dbname = junk;  /* return null filename string */
 myrecp->data = junk;
 myrecp->recnum = result;    /* return position in file
                                 or error (-1) */
 /* update character count */
```

```
 if (myrecp >=0) chars_written += (unsigned long)DBRECLEN;
 return(myrecp);
}

/* return character counts */
void *statfunc(waste)
char    *waste;
{
 static struct stat  status;

 status.chars_read = chars_read;
 status.chars_written = chars_written;
 return(&status);
}


/* create a structure to make registering our procedures easier */
/* the program and version are the same throughout—no sense storing
 those here */

extern int  xdr_status(), xdr_rec();

struct {
 int         proc_num;   /* procedure number */
 void        *(*func)(); /* function to dispatch */
 int         (*xdr_in)(), (*xdr_out)();
} proc_list[] = {
 CARDREAD,   readfunc,   xdr_rec,    xdr_rec,
 CARDWRITE,  writefunc,  xdr_rec,    xdr_rec,
 CARDSTAT,   statfunc,   xdr_void,   xdr_status,
 -1, 0,          0,          0
};

main(argc, argv)
int     argc;
char    **argv;
{
 int                 i, result, dbfd, reclen;
 char                buf[4096];

 /* register procedures corresponding with supported requests */
 for (i = 0; ; i++) {
     if (proc_list[i].proc_num < 0)  /* marks end of list */
         break;
     result = registerrpc(CARDPROGRAM, CARDVERSION,
         proc_list[i].proc_num, proc_list[i].func,
         proc_list[i].xdr_in, proc_list[i].xdr_out);
     if (result != 0) {  /* failed */
```

```
            fprintf(stderr, "registerrpc: Cannot register service\n");
            exit(1);
        }
    }
    svc_run();
}
```

You can see how blissfully simple the server becomes with RPC. The svc_run routine dispatches readfunc(), writefunc(), and statfunc() when the client requests come in. The data is encoded and decoded transparently; the non-RPC-involved functions deal with an ordinary structure, oblivious to the greasy goings-on needed to get the data across the channel.

As for the client, the changes required there were of an even simpler nature. Again, the interface portion of the code can stay the same (and, thus, the modifications you must have made by now are safe); only the database I/O is affected. To add RPC support, it was necessary to change the makefile. The netcards.c file should be copied to rpccards.c, and the following makefile parameters applied:

```
PROGNAME=       rpccards
OBJS=           rpccards.o show_error.o rpcxdr.o
LIBS=           -lform -lmenu -lcurses -lrpc -lsocket
```

Here is the code that should be changed or added in the client module:

```
/* netcards.c: Card file application using ETI and TCP/IP */
/* for chapter 5 */
/* tabs in this file are four spaces apart */

#include "rpccards.h"

#include <unistd.h>
#include <fcntl.h>
#include <stdio.h>
#include <curses.h>
#include <menu.h>
#include <form.h>
#include <rpc/rpc.h>

#define INTR     (MAX_COMMAND + 1)

/* globals */
char     dbfname[255];     /* remember db name once told */
```

```
...
/* ask the server to open a database for us */
int open_db(filename)
char    *filename;
{
 /* the database is opened for each read and write. Unfortunately,
     we can't tell whether the database can be opened or not.
     Perhaps a call should be added to test the database file
     for access rights? */
 strcpy(dbfname, filename);
 return(0);
}

/* read a record from the database */
int read_rec(fd, buf, recnum)
int     fd, recnum;
char    *buf;
{
 return(read_call(dbfname, buf, recnum));
}

/* write record to database. if recnum == 0, append to end of file */
int write_rec(fd, buf, recnum)
int     fd, recnum;
char    *buf;
{
 return(write_call(dbfname, buf, recnum));
}
```

There is one last module: cardstat, a separate client program that queries the server for read and write statistics. Create a makefile with these parameters:

```
PROGNAME=      cardstat
OBJS=          cardstat.o rpcxdr.o
LIBS=          -lrpc -lsocket

/* cardstat.c: get statistics from card server */
/* tabs are four spaces apart */

#include <stdio.h>
#include <rpc/rpc.h>
#include "rpccards.h"

main()
{
 struct stat     status;
 int             result;
```

```
extern int        xdr_status();

result = callrpc("localhost", CARDPROGRAM, CARDVERSION, CARDSTAT,
    xdr_void, NULL, xdr_status, &status);

if (result != 0) {
    fprintf(stderr, "Cannot contact remote server\n");
    exit(1);
}
printf("Card server report: %ld read, %ld written\n",
    status.chars_read, status.chars_written);
}
```

It doesn't get any easier than that.

Because RPC works so well for this application, we'll make this the last change to the cardfile program in this book. By retooling for RPC, we gained several important advantages:

- The server is connectionless and stateless, so there's less worry about losing connections. Our server doesn't need to worry about disappearing clients, and the clients won't even notice if the server is temporarily unavailable, as long as an in-progress request isn't interrupted, and the client doesn't have to wait so long that it times out.

- Each remote call is atomic; when callrpc() returns, you know the data was passed, the call was made, and the data was returned. As long as you did your XDR filters and data handling properly, one call is all it takes. It's almost as simple as a local function call.

- The ability of a single server to register multiple programs, versions, and procedures allows one program to offer a wide variety of services. Servers can be upgraded, even in ways that are incompatible with older clients. As long as the old server procedures are registered under the previous version number, back-leveled clients can still communicate. Also, because only one registerrpc call is required per remote function, it is easy to add new services to existing programs. The structure in rpcserver.c above is one way to build an easily extensible server.

- XDR's versatility makes it possible to package virtually any kind of data. This database could be updated to store a complex mix of numeric, binary, and character data. You would only need to write new XDR filters that matched the database record structure, and specify those filters in the registerrpc and callrpc calls. If you used XDR's ability to work with file data, you could also store your binary and numeric data in a hardware-independent format that could be read by any system supporting RPC.

As mentioned at the start of this section, there are many features of RPC not covered here. Among them are rpcgen, a code generator that can make working with large data structures somewhat easier; complex XDR types including arrays and discriminated unions (a data element that can represent any one of several data types); user authentication (for security); broadcast RPC, in which a client places a call that is answered by every active, registered server on that network. And it goes on. RPC is a rich specification and set of functions, but it's entirely possible to get good use of it with the basic understanding you have gained here.

If you plan to do much serious work with RPC, you should study the documentation carefully. In PC UNIX, the RPC documentation can usually be found in the *NFS Programmer's Guide* and *Reference* manuals. Later releases may make RPC a part of the basic network services; conduct your search accordingly.

This section on RPC concludes the network programming coverage in this book. We'll be moving on to other advanced topics, but there may be the occasional reference back to networking material earlier in the book. Bone up on these chapters, particularly before moving on to the X Window programming chapters that follow.

Chapter 7

X Window and Motif Foundations

This chapter contains material which requires that you have an X Window server installed and running, and are equipped with the libraries and header files needed to produce X Window applications. The Open Desktop Development System from SCO includes everything you need for that environment. You will also need documentation for X Window and OSF/Motif. Specific manuals, titled as in the Open Desktop Development System set, will be called for in the text as needed.

If you haven't worked with X Window before, take the time now to study the graphical interface sections of the *Open Desktop User's Manual* (or the equivalent for your system's X Window software, such as the O'Reilly and Associates *X User's Reference*). Get accustomed to X Window from a user's perspective—this chapter assumes you already know enough about using X Window to survive, and you'll find that we slam pretty quickly into programming.

Examples have been important throughout this book, but in the following two chapters on X Window applications programming, the examples are absolutely essential to understanding the concepts. Some of the examples are lengthy; you can save time by sending for the source code disk with the form in the back of this book.

Why X?

Even with all the recent developments in networking and graphical environments, there is still no match for the power and versatility offered by the suite of programs known as the X Window System. It remains the most elegant way to share applications, text, and graphical data across systems of different types. Today, it is possible to plug DOS-based PC systems, Macintoshes, Amigas, PCs running Microsoft Windows, and other systems of almost every size and description into graphical applications that run predictably, regardless of machine or operating system type. And the X terminal, the X Window equivalent of the "dumb terminal," has no equal in any other environment, allowing users to tap into powerful, demanding graphical applications with no more than the expense of a typical desktop PC.

Even if you have a room full of systems of the same type, X Window still offers unique capabilities. Although X Window does not include a cross-platform binary standard, and you still need to run applications on the hardware and OS for which they were compiled, application code can run on any machine on the network, and route all of its display output and keyboard/mouse input to any other machine on the network.

As you may have learned from picking up the needed X user skills, the traditional concept of client and server might seem reversed when applied to X. While the term "server" is normally used to describe programs (like database management servers) that have little or no direct interaction with users, the most basic definition of a network server—a program that offers a service through a network connection—certainly applies. The service provided by the X server is that of an interface to the user. Graphics and text are displayed, and keyboard and mouse (or touchscreen, or graphics tablet, or what-have-you) input are collected. Client programs link into the X server through a network connection, and request I/O services and services which support user I/O.

Throughout the X Window chapters, you'll find several references to networks and network connections. Like any well-designed client/server package, X Window supports clients that reside on the same machine as the server. Many X Window implementations use shared memory, or some other scheme, to bypass TCP/IP (or whatever networking protocol is being used), and improve the performance of local connections. The main point here is that the X Window applications you write, including the examples here, don't need to worry about whether a connection is local or remote.

The X Window System has a rich history, and is itself a fascinating study in the design and development of client/server software. We won't take time for that here, but you might eventually take the time to read up on the details of the lower levels of X programming. To get you going as quickly as possible, this chapter and the next will focus strictly on the topmost layers available to X Window C programmers: the X toolkit and OSF/Motif.

Please note that OSF/Motif (we'll just call it "Motif" from now on), while it is commonly included in commercial X Window packages (including Open Desktop), is *not* part of the X Window System. X itself is freely available, even in source-code form, while Motif is a commercial product produced under license from the Open Software Foundation. Except for the libraries and header files, which become part of your compiled application, you cannot legally redistribute any portion of the Motif software unless you purchase a license from the OSF. Keep in mind, too, that even though the basic X source code is freely available, a vendor's binary version, like the executables in Open Desktop, can *not* be redistributed. However, you can use the X Window header files and libraries as part of programs you distribute. If you have questions about what your redistribution rights are, get in touch with your vendor before you make assumptions that might get you into trouble.

In the lower layers exists the software that makes and maintains client network connections to servers. The lowest level is contained in a library called "Xlib." Xlib must be linked with every X Window application you produce: Each of the layers up the chain is dependent on all of the layers below it. In addition to managing network connections, Xlib provides the basic translation between requests (like "open a window") and data packets sent to the server. Requests are queued and sent at an arbitrary time. A queue might be flushed for reaching a high-water mark (nearly out of memory), or perhaps a user input request is received that requires that output be brought up to date, or you can make an Xlib call that flushes the queue manually. In any case, a key objective of the link between client and server is the conservation of network traffic. If every request were sent immediately to the server, the network would be loaded with tiny packets, and performance would be very poor. Queueing solves this problem, but it creates another: Your application can never make assumptions about what's on the display. At any point in your application, the X server can be dozens of requests behind. Almost none of the X Window function calls block until the server acknowledges the request.

Another interesting aspect of programming in X is how little control you really have over what the user's screen looks like. The size, position, stacking order, iconified state—you name it, the user can change it. The user can make a window too small to hold any data, or make your program's font so large that it runs off the window's edge. You should let them do it. One of the wonderful things about X is its configurability, and how much of that power it places in the user's hands. Giving up this much control makes some developers unhappy. After all, one of the reasons programming is so thrilling is that sense of ultimate control. Luckily, X Window programming is fun enough, and produces such great-looking results that you soon quit sulking over giving your users the power to shoot themselves.

The user's main weapon in this endeavor is the *window manager*. When the windows that are part of an X application come into the world, they are naked. The frames, resizing handles, and title bars you're accustomed to seeing (or soon will be) are all added by the window manager. This is a special class of X Window application that provides users with the tools they need to manipulate windows. Without a window manager, even the simplest resizing and moving of windows is impossible at the user level. The window manager with which you'll most likely be working is called "mwm", the Motif Window Manager. When your application opens a window, mwm goes through a process called "reparenting." It's a simple idea once you understand how windows are arranged.

Everything in X Window is a window (or, at least, it can be treated like one). The buttons you push, the scrollbars you operate, even the window manager's resizing handles and title bars are all windows. Each falls into a hierarchy at a place determined at the time of the window's creation. So, if you have a window "A", and you create a button inside that window called "B", then "B" is said to be a child of "A". A window can have many child windows, and those children can have children, and so on. That's how the tree is made. Under normal circumstances, the children's behavior is dictated by the parent. If the parent moves or changes size, the child windows can move and resize, too. If the parent window is destroyed (as when the application exits), the destruction ripples down the tree until all the children are gone as well.

Most applications have what's called a top-level window, the window that is the super-parent, the anchor for the windows that are created later. The parent of a top-level window is usually the root window, the X Window background. When a window manager starts running, it asks the server to tell it when new windows are created. Each new top-level window (or any other window that would have the root window as its parent), unless the application specifically requests otherwise, is reparented so that it is actually a child of the graphical frame the window manager paints around it. That's why a window moves when you drag the title bar, and changes size when you drag one of the resizing handles at the corners. The parent, the window manager frame, is controlling the behavior of its child, the application window. The application window, in turn, ripples the changes down to its children, and so on.

The first, best rule of X programming is "never assume anything." Your window won't necessarily end up where you put it, might not be the size you requested, may not use the fonts and colors you tested with, and could be obscured or obliterated at any time by the window manager or another X client. Designing an X application must always include a round of "what if" testing. Don't assume "the user would never be stupid enough to do *that*;" they may have reasons of their own, sensible or not, for taking your program in directions you didn't plan for.

Even if the user is happy to leave your application's windows and fonts and such just as you planned them, the window manager can be an unruly master. If you want to resize your top-level window, for instance, you don't just resize it. You must *ask* the window manager if it's okay. The window manager usually says "Fine," but it can say "No," or it can say "Yes, but use this size instead." Requests to alter fonts, colors, and other resources can also be denied for various reasons by either the window manager or the X server.

The reason you're giving up all this control is simple: Your application is probably sharing the screen with a load of other X clients. They all have needs, too. The X server and window manager reign over this lot because *something* has to keep the peace. Fortunately, X and Motif give you all the tools you need to write programs that make no assumptions, and place no restrictions on the user. The best X clients are those that do just that. In your designs, plan on providing a workable set of defaults, and make *everything* (within reason) user-tunable.

There are some things you have to worry about yourself. Color is a major issue. If you're dead certain that your application will never run on anything different from the hardware, operating system, and version of X Window that you tested with, no problem. Just get it to run on your system and you're fine. But most of us aren't so lucky. If you write for color, what happens if someone runs your program on a monochrome display? If your application uses 27 colors, how will it run on a 16-color display? What about gray-scale? These issues are not resolved for you; you should develop your application with display type independence in mind. The same goes for keyboards. Don't assume, for example, that all keyboards have a "help" or a "scroll lock" key. As for mice, however, the three-button mouse is the standard, and most X servers that support mice with fewer buttons have built-in translations that let users run clients written for three-button mice.

These are some of the more challenging issues you encounter in designing an X Window application. In the next section, we'll discuss some ways to address these issues, and we'll look at an important facility that you need to understand in order to write good X Window applications. Don't be too concerned if you don't understand everything that's being explained. As we get closer to the first example, the pieces should begin to come together for you.

X Resources

A crucial part of the services provided by the X server does not directly affect the placing of pixels on the screen. To manage the complex array of multiple clients, connections, and windows, the X server must be something of a database manager. Every interface element, be it a text window, menu, or push button, has associated with it certain data elements that determine its size, color, and other parameters. These parameters are called *resources*, and are stored in the *resource database*. The term "resource" seems a little ambiguous here, but in the context of the resource database, "resource" always means the same thing: a parameter stored in the resource database. Resources for the interface elements that are part of Motif control things like color, window position, labels, and such. They also control aspects of an interface's behavior. Like any database, each entry has a key, and a data element. In this case, the key is an identifier that locates the target resource in the hierarchy. The type and acceptable range of the data depends on the resource. If it helps, you might think of resource database entries as variable/value pairs instead of key/data pairs.

The concept of resources can be difficult to grasp. Because of this, many first-time X Window programmers leave the handling of resources out of their programs. Don't underestimate the importance of resources, even in small programs. With them, you (and your users) can make minor to sweeping changes to your application's appearance *without recompiling*. Without them, your application stands out as a bad example against the backdrop of properly-written X clients. As a general rule, whatever is possible and prudent to store as a resource should be stored that way, instead of being hard-coded into your application.

The hierarchy that X uses to keep track of windows and their children vaguely parallels the UNIX directory structure: A parent window can have any number of children, but a child can have only one parent. Take a look at Figure 7-1. It shows a simple arrangement of windows and the hierarchy that X builds to represent them. The top level of the hierarchy is occupied by a special entry called the *application class*. For now, let's just say this is an arbitrary name you assign to your application. The tree graph at the bottom of Figure 7-1 shows the structure, but how would you show the relationship of "subwin3" to the rest of the hierarchy without resorting to graphs? You might use something like this:

```
exam1.mainwin.subwin1.subwin3
```

Figure 7-1: The X Hierarchy

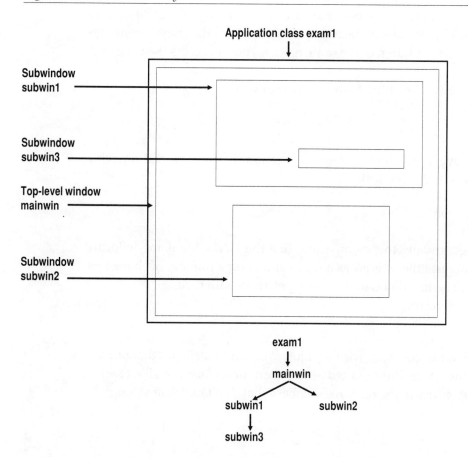

If you understand that each child can have only one parent, then this notation shows clearly that subwin3 is descended directly from subwin1, its grand-
parent is mainwin, and its great-grandparent exam1. As you might have
guessed, this is precisely the notation X uses for resource names in the resource
database.

Wildcards can be used to eliminate any number of tree layers in a resource
name. Consider this:

```
exam1*subwin3
```

Given the hierarchy in Figure 7-1, this is just shorthand for
exam1.mainwin.subwin1.subwin3. But if subwin2 (exam1's other child) also had
a child named subwin3, the resource name above would have matched both children. Is it okay to have two occurrences of the same name in the resource tree? It
is, as long as the path to it is unique. A resource name is considered unique if *any*
of its qualifiers are different. It's possible to have as many subwin3's in your
application as you like. As long as each one is attached to a different parent (one
parent cannot have two children of the same name), you can access them individually.

Finally, we can have the ultimate shortcut to subwin3:

```
*subwin3
```

This matches every subwin3 in your application. If subwin3 had any children, you'd address them, too, with

```
*subwin3*
```

Resist the urge to view this as anything like the UNIX file name wildcard
scheme. You cannot use the asterisk as a replacement for a number of characters,
only entire layers. You could not, for instance, get away with this:

```
*sub*
```

Actually, you *would* get away with it, it just wouldn't match anything unless
a resource with the name "sub" existed somewhere (anywhere, in this case). X
doesn't fuss about entries in the resource database that don't match anything.

So the period defines an explicit path between two layers in the resource tree, and an asterisk matches any number of layers wherever it appears. The two schemes can be combined. In the case of Figure 7-1, subwin3 could also be addressed with:

```
exam1.mainwin.subwin1*
```

This would hit all of the children of subwin1.

When using the resource database for real, you would never construct an address that referred, as in the naming examples given above, to an entire window, or to other interface elements such as a menu or a button. Instead, each window would have a number of resources associated with it that controlled things like size, position, and background color. We're still talking pure theory here—*real* uses for resources are a few paragraphs away—but let's say that we wanted to change the background color of subwin3 in our example. We would need to know the resource name for the background color, and then construct a name that targeted only subwin3's background color resource. If the background color resource was named "background," the full path to it would be:

```
exam1.mainwin.subwin1.subwin3.background
```

But that's only half of a resource database entry. The background color would have a value associated with it, and that value would have an application-defined data type. The application itself would supply an entry for the resource database that reflected the default setting of the background color. If we chose to change it, we would have to construct a new resource database entry, complete with a value matching the data type requirements, and have it added to the resource database.

The resource database is not stored on disk, and you can't manipulate it the way you would a traditional database. However, you can construct a disk file containing new or changed resource database entries, and use an X Window utility to load them into the database of a running X server. An X Window application can, and should, also use resource manager function calls to store and retrieve entries in the resource database. As you'll see later in this chapter, high-level Motif functions take care of some of this for you.

Let's say we wanted to change the background color of subwin3 (remember, we're still dealing in theory—don't try any of this). Let's assume the data type for the background resource permitted the use of named colors. To change the background color of subwin3 to red, we'd use:

```
exam1*subwin3.background:        red
```

I used a shortcut here; you could have spelled it out with the same results.

The above example would make a single change to the resource database. It wouldn't affect any other windows (unless there were multiple subwin3 windows in the application exam1). Let's say, for uniformity's sake, that we wanted all of exam1's window backgrounds to be red. Stop reading for a moment and see if you can construct the correct resource name. Here's one form you could use:

```
exam1*background:        red
```

In the specific case of the simple layout in Figure 7-1, this would work fine. If we had a more complete program with menus, buttons, and such, this resource entry would change the background color of *everything* in the application that kept its background color in a resource named "background," which is, by the way, very common. Your whole application would go red on you, very disconcerting if that's not what you wanted. Assuming our application was more complex and *did* contain buttons and such, we would need a way to construct a resource that changed only the window backgrounds, and left everything else alone. We could resort to separate resource entries for each of the windows, but there is a better way.

Each interface element that is part of an application belongs to a named *class*. A class name can be used wherever a specific resource name is used. When a class name is used, it refers to all interface elements at that level in the tree that are part of that class. Let's say that the menus in our application belonged to the class "Menu", the buttons to the class "Button", and the windows to the class "Window". Resource specifications are case-sensitive, and a leading uppercase letter is traditionally used to signify the use of a class name, rather than a resource. That distinction is not enforced, but it is worth upholding. In the scenario described above, changing the background color of all the windows in our application could go like this:

```
exam1*Window.background:        red
```

This assumes that all of the windows in our application are members of the class Window. Be aware that not only interface elements, but the resources associated with those elements, belong to classes. Our windows could, for instance, each have a pair of background colors: one for morning, and one for afternoon (no one works on computers at night). You couldn't call both resources by the name "background"—this would violate the unique-name rule. But by having both background resources belong to the same class (and they should, since they share the same data type and have very similar purposes), we can address them both by referring to the class to which they both belong:

```
exam1*Window*Background:        red
```

Entries in the resource database are subject to a precedence mechanism that resolves multiple entries that refer to the same resources. The rule is simple: The more explicit the path to the resource, the higher the precedence. Using asterisks and class names will reduce an entry's precedence, while using periods and specific resource names will increase precedence. Let's say we had these two entries in the database at the same time:

```
exam1*Window*Background:        red
exam1*subwin3.am_background: blue
```

The latter entry takes precedence over the former, because it supplies a more explicit path to a specific resource. Sequences of entries similar to the one above are not uncommon. Broad, low-precedence entries can be used to set application-wide defaults, then high-precedence entries can be added to define the exceptions to those defaults.

One Toe in the Water

We're not quite ready yet for full-fledged reality, but let's attach a few of the concepts we've discussed to their specific uses in the X Window system and Motif. We'll start by building on what has already been explained about how X applications are constructed. This is a crash course—hang on tight.

At the head of this chapter we noted that Xlib is at the root of all X Window clients. Xlib provides all the primitives (draw points and lines, change colors, allocate and free client-specific memory in the server, etc.) you need to write any kind of graphical application, but because it is so primitive, you have to do everything "by hand." If you wanted to put a push button in a window, you would have to draw the rectangle, then keep an eye on the mouse to make sure that, when the mouse button is pressed, the button doesn't respond unless the pointer was clicked inside the confines of your button's rectangle. It's even more complicated and tedious than that.

Knowing that application developers would want to have mouse-sensitive objects like windows, buttons, and menus in their programs, the people who crafted the X Window System defined a layer above Xlib called the X Toolkit, or Xt. The toolkit itself doesn't make buttons and menus, but it provides the infrastructure needed to create and manage them. You must stack yet *another* layer above Xt to get full use of it. The Motif library (Xm) is just such a layer. It makes X Toolkit calls that create buttons, menus, windows, and other interface elements.

We've been speaking in vague terms about "interface elements," when what we've been referring to all along is *widgets*. A widget is an interface element, a window that has special properties associated with it. A push button widget, for instance, doesn't need you to figure out when it's been pushed. It knows. Depending on how you set the resources associated with a push button widget, it can change colors when the mouse passes over it, and do other implementation-specific things. Instead of wasting time writing code that manages each of the interface elements in your application, widgets can, to an extent, manage themselves.

The idea of the self-managing widget (called a *managed* widget) needs a little explaining. A push button widget can be created through the facilities of the Motif library, and asked to manage itself. Through resource database entries, you can define *callbacks*, functions that the toolkit calls when certain events occur. Instead of keeping an eye on the push button's region, and doing something when the mouse crosses into it, you can simply define a callback procedure, an ordinary C function that you want executed whenever this takes place. A managed widget also "does the right thing" without your intervention when asked to change size or position, and redraws itself when an overlapping window obscures and then uncovers it. Many elements of a managed widget's behavior can be modified through resources.

Mouse movement, mouse-button presses, keyboard activity, and a host of other things that can require your application's attention, are called *events*. For example, an exposure event is sent to all of the windows (and remember, widgets are windows, too) in your application when something occurs that requires them to redraw themselves. Exposure events are also sent the first time a window appears. In fact, anything you draw into a window prior to the first exposure event is discarded; you must always wait until the first exposure event is received before drawing the contents of a window. That first exposure event is the X server's way of telling you the window is ready. Managed widgets take care of all this for you. If you write an application that uses only managed widgets, you needn't worry about exposure events.

Most Motif applications use the predefined widgets that are part of the Motif library. These cover a wide range of capabilities which we'll discuss in more detail shortly. It is possible to invent your own widgets from scratch, but that's a topic we won't cover here. Instead, we'll focus exclusively on making the best use of the widgets that are provided by Motif.

If you're a student of object-oriented programming, the term "class" probably raised a flag for you. Motif is, in many ways, an object-oriented system. Each type of widget is its own named class, so it shouldn't surprise you that to use a certain class of widget in your application, you must first create an *instance* of it. It can be said that Motif doesn't do widgets, only classes of them. The term "widget," then, can rightly refer to a specific instance of a widget class.

Creating a widget instance is accomplished with a single function call. After creation, you still won't see anything on the screen. Displaying a widget requires that it be *mapped*. Managed widgets, by default, map themselves, but you must first make a separate call after creation to tell your application's widgets to map themselves. Just as widgets can be mapped, they can be unmapped. This doesn't destroy them, it just removes them from the screen.

The ability to create a widget instance that doesn't appear right away brings up two methods of coding Motif applications. Widget instances can be created at any time. Let's say that your application requires a push button that appears only when a particular menu item has been selected. You could write your application to create and remove the push button widget as needed. If the push button isn't needed very frequently, this could be a prudent conservation of resources. But if it is to be activated often, the performance overhead of constantly creating and destroying the push button will be measurable. In the case of a single button, the user probably won't notice, but multiply that for all of the transient widgets in a complex application, and it begins to add up. The tradeoff is this: If you choose to conserve resources by creating and destroying widgets as they are needed, you may be making the user wait while these processes take place. You can, instead, create all of the widgets your application uses before the first window is displayed, but not have them managed until they appear on the screen. To send the widgets away, instead of destroying them, you can simply unmanage (which unmaps) them. The entire widget tree for your application will be in memory, and your application's responsiveness will be *very* snappy. You can make the user wait up front and use up memory, or make them wait each time a widget appears and save memory, or you can use some combination of these two approaches. One popular combination is to create the widget the first time it's called for, then leave it in place (just unmanage it to make it disappear) for the next time. You will see a mix of these methods in the examples to come, and no one of them is intrinsically better than another. It all depends on your style, and what you know about where your application will be run.

There is another aspect to classes that directly relates to a topic discussed earlier: resources. A widget class doesn't exist on its own, it is derived from a line of ancestor classes. Each ancestor in the chain adds some behavior and a set of resources not contained in the class preceding it. At the root of it all is the Core class that defines the most basic requirements of a widget: size, position, and background color, among other things. A single widget class can *inherit* behavior and resources from any number of ancestor classes. The resource set associated with a widget, then, is a combination of its inherited resources *and* its unique resources. The reference manual entry for each Motif widget class lists all of that class's new and inherited resources, and the classes from which resources were inherited. You can easily use widgets in your applications without understanding much (if anything) about how inheritance works. The PushButton widget class, for instance, is descended from the Core, Primitive, and Label classes. You could flip through the manual and look up these classes, but it wouldn't tell you much. Since all of the resources, new and inherited, are listed on each class's manual page, unless the widget behaves in a way you don't understand, you needn't concern yourself with a class's parentage. The exception is when you need to look up the *description* of an inherited resource. For that, you need to flip to the page for the class that defines that resource. However, you'll find that many of the resource names make sense. After looking them up once, the name and data type should be all you need to remind you. Not all classes *do* something. Some exist just for appearance's sake (like the Frame class, which draws a rectangular frame in a window), while others are just containers for holding other widgets.

The First Example

It's been a long, hard road, but you've finally made it to the first example. This is probably the simplest working Motif application you can create: A window with a button in it. Just that description suggests the two widgets we'll need to instantiate: a push button, and a window to stick the push button to. You could have a button floating in space, but it would look strange, and that wouldn't help me reinforce the fact that all applications need a top-level window, a container of some kind. In our case, we'll work with the simplest of the container window classes. The more complex container classes will be covered in the next chapter. For now, we'll use one that just gives us a place to stick a widget: the BulletinBoard.

NOTE: *To locate a particular widget class in the Motif reference manual, you need to add the prefix "Xm" to the raw class name. You can find the manual page for the BulletinBoard widget filed under XmBulletinBoard.*

Type in or load from disk the code for this example.

Here are the makefile parameters:

```
PROGNAME=       button
OBJS=           button.o
LIBS=           -lXm -lXt -lX11 -lsocket
```

Here's the example code:

```c
/* button.c: First Motif example for chapter 7 */
/* tabs are four spaces apart */

#include <X11/Intrinsic.h>
#include <Xm/Xm.h>
#include <Xm/PushB.h>
#include <Xm/BulletinB.h>

main(argc, argv)
int     argc;
char    **argv;
{
    Widget      shell, bulletin_board, push_button;

    /* Initialize the toolkit, set up top-level shell */
    shell = XtInitialize("shell",           /* shell name */
        "Button",                           /* application class */
        NULL,                               /* option list */
        0,                                  /* length of opt list */
```

```
        &argc,                                  /* argument count */
        argv);                                  /* arguments */

    /* create instance of BulletinBoard container widget class */
    bulletin_board =
        XtCreateManagedWidget("bulletin_board",      /* name */
            xmBulletinBoardWidgetClass,     /* class */
            shell,                          /* parent widget */
            NULL,                           /* resource list */
            0);                             /* res count */

    /* create instance of PushButton widget class */
    push_button =
        XtCreateManagedWidget("push_button", xmPushButtonWidgetClass,
            bulletin_board, NULL, 0);

    /* make the whole thing appear */
    XtRealizeWidget(shell);

    /* run the event loop */
    XtMainLoop();
}
```

If you have X Window running, you should be able to run this program now. It doesn't do anything but open a window with a button in it. You can use the mouse to push the button, which should appear to recess into the background. Pushing the button has no effect, because no callbacks were defined. (We'll get to that in the widget breakouts in the next chapter.) To exit the program, you can either move the mouse into the window from which you started the program and press the interrupt key, or if you're running mwm, you should also be able to click on the icon at the upper-left corner of button's window and select "Close" from the menu that appears.

This first example has been kept small so it would be a little easier to describe how a Motif application works. Even though it doesn't do anything, this skeletal program includes all of the procedures needed to get any Motif program rolling.

You may have noticed that the compilation of this short example took a little while. This is due, in part, to the huge header files that must be a part of every Motif application. The first file, "X11/Intrinsic.h", holds the definitions and data structures needed to use the X Toolkit. "Xm/Xm.h" is the main Motif header file. "Xm/PushB.h" and "Xm/BulletinB.h" are the files that set up the PushButton and BulletinBoard widget classes. The first two header files are essential to every Motif program. You also need, as shown in button.c, one header file for each widget class used in the file. The names of the header files are truncated to fit the limited file name size of System V (thankfully, that's changing with Release 4). The file names still map very closely to the class names they cover, but you may have to resort to the occasional ls to figure out how a name is abbreviated. The Motif and toolkit functions that deal with widgets always refer to them through variables of the type Widget.

The first brush that most Motif applications have with widgets is through the XtInitialize call. This one simple function call fires off a number of others that, without XtInitialize(), you would have to call yourself. Among the things XtInitialize does for you is scan the command line used to call your application for toolkit arguments. These arguments give users a shortcut to commonly-modified resources through familiar UNIX-style command line options. Each option that requires an argument has a specific data type. We won't bother to uncover every obscure turn the options and arguments can take, only those that are most useful to the average installation. Here they are:

-background *color*   **Synonym:** -bg
Affected resource: Background

Changes the default background color to *color*. The *color* argument can be a color name (found in /usr/lib/X11/rgb.txt) or a "#" character followed by a hexadecimal string containing the values of the red, green, and blue components of the color.

Examples: xclock -bg LightBlue
           xclock -bg "midnight blue" # spaces must be quoted
           xclock -bg #ff0077   # obnoxious pink

-display *display*   **Synonym:** None
Affected resource: Display

Causes the application to appear on a specified display. You must have authorization to connect to the host to which the display is connected. Authorized host names are usually listed in /etc/X0.hosts, with the 0 changing to reflect the display number for hosts with multiple displays. The xhost command can also be used to add a host authorization to a running server. The *display* argument is usually the name of the host, a colon, and the display number. The host's network address can also be used. Setting the DISPLAY environment variable prior to executing an X Window application has the same effect.

Examples: xclock -display cuthbert:0
           xclock -display 192.1.1.17:1

-font *font*   **Synonym:** -fn
Affected resource: Font

Sets the default font. Fonts are usually located in directories under /usr/lib/X11/fonts. A list of fonts recognized by the current server can be obtained with the xlsfonts utility. See the reference manual entry for xset to see how to add and remove fonts from the server.

Examples: xterm -fn '-*-courier-*-*-*-*-14-*'
                # terminal emulator with 14-pixel courier font

---

-foreground *color*   **Synonym:** -fg
Affected resource: Foreground

Changes the default foreground color.

Examples: xclock -bg #ff0077 -fg LightBlue

-geometry *geometry*   **Synonym:** None
Affected resource: Geometry

Sets the initial size and placement of the window. *XXxYY* specifies a window *XX* pixels wide and *YY* high. Placement is specified by a pair of numbers preceded by plus or minus signs. A positive value indicates the distance in pixels from the left (X) or top (Y) of the screen, while a negative value indicates the distance from the right or bottom edge.

Examples: xclock -geometry 100x100+200+125
                # place a 100x100 window at x=200, y=125
                xclock -geometry '-125-140'
                # 125 pixels from the right, 140 from the bottom

---

-iconic   **Synonym:** None
Resource affected: Iconic

Starts the application in an iconified state. How this is handled depends on the window manager settings.

Examples: xclock -iconic

-title *title*   **Synonym:** None
Resource affected: Title

Alter the title used to identify the application. Normally used to change the text that appears in the window manager's title bar.

Examples: xclock -title "Beat The Clock"

These options are available to every application you write that uses the toolkit. When you start your application with XtInitialize() and pass the argv and argc variables to it, the toolkit parses the command line. Each toolkit argument it finds is evaluated, and then removed from the argument list. When XtInitialize() exits, the argument list and count reflect a command line scrubbed of all toolkit options. In other words, everything is handled for you; you don't even have to step around toolkit options when processing your own.

The first argument to XtInitialize is all-important: the application class name. This argument becomes the first qualifier for all your application's entries in the resource database just as exam1 was in Figure 7-1. We'll play around with the example's resources shortly to give you a feel for the resource database.

XtInitialize() returns the Widget value of a special entity called the top-level shell. This is the conduit between your application and the window manager. The top-level shell can have exactly one child, and it is usually a container widget like the BulletinBoard used in the example. The top-level shell is a valid widget, and can have any widget as a child. For instance, we could have attached the push button directly to the top-level shell. The button would have filled the entire window, though, and it wouldn't have been as clear that it was a button.

There's more to say about XtInitialize and the work it does, but we need to digress for a moment to wrap up the description of the example code. The widgets are created with XtCreateManagedWidget calls. Like XtInitialize, this is a convenience function that dispatches several others to get the job done. In our case, there's no reason to step down to a lower level. There are also convenience functions for each of the Motif widget classes, but XtCreateManagedWidget lets you create an instance of *any* widget class, and it's easy enough to use. A widget's place in an application's widget tree is determined at the time of creation by the third argument to XtCreateManagedWidget. You need to specify a parent widget for every new widget instance. The class name for a particular widget is found in that widget's reference manual page under the subheading "Classes." For the XtCreateManagedWidget call, always use the *class pointer*. It usually starts with "xm" and ends with "WidgetClass," except for the top-level shell classes like ApplicationShell.

The last thing we'll discuss before moving on to specific coverage of resource handling is the XtRealizeWidget()/XtMainLoop() pair. Until XtRealizeWidget() is called, none of the widgets you create appear on the display. XtRealizeWidget() maps the entire widget tree, starting from the widget you provide as an argument. For our simple examples, we'll stick with realizing the whole tree at once. XtMainLoop() is a call that never returns, and this, or the combination of low-level functions that XtMainLoop() calls, is a required part of all Motif applications. XtMainLoop() dispatches the functions that watch for events and make sure they're handled properly. In button's case, we didn't set up any callbacks, or define any responses to user actions. The defaults kick in, giving us a button that can be pressed, but which does nothing. If you didn't call the XtMainLoop function, the button wouldn't respond. You'll see what callbacks are about in the widget breakouts in the next chapter.

Now, on to resources. The XtInitialize call takes care of loading text files containing resource database entries. Each application class can have its own separate default resource database entry file. The name of this file must be the same as the application class name specified in XtInitialize(). So, for the most recent example, the application class name Button would require that a file of the same name be used to hold the default resources. Of course, you can read a file containing any number of resource entries into the resource database at any time, even ones that cross application class boundaries. The xrdb command provides this service. But in writing your own applications, you shouldn't require the user to run xrdb. The database entries that define the default operating parameters for your application's widgets can be read in automatically during toolkit initialization. All you need to do is ensure that a file with the right name, i.e., the same name as the application class, is in one of the places the toolkit will look.

The toolkit looks in a number of places for an application class's default resources file. For applications that are made available system-wide, there is the directory /usr/lib/X11/app-defaults. If you ls that directory on your system, you should see an entry named Mwm. (Remember, class names, including application class names, usually start with an uppercase letter.) You can run more on the contents of that file to see what some of this window manager's tunable aspects are. In addition to /usr/lib/X11/app-defaults, the toolkit will search your home directory for a file that matches the name of the current application class. Finally, it will look in the directory pointed to by the environment variable XAPPLRESDIR. If you use this variable, be sure you set it to a full path specification, and that the path points to a directory, *not* to an individual resource file. In this way, a single directory can contain your favorite (and, in some cases, essential) settings for several applications.

We talked earlier about leaving as much power as possible in the hands of the user. In the case of Motif applications, it's also in the developer's best interest to rely heavily on resource files. Remember that resources define virtually everything that governs a widget's appearance and behavior. It's much more than just colors. There are a few things—*very* few—that can only be modified from inside an application. Let's use the most recent example, the button application, to get a feel for how powerful resources really are.

Making a change to the resource database normally won't have an effect on an application until it is started again. So, as we go through the various resource changes in the following examples (and your own experiments), bear in mind that you won't see any changes until you exit the button and run it again.

Perhaps the easiest things for us to change are the colors. The section above that described some of the toolkit command-line options explained the ways in which a color value can be defined. When building a resource file, the same formatting rules apply, so we can either use one of the colors described in /usr/lib/X11/rgb.txt, or we can offer a hex number that reflects the red, green, and blue values of the desired color.

Color is one of the trickiest things about X. Even though colors are easy for the user (and you) to change, there is no guarantee the changes will be accepted. If you're running SCO Open Desktop on an EGA or VGA display, for example, you may only have a total of 16 colors to work with. The window manager reserves many of these colors for its use. It is possible, on a 16-color screen, that some of the following examples may produce strange results, or no results at all. You can tell mwm not to use so many colors by making changes to the mwm default resource file in /usr/lib/X11/app-defaults/Mwm, or by defining overriding resource entries of your own elsewhere. Just be sure you make a safe copy of the unmodified resource file first, and remember that you have to restart the window manager before the changes will take effect. You may also have a file in /usr/lib/X11/app-defaults called Mwm.mono. This file contains resource entries for a monochrome display. Renaming this file to Mwm (which makes it the new default resource file) on a system with a color screen will result in the window manager running in black and white. It's not as attractive, but it will give your color Motif applications more colors to work with. Of course, if you're running on a monochrome display, the color resource changes will have no effect. If you're running on a gray-scale display, you may see results, but they won't have any relation to the colors being described.

Let's use the XAPPLRESDIR variable to allow us keep the examples and their resource files together. For my system, the examples are in a directory called /usr/tyager/examples/chap07. Under the Bourne or Korn shell, I use this command to point the toolkit at this directory:

```
$ XAPPLRESDIR=/usr/tyager/examples/chap07; export XAPPLRESDIR
```

Under the C shell, use this instead:

```
% setenv XAPPLRESDIR /usr/tyager/examples/chap07
```

Time for our first set of resource changes. Use the editor to create a file called Button in the directory pointed to by XAPPLRESDIR. For this first pass, we'll make some sweeping changes:

```
Button*foreground:          white
Button*background:          black
```

Save the file and run the button application. Unless something is horribly wrong, the entire window should appear in black and white.

Now let's make a more specific change. Clear out the current contents of the Button file and replace it with this:

```
Button*bulletin_board.background:    white
```

Run Button again. The color of the bulletin board widget (the widget the button is "stuck" to) changed, but the button reverted to the default background color. Notice how this simple change affected the appearance. Unless you're running with monochrome defaults on a white background the button's 3D shading is more pronounced.

Experiment a little bit with colors. Practice resource naming by both specific widget names and class names. In this application, we used a BulletinBoard widget (the resource file class name is XmBulletinBoard) and a PushButton widget (class name XmPushButton). The widget names were provided in the first arguments to the XtCreateManagedWidget calls. I always set these to match the variable names used to hold the Widget handles, but don't let that confuse you: The Widget variable names and the resource names associated with widgets are unrelated.

Motif chooses default sizes for widgets based on common sense. The PushButton widget in our application is just large enough to hold the text. That text, by default, is set to the widget's resource name (push_button in this case). That's easy to change, but instead of doing this piecemeal, let's define an entire file of default resources for the button application:

```
# Default resources for button Motif example from Chapter 7
Button*bulletin_board.background:       white
Button*geometry:                        75x40+100+75
Button*push_button.labelString:         Push Me!
```

See how simple that is? Fact is, it doesn't get much harder than that. An application with dozens of widgets can require a rather tedious session of typing to fill the default resource file, but the results are worth it.

Before we move on to the next chapter, I invite you to spend more time playing around with the button program's resources. Learning where to find them is an important part of writing Motif applications. You already know where resources are listed in the reference manual, but in case you need a refresher, the resources for the widgets used in this example can be found under XmBulletinBoard and XmPushButton. Many of the resources won't apply to our ultra-simple example; we made only the smallest use of these widgets' abilities. But experimentation won't harm anything, so go wild.

In the next chapter, we'll see some of the Motif widgets in stand-alone examples that demonstrate their use. Keep your *Motif Reference Manual* handy, since we will not repeat very much of the material contained there. In the final chapter, we'll build working applications with combinations of these widgets.

Chapter 8

Meet the Motif Widgets

Most of what makes Motif useful is the set of graphical interface elements—widgets—that it defines. Using them, you can create applications that not only look great, but are easy to understand and use. The ease is thanks to the fact that Motif is not only a set of widgets, but a presentation style. All properly-written Motif applications share certain predictable behavioral traits. A pull-down menu, for instance, should always pull down from the menu bar with the left mouse button (mouse button 1). Also, a menu bar is expected to be at the top of an application's window. While it is possible to attach the menu bar to the bottom of the window, or fix the menu to pull down with mouse button 3, design choices like these limit users' ability to move from one Motif program to the next with minimal hassle. What made the Macintosh interface such a success was not its superiority, but its predictability.

Even though it is possible to "break" Motif's predictable behavior, the defaults built into most Motif widgets make it more difficult to bend the rules than to simply abide by them. This, plus the overwhelming moral obligation to follow the standard, should drive you to design Motif applications based on the behavior Motif users expect.

This chapter is intended to give you a look at the more useful Motif widget types, and to give you examples that have been written "generically" enough to be boilerplates for your initial original work involving Motif. Each example stands alone. Each allocates its own top-level shell, and contains the code required to get the widget to appear and, when appropriate, to retrieve its state.

These examples are unlike anything you'll ever write; they don't do anything but demonstrate the widgets. They also help introduce some X Window and Motif concepts we haven't wrestled with yet.

This chapter is arranged alphabetically, after a fashion (some widgets' sample code is embedded in other examples). It may look a little like a reference section, which it isn't, mostly because the Open Software Foundation's own documentation covers that ground nicely. The previous chapter gave you some hints about locating *Motif Programmer's Reference Manual* page entries, and of course you'll have that manual close by as you work through these examples. This saves having to repeat a lot of information you already have on hand, and makes it possible to devote more space to examples and practical discussion.

Before we get underway, one final point: This chapter is far from a complete coverage of the Motif widgets: it covers those widgets and techniques Motif programmers encounter most frequently. This chapter will give you a basic understanding of Motif, and will teach you enough about widgets to enable you to build a wide variety of graphical applications. However, there's more to Motif than the few chapters in this book.

Each section has its own figure, descriptive text, sample code, and default resource file. Don't forget to set the XAPPLRESDIR environment variable to the directory in which the resource files are stored.

ArrowButton

Include file: Xm/ArrowB.h

Class name (for resource file): XmArrowButton

Creation examples:

```
Widget     arrow_button;
Arg        *args;
int        argcnt;

arrow_button = XtCreateManagedWidget("widget_name",
    xmArrowButtonWidgetClass, parent_widget, args, argcnt);
```

or

```
arrow_button = XmCreateArrowButton(parent_widget, "widget_name",
    args, argcnt);
XtManageChild(arrow_button);
```

Figure 8-1: Four ArrowButton widgets, with
a Separator (the etched line) and a PushButton ("Quit")

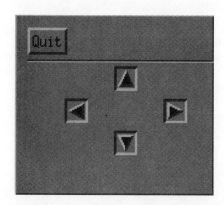

The following widgets are also discussed here and demonstrated in the example:

PushButton

Include file: Xm/PushB.h

Class name: XmPushButton

Creation examples:

```
Widget      push_button;
Arg         *args;
int         argcnt;

push_button = XtCreateManagedWidget("widget_name",
    xmPushButtonWidgetClass, parent_widget, args, argcnt);
```

or

```
push_button = XmCreatePushButton(parent_widget, "widget_name",
    args, argcnt);
XtManageChild(push_button);
```

Separator

Include file: Xm/Separator.h

Class name: XmSeparator

Creation examples:

```
Widget      separator;
Arg         *args;
int         argcnt;

separator = XtCreateManagedWidget("widget_name",
    xmSeparatorWidgetClass, parent_widget, args, argcnt);
```

or

```
separator = XmCreateSeparator(parent_widget, "widget_name",
    args, argcnt);
XtManageChild(separator);
```

BulletinBoard

Include file: Xm/BulletinB.h

Class name: XmBulletinBoard

Creation examples:

```
Widget      bulletin_board;
Arg         *args;
int         argcnt;

bulletin_board = XtCreateManagedWidget("widget_name",
    xmBulletinBoardWidgetClass, parent_widget, args, argcnt);
```

or

```
bulletin_board = XmCreateBulletinBoard(parent_widget, "widget_name",
    args, argcnt);
XtManageChild(bulletin_board);
```

The ArrowButton widget is a square button with an arrowhead drawn on it. Clicking inside the button with the mouse (mouse button 1 by default) causes the function you define as the activation *callback* to be called. The button's shading changes when "pressed," so that it appears to recede into the window's surface.

The button points in the direction specified by the XmNarrowDirection resource, which should be set to XmARROW_UP, XmARROW_DOWN, XmARROW_LEFT, or XmARROW_RIGHT.

Callbacks

Most Motif widgets offer callbacks as the primary mechanism of notifying your program of state changes. The ArrowButton and PushButton described here, for instance, can trigger callbacks in response to three distinct events: When the pointer crosses into the button's area (called "arming"), when the pointer crosses out (called "disarming"), and when the mouse button is pressed within the confines of the button ("activation"). By default, these user actions do nothing. If you don't register a callback for an action, it is generally permitted but ignored.

A callback is a call to an ordinary function inside your application, and Motif defines three arguments that are passed to your callback function each time it is called. The head of the ArrowsCallback function is used in the next example:

```
void ArrowsCallback(widget, client_data, call_data)
Widget                  widget;
void                    *client_data;
XmAnyCallbackStruct     *call_data;
```

The widget ID is passed to give your callback function access to the widget without requiring that it be defined as a global variable. This also permits the same callback function to be registered for several widgets. The client_data argument (the names are unimportant, but these are commonly used) is an arbitrary data pointer that you provide at the time the callback function is registered. You can use this, as the next example does, to determine which widget placed the call.

While the client_data argument can be a pointer to any type of data, the call_data pointer points to a structure associated with the widget that dispatched the callback. Most widgets have their own call_data structure types, and the *Motif Programmer's Reference Manual* describes each widget's call_data structure and the type name used to reference it. This structure is used to return data about the widget's state and about the event that caused the callback to occur. In the case of the ArrowButton example, there isn't much more to say than, "It was pushed," and the callback code can assume that's what happened. More complex widgets, like Text and FileSelectionBox, pass more informative data through the call_data pointer.

The pointer to a callback function is one of a widget's resources, and it can be manipulated like any resource, with one limitation: It can't be set from an external resource file. Functions and widgets cannot occupy the right side of an expression in a resource file, so they must always be set from inside your application. There is a convenience function, XtAddCallback, that registers a callback function with a widget. Here's one of the XtAddCallback calls from the coming example:

```
XtAddCallback(arrow_button_up,      /* existing widget handle */
    XmNactivateCallback,            /* action that triggers callback */
    ArrowsCallback,                 /* function to call */
    "u");                           /* client_data pointer */
```

The second argument, the callback type, is a resource name listed in the Resources section of each widget's reference manual entry. Each callback type also has a reason code associated with it (the code for the above callback type is XmCR_ACTIVATE) that is passed to your callback routine as part of the call_data structure. You can use a single callback function to handle a number of callback types for a single widget. And beyond that, there are no limitations to the use of XtAddCallback. You can register multiple callbacks for one widget, have one callback function handle multiple reason codes and/or widgets, whatever you like. Multiple callbacks registered for a single widget are executed serially.

Callback functions return no data directly (they should always be defined as type "void"), although they can change the widget through the pointer provided. In some cases, the callback can modify some element of the structure passed through call_data, which has an effect on the widget's behavior. Of course, you are free to do with the client_data pointer whatever you like.

The ArrowButton widget is most frequently seen at the ends of ScrollBar widgets, but it can be used wherever your interface needs an intuitive way to represent "up" or "down," "left" or "right," "more" or "less." For the representation of user-changeable numeric values, you might consider the Scale widget.

Throughout Motif, behavior is geared to give users ample opportunity to cancel an action in progress. For most kinds of buttons, an activation callback is not dispatched until the mouse pointer is positioned inside a button's region, and the appropriate button pressed *and released*. If the mouse pointer is moved outside the button's region before the button is released, it is not activated.

There are three other widgets demonstrated in this example: PushButton, Separator and BulletinBoard. The PushButton is just like the ArrowButton, except that by default, its face is text instead of an arrow head. A PushButton's text is defined by its XmNlabelString resource. The button resizes itself as needed to contain the text.

The Separator widget is a horizontal or vertical line of arbitrary length that is drawn on its parent widget. By default, a thin, solid line is drawn with a 3-D shading that makes it appear etched into the window surface. The Separator can be drawn in a variety of styles, depending on the setting of the XmNseparator-Type resource. A Separator can be used for purely cosmetic reasons, but it can also dramatically improve the clarity of interfaces with multiple widgets. Don't use multiple Separators to draw a box around something—use the Frame widget for that.

Finally, the BulletinBoard is one of the simpler container widgets. In short, a widget that is created with a BulletinBoard as a parent is simply "stuck" to the BulletinBoard. The child widget's position and size are not affected by the BulletinBoard. If the window containing a BulletinBoard widget is made too small to show all the child widgets, the children are not moved or destroyed, but merely obscured. By default, areas of the BulletinBoard (and other container widgets) not occupied by a widget's graphical image are set to the color defined in the BulletinBoard's XmNbackground resource.

The following example requires these changes to the makefile boilerplate:

```
PROGNAME=    arrowb
OBJS=        arrowb.o
LIBS=        -lXm -lXt -lX11 -lsocket
```

Remember, the LIBS setting applies to SCO UNIX and Open Desktop; adjust it as needed for your environment.

NOTE: *As with all the examples in this chapter, this program outputs its status to the terminal or window from which it is launched. Any X Window program may still use the standard I/O mechanism for handing text, but be aware that neither X nor Motif create a new window to contain this text: Unless it is redirected, the terminal or window used to launch the application is where the standard I/O output will appear.*

The default resource file for this application is ArrowB, and must be placed in the directory pointed by the XAPPLRESDIR environment variable, or in /usr/lib/X11/app-defaults. This resource file is essential: Without it, all of the buttons will be drawn over the top of one another in the upper-left of the application window.

Resource file (named "ArrowB"):

```
# ArrowB: default resources for arrowb.c example in chapter 8
# make sure XAPPLRESDIR environment variable points to the
#   directory in which this file resides

ArrowB*geometry:                  160x140
ArrowB*quit_button.labelString:   Quit

#resources to place the separator
ArrowB*separator.orientation:     HORIZONTAL
ArrowB*separator.y:               35
ArrowB*separator.width:           160
#resources for each of the arrow buttons
ArrowB*arrow_button_up.arrowDirection:  ARROW_UP
ArrowB*arrow_button_up.x:     80
ArrowB*arrow_button_up.y:     40

ArrowB*arrow_button_down.arrowDirection:    ARROW_DOWN
ArrowB*arrow_button_down.x: 80
ArrowB*arrow_button_down.y: 90

ArrowB*arrow_button_left.arrowDirection:    ARROW_LEFT
ArrowB*arrow_button_left.x: 40
ArrowB*arrow_button_left.y: 65

ArrowB*arrow_button_right.arrowDirection:   ARROW_RIGHT
```

```
ArrowB*arrow_button_right.x:      120
ArrowB*arrow_button_right.y:      65
```

Sample application:

```
/* arrowb.c: ArrowButton Motif example for chapter 8 */
/* also demonstrates Separator, PushButton and
    BulletinBoard widgets */
/* tabs are four spaces apart */

#include <X11/Intrinsic.h>
#include <Xm/Xm.h>
#include <Xm/BulletinB.h>
#include <Xm/ArrowB.h>
#include <Xm/PushB.h>
#include <Xm/Separator.h>
#include <stdio.h>

/* first, set up the callback routine */
/* one function is used for all four arrows. The client_data argument
    (set by the XtAddCallback function) will indicate which arrow
    was affected. */
void ArrowsCallback(widget, client_data, call_data)
Widget                  widget;
void                    *client_data;
XmAnyCallbackStruct *call_data;
{
    char     report[80];

    /* tell the user which button was activated */
    switch (*(char *)client_data) { /* first char tells us direction */
        case 'u':
            strcpy(report, "Up ");
            break;
        case 'd':
            strcpy(report, "Down ");
            break;
        case 'l':
            strcpy(report, "Left ");
            break;
        case 'r':
            strcpy(report, "Right ");
            break;
    }
    /* display the result */
    strcat(report, "arrow button activated");
    fprintf(stderr, "%s\n", report);
```

```
}

/* define a handler for the "quit" convenience push button */
void QuitCallback(widget, client_data, call_data)
Widget                widget;
void                  *client_data;
XmAnyCallbackStruct *call_data;
{
    /* just leave */
    exit(0);
}

main(argc, argv)
int     argc;
char    **argv;
{
    Widget        shell, bulletin_board, arrow_button_up,
                  arrow_button_down, arrow_button_left,
                  arrow_button_right, quit_button,
                  separator;

    /* Initialize the toolkit, set up top-level shell */
    shell = XtInitialize("shell", "ArrowB", NULL, 0, &argc, argv);

    /* create instance of BulletinBoard container widget class */
    bulletin_board =
        XtCreateManagedWidget("bulletin_board",
            xmBulletinBoardWidgetClass, shell, NULL, 0);

    /* create four ArrowButton instances */
    arrow_button_up =
        XtCreateManagedWidget("arrow_button_up",
            xmArrowButtonWidgetClass, bulletin_board, NULL, 0);

    arrow_button_down =
        XtCreateManagedWidget("arrow_button_down",
            xmArrowButtonWidgetClass, bulletin_board, NULL, 0);

    arrow_button_left =
        XtCreateManagedWidget("arrow_button_left",
            xmArrowButtonWidgetClass, bulletin_board, NULL, 0);

    arrow_button_right =
        XtCreateManagedWidget("arrow_button_right",
            xmArrowButtonWidgetClass, bulletin_board, NULL, 0);

    /* create a separator */
    separator =
```

```
    XtCreateManagedWidget("separator",
        xmSeparatorWidgetClass, bulletin_board, NULL, 0);

/* create the Quit PushButton */
quit_button =
    XtCreateManagedWidget("quit_button",
        xmPushButtonWidgetClass, bulletin_board, NULL, 0);

/* link in the callbacks for the arrow buttons */
XtAddCallback(arrow_button_up, XmNactivateCallback,
    ArrowsCallback, "u");
XtAddCallback(arrow_button_down, XmNactivateCallback,
    ArrowsCallback, "d");
XtAddCallback(arrow_button_left, XmNactivateCallback,
    ArrowsCallback, "l");
XtAddCallback(arrow_button_right, XmNactivateCallback,
    ArrowsCallback, "r");

/* set up the quit button callback */
XtAddCallback(quit_button, XmNactivateCallback,
    QuitCallback, NULL);

/* make the whole thing appear */
XtRealizeWidget(shell);

/* run the event loop */
XtMainLoop();
}
```

Command

Include file: Xm/Command.h
Class name (for resource file): XmCommand
Creation examples:

```
Widget      command;
Arg         *args;
int         argcnt;

command = XtCreateManagedWidget("widget_name",
    xmCommandWidgetClass, parent_widget, args, argcnt);
```

or

```
command = XmCreateCommand(parent_widget, "widget_name",
    args, argcnt);
XtManageChild(command);
```

Figure 8-2: Command widget, with a Label (to the left of the Command widget)

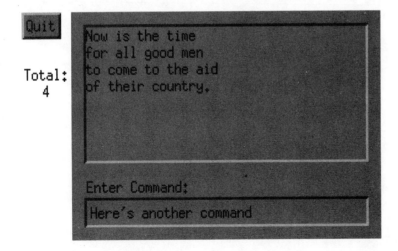

There is also discussion and an example of the following widget class:

Label

Include file: Xm/Label.h
Class name (for resource file): XmLabel
Creation examples:

```
Widget     label;
Arg        *args;
int        argcnt;

label = XtCreateManagedWidget("widget_name",
    xmLabelWidgetClass, parent_widget, args, argcnt);
```

or

```
label = XmCreateLabel(parent_widget, "widget_name",
    args, argcnt);
XtManageChild(label);
```

The Command widget is a compound widget that contains two areas: a command window and a history window. The command window is an editable Text widget that accepts a single line of text terminated by a Return key press. When Return is pressed, that text is returned to your application through the XmNcommandEnteredCallback callback and the XmCommandCallback call_data structure, and a line is added to the list of commands in the history window. Scrollbars appear around the history window whenever the text contained there runs off the right or bottom of the window.

The contents of the history window cannot be directly modified by the user although you can change them from within your application, but the mouse can be used to bring a line from the history window into the command window for editing. By default, a single mouse button click on an entry in the history window brings that entry into the command window. A double click (two rapid presses) will copy that history entry into the command window, and activate the XmNcommandEnteredCallback function.

The history list has an application-defined maximum size (the default is 100). When the number of entries exceeds that size, entries are dropped from the top of the history list as new ones are added at the bottom.

The Command is one of Motif's more obscure widgets, but it is included because it can be useful when turning text-based applications into graphical ones. You might use a Command widget to give the user a history of shell commands executed from within your application, queries to a database, or wherever the user would benefit from being able to repeat a line of text with a mouse button press.

The command line is available to the application through the XmCommandCallbackStruture passed to your callback function. It does not return ordinary null-terminated text strings, but a Motif compound string, which requires special handling. Also, certain Command widget resources are worth querying from within the application. These two techniques are described below.

Compound Strings

Computers are used around the world, often in nations whose representation of language doesn't fit into the ASCII mold. Motif was thoughtfully engineered to permit developers to add support for differing character representations. Some widget text that is shown to the user is not defined using the familiar null-terminated ASCII string, but with Motif's compound string facility. As much as it is capable of, Motif's internationalization is beyond the scope of this book.

Because compound strings are so prevalent in Motif, you do need to know how to convert an ordinary null-terminated string to and from Motif's compound string (XmString) format. Fortunately, this is easy. For short strings, you can often use an external resource file entry. Strings entered there in ASCII (like the "labelString" entry in the previous example's resource file) are silently converted to compound strings before they are stored as resources. For use inside your application, a couple of convenience functions exist for those of us who use 8-bit, left-to-right reading text:

```
XmString    label_string;
int         result;
char        *str;

/* convert from null-terminated ASCII to compound string */
label_string = XmStringCreate("some text", XmSTRING_DEFAULT_CHARSET);

/* convert from compound string to ASCII */
result = XmStringGetLtoR(label_string, XmSTRING_DEFAULT_CHARSET,
    &str);
```

Note that XmStringGetLtoR() requires a *pointer to a pointer* to a character. You provide the address of a character pointer, and XmStringGetLtoR() reaches through that address to change the pointer to point to the ASCII text representation of a compound string. You should modify only a copy of the string, that is, copy the string, not the pointer.

Each time XmStringCreate() is called, it allocates memory that can be freed with XmStringFree(). If your application makes repeated compound "string create" requests, you should consider freeing strings that are no longer needed.

Changing and Retrieving Resources Within an Application

We've discussed the modification of resources through the external resource file. That's an attractive method because it doesn't require recompilation, it's easily read and understood, and data type issues are smoothed over as with compound strings. There are, however, times when it is appropriate to set a resource from inside an application. Also, external resource files don't provide you with any way to query an existing resource.

The Arg data type seen in each of the "Creation examples" is the toolkit's way of passing resource data to and from your applications. Resource function calls that set or get resource values expect a pointer to an Arg structure, but the functions are built to deal with arrays of Arg structures. These arrays are loaded, an element at a time, by the XtSetArg function. As you add elements to an Arg array, you must track the total number of elements yourself. A common method has emerged to handle this, and it has the added benefit of making it easier for you to add or remove XtSetArg calls as your application takes shape.

```
Arg        args[5];
int        nargs;

nargs = 0;
XtSetArg(args[nargs], XmNlabelString, XmStringCreateLtoR("foo",
    XmSTRING_DEFAULT_CHARSET)); nargs++;
XtSetArg(args[nargs], XmNx, 12); nargs++;
XtSetValues(widget, args, nargs);
```

The second argument to XtSetArg() is a resource name found in the reference manual. Inherited and original resources can be addressed by XtSetArg() without regard for their origin. The third argument is technically typeless, but it is expected to match the resource's data type requirement, also listed in the Reference Manual.

When a list of resource entries is constructed, it is not associated with a widget or widget class. The XtSetValues call applies an array of resource names and values to a specific widget's resource list. Unlike the setting of resources through an external resource file, XtSetValues() can trigger error messages if a data type doesn't match, is outside a permissible range, or is otherwise unfit. Also, while resource file references to nonexistent resource names are ignored, the compiler will generate errors for XtSetArg() resource names that don't exist.

Resources can be retrieved with a similar method:

```
Arg      args[5];
int      nargs, hist_count, max_items;

nargs = 0;
XtSetArg(args[nargs], XmNhistoryItemCount, &hist_count); nargs++;

XtSetArg(args[nargs], XmNhistoryMaxItems, &max_items); nargs++;
XtGetValues(widget, args, nargs);
```

XtGetValues() always expects a pointer for its third argument. It is particularly important to make sure that you have allocated sufficient storage behind that pointer, and that it matches the type of the resource you are querying.

The lists created by XtSetArg() are not ruined by XtGetValues() or XtSetValues() calls. They can be reused as long as pointers passed in the third argument remain valid.

The Label widget simply displays the compound string contained in its XmNlabelString resource as text on its parent widget. It does not appear in a window or with a border around it. If you want to set it apart from the rest of your window, you should use the Separator or Frame widget.

The makefile boilerplate should be modified to read:

```
PROGNAME=    command
OBJS=        command.o
LIBS=        -lXm -lXt -lX11 -lsocket
```

The default resource file must be named Command:

```
*bulletin_board.background: White
*command.x:       50
*quit_button.labelString:   Quit
*geometry:        300x200
*command.width: 250
*promptString:  Enter Command:
*history_label.y:    50
*history_label.background:  White
*history_label.labelString: Total:
```

Example source code:

```
/* command.c: Command Motif example for chapter 8 */
/* also example for Label widget */
/* tabs are four spaces apart */

#include <X11/Intrinsic.h>
#include <Xm/Xm.h>
#include <Xm/BulletinB.h>
#include <Xm/Command.h>
#include <Xm/PushB.h>
#include <Xm/Label.h>
#include <stdio.h>

/* globals */
Widget       history_label;

/* callback routine for command widget */
void CommandCallback(widget, client_data, call_data)
Widget                  widget;
void                    *client_data;
XmCommandCallbackStruct *call_data;
{
    char        *cmd_str, hist_str[25];
    XmString    hist_label;
    int         result, hist_count;
    Arg         args[2];

    /* decipher the string passed back to us */
    result = XmStringGetLtoR(call_data->value,
        XmSTRING_DEFAULT_CHARSET, &cmd_str);
    printf("Command: %s\n", cmd_str);
    if (strcmp(cmd_str, "quit") == 0)   /* just for grins */
        exit(0);

    /* show the XmCommandError function in action */
    if (cmd_str[0] == 'a') {
```

```
            strcpy(hist_str, "XmCommandError Called!");
            hist_label = XmStringCreateLtoR(hist_str,
                XmSTRING_DEFAULT_CHARSET);
            XmCommandError(widget, hist_label);
    }

    /* find out how many commands there are in the history area */
    XtSetArg(args[0], XmNhistoryItemCount, &hist_count);
    XtGetValues(widget, args, 1);

    printf("Length of history list: %d\n", hist_count);

    /* change the Label widget to show the number of history
        window entries */
    sprintf(hist_str, "Total:\n%d", hist_count);
    hist_label = XmStringCreateLtoR(hist_str,
        XmSTRING_DEFAULT_CHARSET);

    /* Set the label widget's labelString resource */
    /* The change will be reflected quickly */
    XtSetArg(args[0], XmNlabelString, hist_label);
    XtSetValues(history_label, args, 1);
}

/* define a handler for the "quit" convenience push button */
void QuitCallback(widget, client_data, call_data)
Widget              widget;
void                *client_data;
XmAnyCallbackStruct *call_data;
{
    exit(0);
}

main(argc, argv)
int     argc;
char    **argv;
{
    Widget      command, shell, bulletin_board, quit_button;
    int         i;
    char        button_name[15];

    /* Initialize the toolkit, set up top-level shell */
    shell = XtInitialize("shell", "Command", NULL, 0, &argc, argv);

    /* create instance of BulletinBoard container widget class */
    bulletin_board =
        XtCreateManagedWidget("bulletin_board",
            xmBulletinBoardWidgetClass, shell, NULL, 0);
```

```
/* create Command widget */
command =
    XtCreateManagedWidget("command",
        xmCommandWidgetClass, bulletin_board, NULL, 0);

/* set up the Command widget's callback (triggered when a command
    is entered or double-clicked with the mouse) */
XtAddCallback(command, XmNcommandEnteredCallback,
    CommandCallback, NULL);

/* create the history label */
history_label =
    XtCreateManagedWidget("history_label",
        xmLabelWidgetClass, bulletin_board, NULL, 0);

/* build the quit button */
quit_button =
    XtCreateManagedWidget("quit_button",
        xmPushButtonWidgetClass, bulletin_board, NULL, 0);

/* set up the quit button callback */
XtAddCallback(quit_button, XmNactivateCallback,
    QuitCallback, NULL);

/* make the whole thing appear */
XtRealizeWidget(shell);

/* run the event loop */
XtMainLoop();
}
```

FileSelectionBox

Include file: Xm/FileSB.h
Class name (for resource file):   XmFileSelectionBox
Creation examples:

```
Widget     file_box;
Arg        *args;
int        argcnt;

file_box = XtCreateManagedWidget("widget_name",
    xmFileSelectionBoxWidgetClass, parent_widget, args, argcnt);
```

Figure 8-3: FileSelectionBox widget, enclosed in a Frame to set it apart from the background

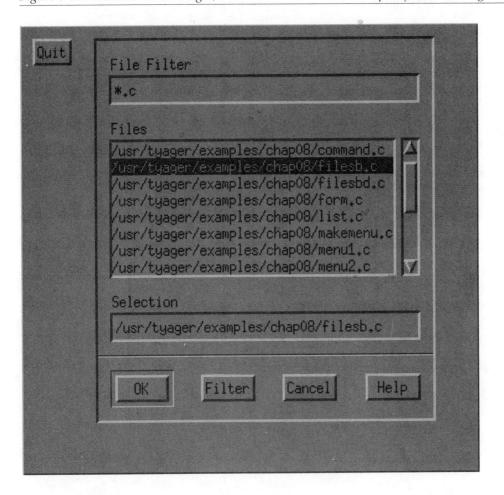

or

```
file_box = XmCreateFileSelectionBox(parent_widget, "widget_name",
    args, argcnt);
XtManageChild(file_box);
```

Figure 8-4: FileSelectionBox widget as a popup (a separate, movable window)

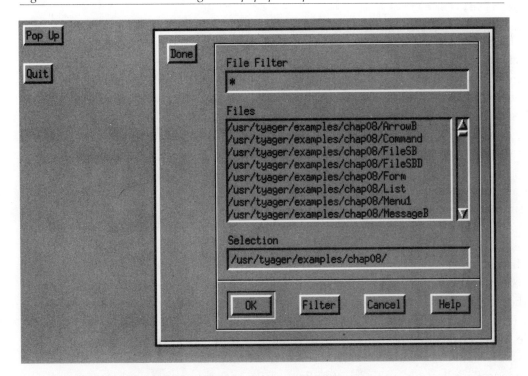

The following widget is also discussed and demonstrated:

Frame

Include file: Xm/Frame.h
Class name (for resource file):   XmFrame
Creation examples:

```
Widget    frame;
Arg       *args;
int       argcnt;
```

```
frame = XtCreateManagedWidget("widget_name",
    xmFrameWidgetClass, parent_widget, args, argcnt);
```

or

```
frame = XmCreateFrame(parent_widget, "widget_name",
    args, argcnt);
XtManageChild(frame);
```

The FileSelectionBox makes much easier the tedious duty of allowing the user to choose from a list of files. This compound widget includes an editable Text widget for a filename wildcard string (the *File Filter*), a scrollable list of files matching that wildcard, and an editable Text widget for the selected file name. Four Pushbuttons across the bottom—OK, Filter, Cancel, and Help—act on the widget's current state. The OK PushButton dispatches the XmNokCallback, passing the current selection through the XmFileSelectionBoxCallbackStruct's value member, which is an XmString. Pressing Filter refreshes the file list, and typically follows a change to the wildcard in the filter window. A Filter PushButton press is also simulated when you press Return in the File Filter window. The Cancel and Help PushButtons dispatch the XmNcancelCallback and XmNhelpCallback functions, respectively.

By default, the FileSelectionBox opens with a complete list of files in the current directory. You can specify a different directory, or provide a wildcard that limits the scope of the search to, say, files with a ".c" extension, through the XmNdirMask resource. This is an XmString that holds the wildcard displayed in the File Filter window. A convenience function, XmFileSelectionDoSearch, changes this resource for you and triggers a search based on the new wildcard.

In practical application, a FileSelectionBox would probably appear only temporarily, and disappear after the user pressed the OK PushButton. There are two FileSelectionBox examples. The first creates the FileSelectionBox as a child of a BulletinBoard widget, just as the preceding examples have done. The second example creates the FileSelectionBox with the XmCreateFileSelectionDialog function. This function creates a new DialogShell widget, and places a FileSelectionBox widget inside it. The DialogShell is a container widget that appears in a window of its own. Such widgets are referred to as "pop-up" widgets, because they are made to appear and disappear as needed.

Pop-up Widgets

The examples in this chapter, with the exception of the second of the two examples that follow, create a window that remains on the screen until the application exits. An application's main window should be handled this way, but it is often useful to have transient windows, windows that appear when needed, and disappear when the user is done with them. Such windows are called pop-ups, and both the X Toolkit and Motif have special facilities for creating and managing them.

A pop-up is really a new top-level widget, because its parent (visually, at least), is the root window or display background. Pop-ups "float" above the root window just like top-level application windows, rather than being attached to some widget in the application's main window. The FileSelectionBox is only one of several Motif widgets that are frequently used as pop-ups. Motif also provides XmCreate...Dialog functions that build pop-up BulletinBoard, SelectionBox, MessageBox, and Form dialogs. In every case, the widget is created as a child of a DialogShell widget which the convenience function creates for you as well.

The XmCreate...Dialog calls create windows which, even though they may move about freely, still must be parented by some widget in your application's hierarchy. PushButtons are typical parents for pop-up dialogs, since a pop-up is usually made to appear when the user presses a button, or selects an item (which is also a PushButton), from a menu .

The XmCreateBulletinBoardDialog and XmCreateFormDialog functions give you the freedom to turn any widget hierarchy into a pop-up. In the case of the second example, the code required only slight modification to turn the FileSelectionBox's parent BulletinBoard widget into one created by the XmCreateBulletinBoardDialog function. The main BulletinBoard application window holds a pair of PushButtons: Pop Up and Done. Pushing the Pop Up PushButton dispatches a call to PopUpCallback(), which in turn calls XtManageChild() to make the BulletinBoardDialog and its children (the FileSelectionBox and the Done PushButton) appear. The Done PushButton calls PopDownCallback, which uses XtUnmanageChild() to "pop down" the BulletinBoardDialog.

Even on a fast machine, there can be several seconds between the calling of XtManageChild() and the appearance of the pop-up window. This is particularly true if a pop-up is remanaged immediately after being unmanaged.

The Frame widget, also used in these examples, draws a 3-D shaded box on its child widget. The 3-D shading style can be modified through the XmNshadowType resource. The default, XmSHADOW_ETCHED_IN, gives the appearance of a rectangle etched into the parent widget's surface. XmSHADOW_ETCHED_OUT makes the line appear to jut out from the surface. XmSHADOW_IN and XmSHADOW_OUT respectively make the area inside the Frame appear to sink into, or rise up from, the surface.

Aside from being visually pleasing, the Frame widget is useful for drawing the user's eye toward an important portion of your interface. Like the Separator, the Frame can be used to help unclutter a window with multiple widgets, or to group widgets that might not obviously go together if they're seen as just "floating" in the window.

The FileSelectionBox widget is a descendant of the SelectionBox widget; the two are so similar that we won't give the SelectionBox separate coverage. The SelectionBox is a useful widget, though. After you've worked with the FileSelectionBox example below, take the time to read through the Reference Manual section on XmSelectionBox.

The makefile boilerplate for the first example should be modified as follows:

```
PROGNAME=       filesb
OBJS=           filesb.o
LIBS=           -lXm -lXt -lX11 -lsocket
```

This sample resource file should be stored under the name FileSB:

```
FileSB*geometry:                370x350
FileSB*quit_button*labelString: Quit
FileSB*frame.x:                 60

# try uncommenting one of these:
#FileSB*frame.shadowType:        SHADOW_OUT
#FileSB*frame.shadowType:        SHADOW_ETCHED_OUT
#FileSB*frame.shadowType:        SHADOW_IN
```

Here's the FileSelectionBox example:

```
/* filesb.c: FileSelectionBox Motif example for chapter 8 */
/* also example for Frame widget */
/* tabs are four spaces apart */
```

```c
#include <X11/Intrinsic.h>
#include <Xm/Xm.h>
#include <Xm/BulletinB.h>
#include <Xm/FileSB.h>
#include <Xm/Frame.h>
#include <Xm/PushB.h>
#include <stdio.h>

/* the FileSelectionBox callback routine */
/* all of the widgets that are part of the FileSelectionBox are
   wired into this callback. The call_data structure tells us
   why this callback was triggered. */
void FSBoxCallback(widget, client_data, call_data)
Widget                            widget;
void                              *client_data;
XmFileSelectionBoxCallbackStruct  *call_data;
{
    char        *sfptr;
    int         result;

    /* handle this based on the reason for the callback */
    /* the reason types are listed on the XmSelectionBox manual
       page */
    switch (call_data->reason) {
        case XmCR_OK:   /* OK button was pressed */
            fprintf(stderr, "OK button pressed\n");
            if (call_data->length == 0)
                fprintf(stderr, "No file selected\n");
            else {
                /* selected file is returned as compound string;
                   it must be converted to an ordinary null-terminated
                   string */
                result = XmStringGetLtoR(call_data->value,
                    XmSTRING_DEFAULT_CHARSET, &sfptr);
                printf("Selected filename: %s\n", sfptr);
                XmStringFree(call_data->value);
            }
            break;

        case XmCR_CANCEL:
            fprintf(stderr, "Cancel button pressed\n");
            break;

        case XmCR_HELP:
            fprintf(stderr, "Help button pressed\n");
            break;
    }
}
```

```
/* define a handler for the "quit" convenience push button */
void QuitCallback(widget, client_data, call_data)
Widget              widget;
void                *client_data;
XmAnyCallbackStruct *call_data;
{
    exit(0);
}

main(argc, argv)
int     argc;
char    **argv;
{
    Widget      shell, bulletin_board, file_box, quit_button, frame;

    /* Initialize the toolkit, set up top-level shell */
    shell = XtInitialize("shell", "FileSB", NULL, 0, &argc, argv);

    /* create instance of BulletinBoard container widget class */
    bulletin_board =
        XtCreateManagedWidget("bulletin_board",
            xmBulletinBoardWidgetClass, shell, NULL, 0);

    /* build Frame for FileSelectionBox */
    frame =
        XtCreateManagedWidget("frame",
            xmFrameWidgetClass, bulletin_board, NULL, 0);

    /* create FileSelectionBox instance */
    file_box =
        XtCreateManagedWidget("file_box",
            xmFileSelectionBoxWidgetClass, frame, NULL, 0);

    /* create quit button */
    quit_button =
        XtCreateManagedWidget("quit_button",
            xmPushButtonWidgetClass, bulletin_board, NULL, 0);

    /* link in the callbacks for buttons in file_box */
    XtAddCallback(file_box, XmNokCallback,  /* OK button */
        FSBoxCallback, NULL);
    XtAddCallback(file_box, XmNcancelCallback,  /* Cancel */
        FSBoxCallback, NULL);
    XtAddCallback(file_box, XmNhelpCallback,    /* Help */
        FSBoxCallback, NULL);

    /* set up the quit button callback */
```

```
    XtAddCallback(quit_button, XmNactivateCallback,
        QuitCallback, NULL);

    /* make the whole thing appear */
    XtRealizeWidget(shell);

    /* run the event loop */
    XtMainLoop();
}
```

The second example (which uses the BulletinBoardDialog to create a pop-up FileSelectionBox window) should have the following makefile parameters:

```
PROGNAME=    filesbd
OBJS=        filesbd.o
LIBS=        -lXm -lXt -lX11 -lsocket
```

Here is the sample resource file, called FileSBD:

```
FileSBD*bulletin_board.geometry:        70x90
FileSBD*quit_button.labelString:        Quit
FileSBD*popup_button.labelString:       Pop Up
FileSBD*done_button.labelString:        Done
FileSBD*quit_button.y:                  50

FileSBD*frame.x:                        60

# try uncommenting one of these:
#FileSBD*frame.shadowType:              SHADOW_OUT
#FileSBD*frame.shadowType:              SHADOW_ETCHED_OUT
#FileSBD*frame.shadowType:              SHADOW_IN
```

Here's the source code for the second FileSelectionBox example:

```
/* filesbd.c: FileSelectionBox pop-up Motif example for chapter 8 */
/* tabs are four spaces apart */

#include <X11/Intrinsic.h>
#include <Xm/Xm.h>
#include <Xm/BulletinB.h>
#include <Xm/FileSB.h>
#include <Xm/Frame.h>
#include <Xm/PushB.h>
#include <stdio.h>
```

```
/* the FileSelectionBox callback routine */
/* all of the widgets that are part of the FileSelectionBox are
   wired into this callback. The call_data structure tells us
   why this callback was triggered. */
void FSBoxCallback(widget, client_data, call_data)
Widget                              widget;
void                                *client_data;
XmFileSelectionBoxCallbackStruct    *call_data;
{
    char            *sfptr;
    int             result;

    /* handle this based on the reason for the callback */
    /* the reason types are listed on the XmSelectionBox manual
       page */
    switch (call_data->reason) {
        case XmCR_OK:    /* OK button was pressed */
            fprintf(stderr, "OK button pressed\n");
            if (call_data->length == 0)
                fprintf(stderr, "No file selected\n");
            else {
                /* selected file is returned as compound string;
                   it must be converted to an ordinary null-terminated
                   string */
                result = XmStringGetLtoR(call_data->value,
                    XmSTRING_DEFAULT_CHARSET, &sfptr);
                printf("Selected filename: %s\n", sfptr);
                XmStringFree(call_data->value);
            }
            break;

        case XmCR_CANCEL:
            fprintf(stderr, "Cancel button pressed\n");
            break;

        case XmCR_HELP:
            fprintf(stderr, "Help button pressed\n");
            break;
    }
}

/* This callback pops up the BulletinBoardDialog */
void PopUpCallback(widget, bb_dialog, call_data)
Widget                widget;
Widget                bb_dialog;
XmAnyCallbackStruct *call_data;
```

```
{
    /* the widget handle for the BulletinBoardDialog is passed
        as the bbdialog; use it to pop up the window */
    XtManageChild(bb_dialog);
}

/* make the BulletinBoardDialog disappear */
void PopDownCallback(widget, bb_dialog, call_data)
Widget              widget;
Widget              bb_dialog;
XmAnyCallbackStruct *call_data;
{
    /* pop down the BulletinBoardDialog widget passed as
        bbdialog */
    XtUnmanageChild(bb_dialog);
}

/* define a handler for the "quit" convenience push button */
void QuitCallback(widget, client_data, call_data)
Widget              widget;
void                *client_data;
XmAnyCallbackStruct *call_data;
{
    exit(0);
}

main(argc, argv)
int     argc;
char    **argv;
{
    Widget      shell, bulletin_board, file_box, quit_button, frame;
    Widget      bb_dialog, done_button, popup_button;

    /* Initialize the toolkit, set up top-level shell */
    shell = XtInitialize("shell", "FileSBD", NULL, 0, &argc, argv);

    /* create instance of BulletinBoard container widget class */
    bulletin_board =
        XtCreateManagedWidget("bulletin_board",
            xmBulletinBoardWidgetClass, shell, NULL, 0);

    /* create Pop Up and Quit buttons */
    quit_button =
        XtCreateManagedWidget("quit_button",
            xmPushButtonWidgetClass, bulletin_board, NULL, 0);
```

```
    popup_button =
        XtCreateManagedWidget("popup_button",
            xmPushButtonWidgetClass, bulletin_board, NULL, 0);

    /* link in callback for Quit PushButton */
    XtAddCallback(quit_button, XmNactivateCallback,
        QuitCallback, NULL);

    /* create pop-up BulletinBoardDialog to hold FileSelectionBox and
        the "Done" PushButton */
    bb_dialog =
        XmCreateBulletinBoardDialog(popup_button, "bb_dialog",
            NULL, 0);
    /* don't call XtManageChild for the bb_dialog widget here unless
        you want the application to open with the pop-up window present
        at the start */

    /* link in callback for PopUp button in main window (we had to have
        the bb_dialog created first) */
    XtAddCallback(popup_button, XmNactivateCallback,
        PopUpCallback, bb_dialog);

    /* create Done PushButton, link in callback */
    done_button =
        XtCreateManagedWidget("done_button",
            xmPushButtonWidgetClass, bb_dialog, NULL, 0);
    XtAddCallback(done_button, XmNactivateCallback,
        PopDownCallback, bb_dialog);

    /* build Frame for FileSelectionBox */
    frame =
        XtCreateManagedWidget("frame",
            xmFrameWidgetClass, bb_dialog, NULL, 0);

    /* create FileSelectionBox instance */
    file_box =
        XtCreateManagedWidget("file_box",
            xmFileSelectionBoxWidgetClass, frame, NULL, 0);

    /* link in the callbacks for buttons in file_box */
    XtAddCallback(file_box, XmNokCallback,  /* OK button */
        FSBoxCallback, NULL);
    XtAddCallback(file_box, XmNcancelCallback,  /* Cancel */
        FSBoxCallback, NULL);
    XtAddCallback(file_box, XmNhelpCallback,     /* Help */
```

```
        FSBoxCallback, NULL);

    /* make the main window and buttons appear--the BulletinBoardDialog
        and its PushButton and FileSelectionBox widgets will not appear
        until the Pop Up button in the main window is pressed */
    XtRealizeWidget(shell);

    /* run the event loop */
    XtMainLoop();
}
```

Form

Include file: Xm/Form.h
Class name (for resource file):   XmForm
Creation examples:

```
Widget      form;
Arg         *args;
int         argcnt;

form = XtCreateManagedWidget("widget_name",
    xmFormWidgetClass, parent_widget, args, argcnt);
```

or

```
form = XmCreateForm(parent_widget, "widget_name",
    args, argcnt);
XtManageChild(form);
```

Figure 8-5: Five PushButtons in a Form widget using absolute positioning

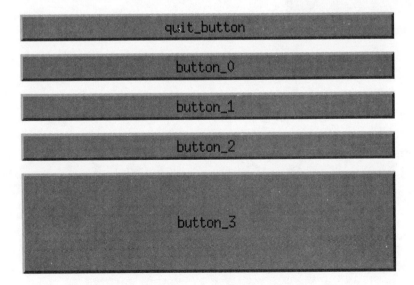

Figure 8-6: PushButtons in a Form widget using relative positioning

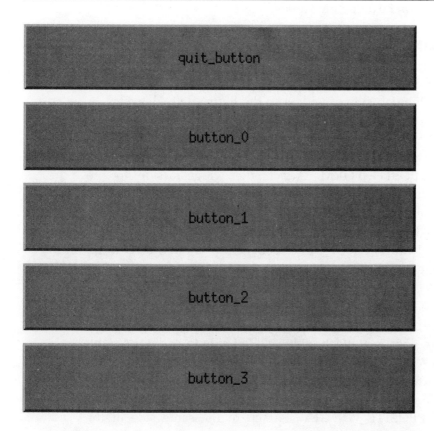

Form is a container widget that can be configured to rearrange and/or resize its child widgets as the widget containing the form is resized. With it, you can build interfaces that automatically adjust themselves to account for the size of the window.

Like the BulletinBoard widget, the Form accepts any number of child widgets, and displays them according to their positional resources XmNx, XmNy, XmNwidth, and XmNheight. But when a widget is given a Form widget for a parent, that widget is endowed with several new positional resources. In addition to the standard resources that allow you to position the widget's upper-left corner within the parent, the Form widget gives you more control over where the widget's top, bottom, left, and right sides will be placed. Each side has a resource associated with it: XmNtopAttachment,

XmNbottomAttachment, XmNleftAttachment, and XmNrightAttachment. These resources can be set to one of the following values:

- **XmATTACH_NONE.** This side of the widget will not be affected by the Form widget
- **XmATTACH_FORM.** Attach the widget's side to the Form widget's corresponding edge (left side of widget to the Form's left edge, etc.). A margin between the Form edge and the widget's side can be established with XmN*side*Offset, where *side* is replaced with top, bottom, left, or right. The offset value is in pixels (by default).
- **XmATTACH_OPPOSITE_FORM.** Attach the widget's side to the opposite of the Form widget's corresponding side. Setting XmNrightAttachment to XmATTACH_OPPOSITE_FORM will attach the widget's right side to the Form's left edge. The XmN*side*Offset works here as well, and XmATTACH_OPPOSITE_FORM is often used to fix one side of a widget so that it does not move.
- **XmATTACH_WIDGET.** Attach the widget's side to the widget specified in the XmN*side*Widget resource. A link between widgets should only be done in one direction. Don't, for example, attach widget1's right side to widget2's left, and then attach widget2's left side to widget1's right. Only one of these associations is needed. Again, the XmN*side*Offset can be used to set a fixed space between the widgets. (The XmN*side*Widget resource must be set from within the application.)
- **XmATTACH_OPPOSITE_WIDGET.** Attach to the same side of the widget specified in the XmN*side*Widget resource. The left side of the current widget attaches to the left side of the specified widget, right to right, and so on. The XmN*side*Offset lets you specify a fixed distance from the specified widget's side.
- **XmATTACH_POSITION.**   Attach the widget's side to a relative position on the Form according to the XmN*side*Position resource. The position is, by default, specified as a percentage toward the bottom or right of the Form. As the Form resizes, the widget's side will be adjusted to maintain its relative position in the form.
- **XmATTACH_SELF.** Fix the widget's side to its initial position on the Form.

A typical Form widget contains a mix of widgets; some that benefit from resizing, and some that don't. A Text widget, for example, should resize with the window. A larger window makes room for more visible text. But a single-line Text widget shouldn't be resized vertically, so either the bottom or top edge of such a widget should be set so that it is not moved (XmATTACH_NONE). Resizing of a widget within a Form occurs only when one edge of the widget is moved toward, or away from, the opposite edge. A widget that benefits from a larger space, like a multi-line Text Widget or a FileSelectionBox, can reasonably be resized in all directions with pleasing results.

While the Form widget will change the size of widgets, it has no effect on text or graphics displayed inside them. Text inside a widget resized by a Form widget does not change size or shape. Until X Window is endowed with scalable fonts, there is no easy way to grow or shrink text.

Laying out widgets in a Form, and getting the XmN*side*Attachment and corresponding resources set properly usually requires some experimentation. The behavior of a Form widget is much more easily demonstrated than explained, so let's move to the example.

The makefile boilerplate should be modified as follows:

```
PROGNAME=      form
OBJS=          form.o
LIBS=          -lXm -lXt -lX11 -lsocket!
```

The resource file, named Form, is the main basis for your experimentation. The one that follows is only a start; read the Reference Manual entry for XmForm, and test the resources until you feel confident that you understand the Form's behavior. Remember, as you work with the XmATTACH_WIDGET attachment type, that the widget resource (XmN*side*Widget) cannot be specified in a resource file. Study and run the example with the settings provided, and then add your own. Resources in the external file will override those set inside the application.

```
# settings for Form widget example

*form.background:       White

## custom settings--uncomment to activate (overrides resources
##    set inside form program)
```

```
## global settings first
*form*geometry:                     300x300
*form*XmPushButton.leftAttachment:  ATTACH_FORM
*form*XmPushButton.rightAttachment: ATTACH_FORM
*form*XmPushButton.leftOffset:      5
*form*XmPushButton.rightOffset:     5

## Comment/uncomment from here down to see effect

## top and bottom positions for each of the widgets
#*form*quit_button.topAttachment:    ATTACH_FORM
#*form*quit_button.topOffset:        5
#*form*quit_button.bottomAttachment:     ATTACH_POSITION
#*form*quit_button.bottomPosition:   18
#
#*form*button_0.topAttachment:       ATTACH_POSITION
#*form*button_0.bottomAttachment:    ATTACH_POSITION
#*form*button_0.topPosition:            20
#*form*button_0.bottomPosition:      38
#
#*form*button_1.topAttachment:       ATTACH_POSITION
#*form*button_1.bottomAttachment:    ATTACH_POSITION
#*form*button_1.topPosition:            40
#*form*button_1.bottomPosition:      58
#
#*form*button_2.topAttachment:       ATTACH_POSITION
#*form*button_2.bottomAttachment:    ATTACH_POSITION
#*form*button_2.topPosition:            60
#*form*button_2.bottomPosition:      78
#
#*form*button_3.topAttachment:       ATTACH_POSITION
#*form*button_3.bottomAttachment:    ATTACH_FORM
#*form*button_3.topPosition:            80
#*form*button_3.bottomOffset:        5
```

Here's the source code:

```
/* form.c: Form Motif example for chapter 8 */
/* tabs are four spaces apart */

#include <X11/Intrinsic.h>
#include <Xm/Xm.h>
#include <Xm/Form.h>
#include <Xm/PushB.h>
#include <stdio.h>

/* define a handler for the "quit" convenience push button */
```

```
void QuitCallback(widget, client_data, call_data)
Widget                 widget;
void                   *client_data;
XmAnyCallbackStruct *call_data;
{
    exit(0);
}

main(argc, argv)
int     argc;
char    **argv;
{
    Widget        shell, buttons[4], quit_button, form;
    int           i, narg;
    char          button_name[20];
    Arg           args[10];

    /* Initialize the toolkit, set up top-level shell */
    shell = XtInitialize("shell", "Form", NULL, 0, &argc, argv);

    /* create the Form instance */
    form =
        XtCreateManagedWidget("form",
            xmFormWidgetClass, shell, NULL, 0);

    /* create four buttons to show form widget's behavior */
    for (i = 0; i < 4; i++) {
        sprintf(button_name, "button_%d", i);
        buttons[i] =
            XtCreateManagedWidget(button_name,
                xmPushButtonWidgetClass, form, NULL, 0);
    }

    quit_button =
        XtCreateManagedWidget("quit_button",
            xmPushButtonWidgetClass, form, NULL, 0);

    narg = 0;
    /* attach all widgets to left and right sides of form */
    XtSetArg(args[narg], XmNleftAttachment, XmATTACH_FORM); narg++;
    XtSetArg(args[narg], XmNrightAttachment, XmATTACH_FORM); narg++;
    for (i = 0; i < 4; i++)
        XtSetValues(buttons[i], args, narg);
    XtSetValues(quit_button, args, narg);

    /* position widget top and bottom edges */
    narg = 0;
    /* quit button at top */
```

```
    XtSetArg(args[0], XmNtopAttachment, XmATTACH_FORM);
    XtSetValues(quit_button, args, 1);
    /* buttons stacked beneath */
    XtSetArg(args[narg], XmNtopAttachment, XmATTACH_WIDGET); narg++;
    XtSetArg(args[narg], XmNtopOffset, 10); narg++;
    XtSetArg(args[narg], XmNtopWidget, quit_button); narg++;
    XtSetValues(buttons[0], args, narg);

    for (i = 1; i < 4; i++) {
        narg = 2;   /* reuse first two resources from above */
        XtSetArg(args[narg], XmNtopWidget, buttons[i - 1]); narg++;
        XtSetValues(buttons[i], args, narg);
    }

    /* fix last button to bottom of form */
    XtSetArg(args[0], XmNbottomAttachment, XmATTACH_FORM);
    XtSetValues(buttons[3], args, 1);

    /* set up the quit button callback */
    XtAddCallback(quit_button, XmNactivateCallback,
        QuitCallback, NULL);

    /* make the whole thing appear */
    XtRealizeWidget(shell);

    /* run the event loop */
    XtMainLoop();
}
```

List

Include file: Xm/List.h

Class name (for resource file): XmList

Creation examples:

```
Widget      list;
Arg         *args;
int         argcnt;

list = XtCreateManagedWidget("widget_name",
    xmListWidgetClass, parent_widget, args, argcnt);
```

or

```
list = XmCreateList(parent_widget, "widget_name",
    args, argcnt);
XtManageChild(list);
```

or

```
list = XmCreateScrolledList(parent_widget, "widget_name",
    args, argcnt);
XtManageChild(list);
```

Figure 8-7: ScrolledList widget with three items selected

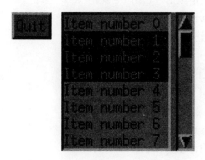

The List widget puts up a window with an application-defined list of text items, and the user can select one or more items from the list with the mouse or keyboard. The List widget's list window can be scrolled if the XmCreateScrolledList convenience function is used, to reveal text items that extend past the bottom of the window. The selection mechanism is robust, and is configured through the XmNselectionPolicy resource. This can be set to one of the following (described behavior is based on List widget defaults):

- **XmSINGLE_SELECT.**   One item at a time may be selected from the list. A single mouse click on an item, or positioning the highlight cursor and pressing Return, will dispatch the XmNsingleSelectionCallback. Any previously-selected item is deselected.

- **XmBROWSE_SELECT.**   If the XmNautomaticSelection resource is set to False, it behaves exactly like XmSINGLE_SELECT mode, except that the XmNbrowseSelectionCallback is dispatched when a selection is made. If XmNautomaticSelection is True, then each item over which the mouse is drawn while the button is pressed generates a new callback to XmNbrowseSelectionCallback. This is not multiple selection: only one item at a time is highlighted and passed to the callback routine.

- **XmMULTIPLE_SELECT.** Multiple items may be independently selected or deselected with mouse button presses or the Return key. The entire list of selected items is passed to the application (through the XmNmultipleSelectionCallback) with each new selection. Selecting a highlighted (selected) item again deselects it, and removes it from the selected item list.

- **XmEXTENDED_SELECT.**   In this mode, a range of items can be selected or deselected by dragging the mouse over them with the button pressed. This action dispatches a call to the XmNextendedSelectionCallback with a selection_type of XmINITIAL, passing the list of items selected in that operation. selection_type is a member of the XmListCallbackStruct structure passed to the callback routine. The range of selected items can be extended by pressing the Shift key, moving to a new end-point, and selecting it with the mouse button or Return. The new selection list then includes everything from the original start position, where the mouse button was first pressed in selecting the XmINITIAL list, to the new end-point. Any previously selected items in the chosen range will be deselected. Extending a selection causes a call to the XmNextendedSelectionCallback with a selection_type of XmMODIFICATION. Again, the entire list of selected items is passed to the callback. A group of items can be added to the list by holding the Control key and selecting them individually, or dragging through a range of items with the Control key held down. The callback is dispatched with a selection_type of XmADDITION. Selected items are deselected in the same manner, and the selection_type is still XmADDITION.

If the XmNautomaticSelection resource is set in XmMULTI-PLE_SELECT mode, then the XmNextendedSelectionCallback is dispatched for each item selected or deselected by the user.

In all modes, a double-click on a single item will result in a call to the XmNdefaultActionCallback function. Also, modes that return a single selection also return that selection's position, or index, in the list.

The XmCreateScrolledList convenience function returns the widget ID for the List widget, but the function creates an encompassing ScrolledWindow widget as a parent. Sizing and positioning should be carried out against the parent ScrolledWindow widget, whose resource name is derived by adding the suffix SW to the end of the name provided to the XmCreateScrolledList function. Direct manipulation inside the application can be carried out by using the XtParent function to obtain the List widget's ScrolledWindow parent. Note that the List widget resources that modify the behavior of scrollbars apply only to the ScrolledList type of List widget.

Not all members of the XmListCallbackStruct structure hold valid information for all types of callbacks and values of XmNselectionPolicy; consult the Reference Manual for details. See the example for techniques of extracting the selected item list from the structure passed to the callback routines.

The List, like the Command and SelectionBox widgets, provides users with graphical shortcuts for manipulating textual information. A sample use for the List widget would be a database manager's report generator. A list of available fields could be placed in a List widget, the XmMULTIPLE_SELECT, or XmEXTENDED_SELECT mode set, and the user would have a very simple interface for choosing the fields to include in his or her report. It might also be appropriate for maintaining a list of users to which a piece of electronic mail should be directed.

The makefile boilerplate should be modified as follows:

```
PROGNAME=     list
OBJS=         list.o
LIBS=         -lXm -lXt -lX11 -lsocket
```

The default resource file, List, can start with this information:

```
# resources for List widget example
*bulletin_board.background: white
*list_boxSW.x:                  50
*quit_button.labelString:   Quit
*geometry:       300x200

# uncomment only one of the following:
#*selectionPolicy:          SINGLE_SELECT
#*selectionPolicy:          MULTIPLE_SELECT
*selectionPolicy:           EXTENDED_SELECT
#*selectionPolicy:          BROWSE_SELECT
```

Here's the code for the example:

```
/* list.c: List Motif example for chapter 8 */
/* tabs are four spaces apart */

#include <X11/Intrinsic.h>
#include <Xm/Xm.h>
#include <Xm/BulletinB.h>
#include <Xm/PushB.h>
#include <Xm/List.h>
#include <stdio.h>

void ListCallback(widget, client_data, call_data)
Widget                  widget;
void                    *client_data;
XmListCallbackStruct    *call_data;
{
    char    *select_str;
    int     multiple = 0;   /* set if multiple selection active */
    int     i;

    /* handle the callback based on the reason code */
    switch (call_data->reason) {
        case XmCR_BROWSE_SELECT:
            printf("BROWSE_SELECT\n");
            break;

        case XmCR_SINGLE_SELECT:
            printf("SINGLE_SELECT\n");
            break;

        case XmCR_DEFAULT_ACTION:
```

```
            printf("DEFAULT_ACTION\n");
            break;

    case XmCR_MULTIPLE_SELECT:
            printf("MULTIPLE_SELECT\n");
            multiple = 1;
            break;

    case XmCR_EXTENDED_SELECT:
            printf("EXTENDED_SELECT\n");
            multiple = 2;
            break;

    default:
            printf("Callback reason unknown!\n");
            return;
}
if (multiple == 0) {
    XmStringGetLtoR(call_data->item, XmSTRING_DEFAULT_CHARSET,
        &select_str);
    printf("String: %s\nPosition: %d\n", select_str,
        call_data->item_position);
}
if (multiple == 2) {
    /* display selection type */
    printf("Selection type: ");
    switch (call_data->selection_type) {
        case XmINITIAL:
            printf("INITIAL\n");
            break;

        case XmMODIFICATION:
            printf("MODIFICATION\n");
            break;

        case XmADDITION:
            printf("ADDITION\n");
            break;

        default:
            printf("Unknown\n");
            break;
    }
    --multiple;      /* now handle as normal multiple selection */
}

if (multiple == 1) {
    if (call_data->selected_item_count == 0) {
```

```
            printf("Nothing selected!\n");
        } else {
            for (i = 0; i < call_data->selected_item_count; i++) {
                XmStringGetLtoR(call_data->selected_items[i],
                    XmSTRING_DEFAULT_CHARSET, &select_str);
                printf("String [%d]: %s\n", i, select_str);
            }
        }
    }
    printf("\n");
}

/* define a handler for the "quit" convenience push button */
void QuitCallback(widget, client_data, call_data)
Widget                widget;
void                  *client_data;
XmAnyCallbackStruct *call_data;
{
    exit(0);
}


main(argc, argv)
int      argc;
char     **argv;
{
    Widget      shell, bulletin_board, list_box, quit_button;
    XmString    item_list[30];
    char        item_string[25];
    Arg         args[5];
    int         i, n;

    /* Initialize the toolkit, set up top-level shell */
    shell = XtInitialize("shell", "List", NULL, 0, &argc, argv);

    /* create instance of BulletinBoard container widget class */
    bulletin_board =
        XtCreateManagedWidget("bulletin_board",
            xmBulletinBoardWidgetClass, shell, NULL, 0);

    /* create List instance */
    /* notice that the convenience function XmCreateScrolledList is
        used so we don't have to create the scrollbars by hand */
    /* first, build the list box's contents */
    for (i = 0; i < 30; i++) {
        sprintf(item_string, "Item number %d", i);
        item_list[i] = XmStringCreate(item_string,
            XmSTRING_DEFAULT_CHARSET);
    }
```

```
/* set the list box's default resources */
n = 0;
XtSetArg(args[n], XmNitems, item_list); n++;
XtSetArg(args[n], XmNitemCount, 30); n++;
XtSetArg(args[n], XmNvisibleItemCount, 8); n++;

list_box =
    XmCreateScrolledList(bulletin_board, "list_box", args, n);
XtManageChild(list_box);

quit_button =
    XtCreateManagedWidget("quit_button",
        xmPushButtonWidgetClass, bulletin_board, NULL, 0);

/* link in List widget selection callbacks */
XtAddCallback(list_box, XmNbrowseSelectionCallback,
    ListCallback, NULL);
XtAddCallback(list_box, XmNdefaultActionCallback,
    ListCallback, NULL);
XtAddCallback(list_box, XmNextendedSelectionCallback,
    ListCallback, NULL);
XtAddCallback(list_box, XmNmultipleSelectionCallback,
    ListCallback, NULL);
XtAddCallback(list_box, XmNsingleSelectionCallback,
    ListCallback, NULL);

/* set up the quit button callback */
XtAddCallback(quit_button, XmNactivateCallback,
    QuitCallback, NULL);

/* make the whole thing appear */
XtRealizeWidget(shell);

/* run the event loop */
XtMainLoop();
}
```

PulldownMenu

Include files: Xm/RowColumn.h Xm/PushB.h Xm/CascadeB.h
Class name (for resource file):   (none—not a distinct class)
Creation examples: (see text and example)

Figure 8-8: PulldownMenu example (showing
MenuBar, PushButtons, and CascadeButtons) with sub-menu

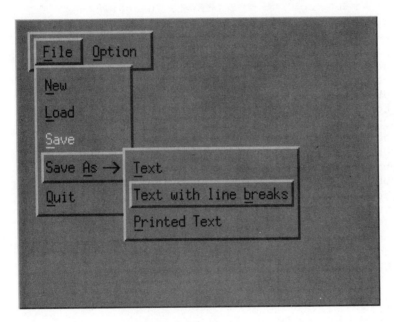

   Also discussed are the following:

PopupMenu

Include files: Xm/RowColumn.h Xm/PushB.h Xm/CascadeB.h
Class name (for resource file): (none—not a distinct class)
Creation examples: (see text and example)

CascadeButton

Include files: Xm/CascadeB.h
Class name (for resource file):   XmCascadeButton
Creation examples:

```
Widget      cascade_button;
Arg         *args;
int         argcnt;

cascade_button = XtCreateManagedWidget("widget_name",
    xmCascadeButtonWidgetClass, parent_widget, args, argcnt);
```

or

```
cascade_button = XmCreateCascadeButton(parent_widget, "widget_name",
    args, argcnt);
XtManageChild(cascade_button);
```

Figure 8-9: PopupMenu example (no MenuBar; appears in parent window when requested)

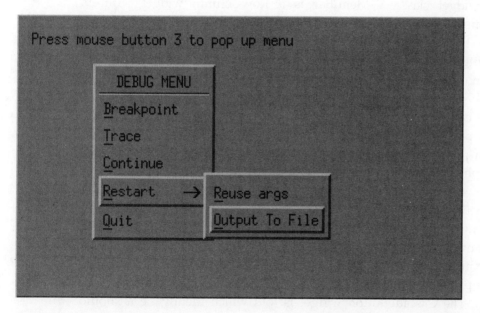

There are three kinds of menus directly supported by Motif: Pulldown, Popup and Option. Within these types, there is a nearly endless variety of configurable options and behavioral settings. To avoid devoting half the book to Motif menus, we will eliminate the Option menu type, and limit coverage of the Pulldown and Popup menu types to their most frequently used capabilities. Nevertheless there's still plenty of ground to cover.

As you saw in this section's opening, neither the Pulldown nor the Popup menu types exist as distinct classes. There are two convenience routines,

XmCreatePulldownMenu and XmCreatePopupMenu, that lay the foundations for the building of Pulldown and Popup menus. That's as far as the "convenience" goes, however: There is no Motif function that will magically build menus for you. The examples to come include functions that build menus based on easily defined data, and you'll find that there is enough complexity to Motif's menu system to make such functions more than a convenience.

Pulldown and Popup menus have a great deal in common, but we'll simplify things a bit by focusing first on the Pulldown, the more common type of menu. An application's Pulldown menu system is a series of widgets, starting with a special type of RowColumn widget called a MenuBar. The RowColumn is a handy widget that provides automatic placement of widgets in rows or columns. In the case of the MenuBar, the placement is along a row (horizontally). There is no MenuBar widget class. A MenuBar is a RowColumn widget with its XmNrowColumnType resource set to XmMENU_BAR.

Attached to the MenuBar is a special type of button called a CascadeButton. The CascadeButton widget class defines a behavior such that, when activated with the left mouse button, the CascadeButton causes a MenuPane to be displayed. (We'll get to the creation of the MenuPane in a moment.) A CascadeButton can have associated with it a single alphanumeric key, called a *mnemonic*, that pops up the MenuPane when the key is pressed in conjunction with the "meta" key: Alt on most keyboards, but it can also be Option, Command, or a graphical symbol such as the diamond key on Sun systems.

The Pulldown MenuPane is created with the XmCreatePulldownMenu convenience function, which creates a RowColumn widget with an XmNrowColumnType of XmMENU_PULLDOWN (MenuPane and Pulldown are terms of convenience, not widget classes). The parent for this MenuPane, as passed to the XmCreatePulldownMenu function, is *not* set to the CascadeButton that pops it up, rather it is set to the MenuBar that is the parent of the CascadeButton. The CascadeButton widget is told which MenuPane it should make visible through the CascadeButton's XmNsubMenuId resource. XmNsubMenuId is set, with XtSetArg(), to the widget ID of the MenuPane created with XmCreatePulldownMenu(). For each menu item on the MenuBar, you need to create one CascadeButton and one Pulldown MenuPane.

The Pulldown menu's choices are made up of child widgets attached to the MenuPane. The MenuPane accepts Label, PushButton, Separator, and CascadeButton children. The MenuPane stacks the children vertically in the order they were added, and sizes itself to accommodate them. If you create a menu too large for your screen, it will run off the bottom: There are no scrolling menus in Motif, but you should use a ScrolledList or SelectionBox if there are that many choices.

A MenuPane is not bound by the limits of your application's window, however. Label and Separator widgets do not respond to the mouse or keyboard, they just provide cosmetic relief. A PushButton child of a MenuPane is sized automatically, and its behavior is modified to be consistent with Motif's style. A CascadeButton child of a MenuPane is used to bring up a submenu. By default, this CascadeButton is drawn with its XmNlabelString text followed by a right-pointing arrow. When the CascadeButton is selected, the MenuPane widget identified in the CascadeButton's XmNsubMenuId resource is made active. As with the CascadeButtons attached to the MenuBar, submenu MenuPanes are not parented by the CascadeButtons that activate them. A Submenu MenuPane, which is created by XmCreatePulldownMenu(), should be parented by the MenuPane on which the CascadeButton resides. There is no arbitrary limit to the number of MenuPane-CascadeButton-MenuPane-CascadeButton... submenu levels you can create, but there is clearly a limit to users' patience.

Since the discussion above is pretty dense, let's looks at a summary of the steps required to build a Pulldown menu. The steps are in the order in which they should be executed by your application, not in widget tree hierarchy order:

- **Create MenuBar.** The MenuBar is a RowColumn widget, a horizontal strip positioned at the top of the widget you specify as the MenuBar's parent. The parent should be a container widget of some kind, like the BulletinBoard as in this example.

```
Widget      menu_bar, bulletin_board;

menu_bar = XmCreateMenuBar(bulletin_board, "menu_bar_name", NULL, 0);
XtManageChild(menu_bar);
```

- **Create a Pulldown MenuPane.** Each Pulldown menu or submenu in your application requires a Pulldown MenuPane. This is a vertical RowColumn widget. *Do not call XtManage() on the widget ID returned by XmCreatePulldownMenu.* It is managed and unmanaged automatically by a CascadeButton. The parent must be either a MenuBar or, in the case of a submenu, another MenuPane.

```
Widget      menu_bar, pulldown;

pulldown = XmCreatePulldownMenu(menu_bar, "pulldown_name", NULL, 0);
```

■ **Create CascadeButton on MenuBar.** Each Pulldown MenuPane must be associated with, but not a child of, a CascadeButton. The MenuBar's CascadeButton needs to have its XmNsubMenuId resource set to the widget ID of the MenuPane that the CascadeButton is intended to make visible. The CascadeButton's XmN mnemonic resource can be set to provide a way to pull down a menu from the keyboard.

```
Arg         args[3];
Widget      cascade_button, pulldown;
char        mnemonic = 'F', *label = "File";
int         nargs;

nargs = 0;
/* tell the CascadeButton which menu to pull down */
XtSetArg(args[nargs], XmNsubMenuId, pulldown); nargs++;
/* provide a keyboard shortcut to the menu */
XtSetArg(args[nargs], XmNmnemonic, mnemonic); nargs++;
/* set the button's label text */
XtSetArg(args[nargs], XmNlabelString, XmStringCreate(label,
    XmSTRING_DEFAULT_CHARSET)); nargs++;

cascade_button = XmCreateCascadeButton(menu_bar, "menu_name",
    args, nargs);
XtManageChild(cascade_button);
```

■ **Add the menu buttons and visuals.** PushButton, CascadeButton, Label and Separator widgets can be children of a Pulldown MenuPane. The MenuPane will arrange and manage them, placing them in the menu in the order of creation. PushButton and CascadeButton widgets can have keyboard shortcut mnemonics associated with them. Creating submenus with CascadeButton widgets is shown in the long example.

```
Widget      buttons[5], label, separator, pulldown;
Arg         args[3];
int         nargs, i;
void        ButtonCallback();
char        temp[25], *mnemonics = "ABCDE";

for (i = 0; i < 5; i++) {
```

```
    sprintf(temp, "menu_button_%d", i);
    nargs = 0;
    XtSetArg(args[nargs], XmNmnemonic, mnemonics[i]); nargs++;
    buttons[i] = XtCreateManagedWidget(temp, xmPushButtonWidgetClass,
        pulldown, args, nargs);
    XtAddCallback(buttons[i], XmNactivateCallback, ButtonCallback,
        temp);

    if (i == 2) {      /* add a separator and label after button 3 */
        nargs = 0;
        XtSetArg(args[nargs], XmNlabelString,
            XmStringCreate("More Buttons", XmSTRING_DEFAULT_CHARSET));
        nargs++;
        label = XtCreateManagedWidget("label", xmLabelWidgetClass,
            pulldown, args, nargs);
        separator = XtCreateManagedWidget("separator",
            XmSeparatorWidgetClass, pulldown, NULL, 0);
    }
}
```

If you don't attach any CascadeButton submenus, that's all it takes to create one pulldown menu. Additional pulldowns start from the "Create Pulldown MenuPane" step.

Motif Pulldown menus are easy to use, as they should be. The default behavior covers most users' expectations, and should only be modified when unavoidable. Pulldown menus are pulled down with the left mouse button (mouse button 1). Clicking once on a MenuBar CascadeButton pulls down its associated MenuPane, and leaves the MenuPane in place until a selection is made. A single mouse click on a PushButton dispatches a call to that button's XmNactivateCallback function, and dismisses the menu. Pressing a CascadeButton in a MenuPane makes visible the submenu associated with it; again, the submenu remains in place until a selection is made. The menu can be dismissed without making a selection by clicking outside the menu's region.

A pulldown menu can also be operated in "spring loaded" mode: Mouse button 1 is pressed over the MenuBar CascadeButton, and the Pulldown MenuPane appears. As long as the button is held down, the pointer highlights each PushButton it passes over. Releasing the mouse button activates the PushButton that was highlighted at the time of the release, unless the pointer was moved outside the PushButton's region. Passing over a CascadeButton with the mouse button pressed will, after a delay, cause CascadeButton's submenu to appear. In spring-loaded mode, releasing the button always dismisses all levels of menus and submenus. If the pointer was positioned over an active PushButton at the time of release, the button is activated.

The keyboard can also be used effectively to navigate menus, provided mnemonics have been applied to at least one of the MenuBar CascadeButtons. A menu is pulled down from the keyboard by positioning keyboard focus in the application's window, usually by moving the mouse pointer into the window or clicking in the window; holding down the Meta key; and pressing the mnemonic associated with that menu's CascadeButton. If the mnemonic is part of the CascadeButton's label (and it should be), the first occurrence of the mnemonic character in the button's label is underlined. You can also pull down the leftmost menu in a MenuBar by pressing the F10 key. Once a menu is pulled down, a button from the visible menu can be activated by pressing the mnemonic key associated with it. The Meta key is not necessary. The arrow keys may also be used to navigate the menu; up and down move vertically through a single menu's buttons, wrapping around after the first or last item. The left and right keys move among MenuPanes attached to MenuBar CascadeButtons. The exception is the pressing of the right arrow when the highlighted button is a submenu CascadeButton: This makes the submenu visible. The submenu is dismissed by pressing the left arrow key. The Return key makes a selection and dismisses all menus: Esc dismisses all menus without making a selection.

Any mix of mouse and keyboard navigation may be used with Motif Pulldown menus, except that actions associated with spring-loaded mode can't be used if the menu is pulled down from the keyboard, since the keyboard posts the menu until a selection is made or it is explicitly dismissed.

Fortunately, Popup menus aren't all that different. Popup menus "float," popping up in a window in response to a mouse button press (typically the rightmost button, or button 3). There is no MenuBar associated with a Popup; the Popup MenuPane created by the XmCreatePopupMenu call is parented by the widget in which you want the menu to appear. The XtAddEventHandler call is used on the Popup MenuPane's parent widget so that it will listen for a mouse button press and dispatch an event handler, a function similar to a callback. Your event handler should use XtManageChild() to make the Popup MenuPane appear. It may call the XmMenuPosition convenience function first so that the Popup MenuPane is positioned as near the mouse pointer as possible. Aside from this, the creation of a Popup menu is just the same as a Pulldown. In fact, any submenus attached to a Popup menu through CascadeButtons must be

Pulldown MenuPanes. The second of the two menu examples shows the creation and management of a Popup menu.

The behavior of a Popup menu is somewhat different from that of a pulldown. When activated with the mouse, a Popup menu is always spring-loaded, and its behavior tracks the description above for spring-loaded Pulldown menus. A Popup MenuPane can be called up from the keyboard, but because there is no MenuBar or CascadeButton, there is no mnemonic associated with the menu. Instead, a resource associated with the Popup MenuPane, called XmNmenuAccelerator, specifies a key sequence that pops up the menu. This is not a single character, but a variant of a *translation string*, a way of tagging user input events with identifiers that can be used as shorthand to reference that event. The X Toolkit Translation Manager is a rich facility worthy of study, but beyond the scope of this book. For now, satisfy yourself with the accelerator specification used in the second example and consult your *X Toolkit Intrinsics Manual* for more information about the Translation Manager. Motif assigns a default accelerator of F4, which pops up the Popup MenuPane for the window that has input focus.

Since menus are one of those concepts best explained by example, here are two:

The first creates a BulletinBoard with a Popup menu system. It defines a convenience function, MakePulldownMenu, that reads data from an array of structures, and creates a CascadeButton and a Pulldown MenuPane. It handles labels, separators, mnemonics, and multiple levels of submenus.

The second example creates a BulletinBoard widget with a Popup MenuPane associated with it. Again, a function, MakePopupMenu, is defined, and eases the creation of Popup menus significantly. The convenience functions are grouped together in makemenu.c.

The makefile boilerplate for the first example (Pulldown menu system) should be modified as follows:

```
PROGNAME=   menu1
OBJS=       menu1.o makemenu.o
LIBS=       -lXm -lXt -lX11 -lsocket
```

Both examples are dependent on the header file makemenu.h and on makemenu.c.

```
/* makemenu.h: structure definition for chapter 8 Motif menu
    examples */

struct menu_struct {
    char        *button_label;  /* appears on button top */
    char        mnemonic;       /* key to activate button */
    void        (*callback)();  /* callback for activation */
    void        *button_name;   /* button name for resource db */
    struct menu_struct  *submenu;
};

extern Widget MakePulldownMenu();
extern Widget MakePopupMenu();



/* makemenu.c: convenience routines for creating Pulldown and Popup
    menus, used in Chapter 8 Motif menu examples */
#include <X11/Intrinsic.h>
#include <Xm/Xm.h>
#include <Xm/RowColumn.h>
#include <Xm/PushB.h>
#include <Xm/CascadeB.h>
#include <Xm/Label.h>
#include <Xm/Separator.h>
#include <stdio.h>
#include <makemenu.h>

/* build a pull-down menu from a menu definition */
Widget MakePulldownMenu(menu_bar, menu, menu_name, menu_label,
    mnemonic)
Widget      menu_bar;
struct menu_struct  *menu;
char        *menu_name, *menu_label, mnemonic;
{
    int         i, nargs;
    Widget      pulldown, button, cascade_button;
    Widget      label, separator;
    Arg         args[5];
    char        temp[80];
    XmString    label_string;

    /* create a Pulldown menu widget */
    sprintf(temp, "%sPD", menu_name);
    pulldown =
        XmCreatePulldownMenu(menu_bar, temp, NULL, 0);

    /* now that the PulldownMenu exists, instantiate the CascadeButton
```

```
    and notify it of its PulldownMenu attachment */
/* make its name the same as the menu name argument */
nargs = 0;
XtSetArg(args[nargs], XmNsubMenuId, pulldown); nargs++;
XtSetArg(args[nargs], XmNmnemonic, mnemonic); nargs++;
label_string =
    XmStringCreateLtoR(menu_label, XmSTRING_DEFAULT_CHARSET);
XtSetArg(args[nargs], XmNlabelString, label_string); nargs++;
cascade_button =
    XmCreateCascadeButton(menu_bar, menu_name, args, nargs);

/* fill the menu */
for (i = 0; ; i++) {
    if (menu[i].button_label == NULL)   /* end of list */
        break;

    /* handle special cases: label and separator */
    if (strncmp(menu[i].button_name, "LBL", 3) == 0) { /* label */
        nargs = 0;
        /* set the label string */
        XtSetArg(args[nargs], XmNlabelString,
            XmStringCreate(menu[i].button_label,
            XmSTRING_DEFAULT_CHARSET)); nargs++;
        label = XtCreateManagedWidget(menu[i].button_label,
            xmLabelWidgetClass, pulldown, args, nargs);
        continue;
    }
    if (strncmp(menu[i].button_name, "SEP", 3) == 0) {
        /* separator requested */
        separator = XtCreateManagedWidget(menu[i].button_name,
            xmSeparatorWidgetClass, pulldown, NULL, 0);
        continue;
    }

    if (menu[i].submenu != NULL) {  /* sub-menu request */
        /* make current pulldown pane parent of new sub-menu. A
           CascadeButton will be created and a new PulldownMenu
           pane associated with it */
        MakePulldownMenu(pulldown, menu[i].submenu,
            menu[i].button_name, menu[i].button_label,
            menu[i].mnemonic);
    } else {     /* regular PushButton */
        nargs = 0;
        /* mnemonic to activate button from keyboard */
        XtSetArg(args[nargs], XmNmnemonic, menu[i].mnemonic);
        nargs++;
        /* label string for button surface */
        XtSetArg(args[nargs], XmNlabelString,
```

```
                    XmStringCreate(menu[i].button_label,
                    XmSTRING_DEFAULT_CHARSET)); nargs++;

            button =
                XmCreatePushButton(pulldown, menu[i].button_name,
                    args, nargs);
            XtAddCallback(button, XmNactivateCallback,
                menu[i].callback, menu[i].button_name);
            XtManageChild(button);
        }
    }
    XtManageChild(cascade_button);
    return(pulldown);
}

/* build a popup menu from a menu definition */
Widget MakePopupMenu(popup_parent, menu, menu_name, accel, post)
Widget      popup_parent;
struct      menu_struct *menu;
char        *menu_name, *accel;
void        (*post)();
{
    int             i, nargs;
    Widget          popup, button, label;
    Widget          submenu, separator;
    Arg             args[5];
    char            temp[80];

    /* define accelerator key to pop menu from keyboard */
    if (accel != NULL)
        XtSetArg(args[0], XmNmenuAccelerator, accel);

    popup =
        XmCreatePopupMenu(popup_parent, menu_name, args, 1);

    /* register the function that posts menu when mouse button is
        pressed */
    XtAddEventHandler(popup_parent, ButtonPressMask, False,
        post, popup);

    /* attach the PushButtons, declare the callbacks */
    for (i = 0; ; i++) {
        if (menu[i].button_label == NULL)   /* end of list */
            break;
        /* handle special cases: label and separator */
        if (strncmp(menu[i].button_name, "LBL", 3) == 0) { /* label */
            nargs = 0;
            /* set the label string */
```

```
            XtSetArg(args[nargs], XmNlabelString,
                XmStringCreate(menu[i].button_label,
                XmSTRING_DEFAULT_CHARSET)); nargs++;
            label = XtCreateManagedWidget(menu[i].button_label,
                xmLabelWidgetClass, popup, args, nargs);
            continue;
        }
        if (strncmp(menu[i].button_name, "SEP", 3) == 0) {
            /* separator request */
            separator = XtCreateManagedWidget(menu[i].button_name,
                xmSeparatorWidgetClass, popup, NULL, 0);
            continue;
        }

        if (menu[i].submenu != NULL) {
            submenu = MakePulldownMenu(popup, menu[i].submenu,
                menu[i].button_name, menu[i].button_label,
                menu[i].mnemonic);
        } else {    /* regular PushButton */
            nargs = 0;
            /* mnemonic to activate button from keyboard */
            XtSetArg(args[nargs], XmNmnemonic, menu[i].mnemonic);
            nargs++;
            /* label string for button surface */
            XtSetArg(args[nargs], XmNlabelString,
                XmStringCreate(menu[i].button_label,
                XmSTRING_DEFAULT_CHARSET)); nargs++;

            button =
                XmCreatePushButton(popup, menu[i].button_name,
                    args, nargs);
            XtAddCallback(button, XmNactivateCallback,
                menu[i].callback, menu[i].button_name);
        }
        XtManageChild(button);
    }
    return(popup);
}
```

Here's the first of the two examples:

```
/* menu1.c: pull-down menu Motif example for chapter 8 */
/* tabs are four spaces apart */

#include <X11/Intrinsic.h>
#include <Xm/Xm.h>
#include <Xm/BulletinB.h>
```

```
#include <Xm/RowColumn.h>
#include <stdio.h>
#include <makemenu.h>

void MenuCallback(widget, client_data, call_data)
Widget              widget;
void                *client_data;
XmAnyCallbackStruct *call_data;
{
    printf("menu callback: %s\n", client_data);

    if (strcmp(client_data, "File_Quit") == 0)
        exit();
}

/* create structures for menus */
struct menu_struct save_as_submenu_struct[] = {
    "Text", 'T', MenuCallback, "Save_As_Text", NULL,
    "Text with line breaks", 'b', MenuCallback, "Save_As_Text_Breaks",
        NULL,
    "Printed Text", 'P', MenuCallback, "Save_As_Printed_Text",
        NULL,
    NULL, 0, NULL, NULL, NULL
};

struct menu_struct file_menu_struct[] = {
    "New",  'N', MenuCallback, "File_New", NULL,
    "Load", 'L', MenuCallback, "File_Load", NULL,
    "Save", 'S', MenuCallback, "File_Save", NULL,
    "Save As", 'A', MenuCallback, "File_Save_As",
        save_as_submenu_struct,
    "Quit", 'Q', MenuCallback, "File_Quit", NULL,
    NULL, 0, NULL, NULL, NULL
};

struct menu_struct option_menu_struct[] = {
    "Document", 'D', MenuCallback, "Option_Document", NULL,
    "Paragraph", 'P', MenuCallback, "Option_Paragraph", NULL,
    "Style", 'S', MenuCallback, "Option_Style", NULL,
    NULL, 0, NULL, NULL, NULL
};

main(argc, argv)
int     argc;
char    **argv;
{
    Widget      shell, bulletin_board, quit_button, menu_bar;
    Widget      file_menu, save_as_submenu, option_menu;
```

```
    setbuf(stdout, NULL);

    /* Initialize the toolkit, set up top-level shell */
    shell = XtInitialize("shell", "Menu1", NULL, 0, &argc, argv);

    /* create instance of BulletinBoard container widget class */
    bulletin_board =
        XtCreateManagedWidget("bulletin_board",
            xmBulletinBoardWidgetClass, shell, NULL, 0);

    /* create the menu bar, two cascade buttons for choices */
    menu_bar =
        XmCreateMenuBar(bulletin_board, "menu_bar", NULL, 0);
    XtManageChild(menu_bar);

    /* create the Pulldown menus */
    file_menu = MakePulldownMenu(menu_bar, file_menu_struct,
        "File", "File", 'F');

    option_menu = MakePulldownMenu(menu_bar, option_menu_struct,
        "Option", "Option", 'O');

    /* make the whole thing appear */
    XtRealizeWidget(shell);

    /* run the event loop */
    XtMainLoop();
}
```

The makefile boilerplate for the second example should be modified as follows:

```
PROGNAME=       menu2
OBJS=           menu2.o makemenu.o
LIBS=           -lXm -lXt -lX11 -lsocket
```

Here's the source code:

```
/* menu2.c: Popup menu Motif example for chapter 8 */
/* also covers AddEventHandler */
/* tabs are four spaces apart */
#include <X11/Intrinsic.h>
#include <Xm/Xm.h>
#include <Xm/BulletinB.h>
#include <Xm/RowColumn.h>
#include <Xm/Label.h>
```

```
#include <stdio.h>
#include <makemenu.h>

void MenuCallback(widget, client_data, call_data)
Widget                widget;
void                  *client_data;
XmAnyCallbackStruct   *call_data;
{
    printf("menu callback: %s\n", client_data);

    if (strcmp(client_data, "Debug_Quit") == 0)
        exit();
}

void PostMenu(widget, menu, event)
Widget          widget, menu;
XButtonEvent    *event;
{
    /* only pay attention to button 3 */
    if (event->button != Button3)
        return;

    /* use a convenience function to position the popup where the
        mouse is */
    XmMenuPosition(menu, event);

    /* make the menu appear */
    XtManageChild(menu);
}

/* create structures for menus */

/* a couple of additions: An element with a label (field 1) but no
    button name (field 4) is interpreted as a menu label and inserted
    at the current position. An element with a label of "SEP" causes
    a horizontal separator to be placed at the current position. */

struct menu_struct restart_menu_struct[] = {
    "Reuse args", 'R', MenuCallback, "Restart_Reuse_Args", NULL,
    "Output To File", 'O', MenuCallback, "Restart_Output_To_File", NULL,
    NULL, 0, NULL, NULL, NULL
};

struct menu_struct debug_menu_struct[] = {
    "DEBUG MENU", '\0', NULL, "LBLdebug_menu", NULL,
    "SEP", '\0', NULL, "SEPdebug_menu", NULL,
    "Breakpoint", 'B', MenuCallback, "Debug_Breakpoint", NULL,
    "Trace", 'T', MenuCallback, "Debug_Trace", NULL,
```

```
    "Continue", 'C', MenuCallback, "Debug_Continue", NULL,
    "Restart", 'R', MenuCallback, "Debug_Restart", restart_menu_struct,
    "Quit", 'Q', MenuCallback, "Debug_Quit", NULL,
    NULL, 0, NULL, NULL, NULL
};

main(argc, argv)
int     argc;
char    **argv;
{
    Widget      shell, bulletin_board, prompt;
    Widget      menu_1;
    Arg         args[2];
    char        *s = {"Press mouse button 3 to pop up menu"};

    /* Initialize the toolkit, set up top-level shell */
    shell = XtInitialize("shell", "Menu2", NULL, 0, &argc, argv);

    /* create instance of BulletinBoard container widget class */
    bulletin_board =
        XtCreateManagedWidget("bulletin_board",
            xmBulletinBoardWidgetClass, shell, NULL, 0);

    /* create a prompt so the user knows what to do */
    XtSetArg(args[0], XmNlabelString, XmStringCreate(s,
        XmSTRING_DEFAULT_CHARSET));
    prompt =
        XtCreateManagedWidget("prompt",
            xmLabelWidgetClass, bulletin_board, args, 1);

    /* create the Pulldown menus */
    menu_1 = MakePopupMenu(bulletin_board, debug_menu_struct, "Debug",
        "Meta <Key> D", PostMenu);

    /* make the whole thing appear */
    XtRealizeWidget(shell);

    /* run the event loop */
    XtMainLoop();
}
```

MessageBox

Include file: Xm/MessageB.h
Class name (for resource file):   XmMessageBox
Creation examples:

```
Widget     message_box;
Arg        *args;
int        argcnt;

message_box = XtCreateManagedWidget("widget_name",
    xmMessageBoxWidgetClass, parent_widget, args, argcnt);
```

or

```
message_box = XmCreateMessageBox(parent_widget, "widget_name",
    args, argcnt);
XtManageChild(message_box);
```

Figure 8-10: MessageBox widget (XmNdialogType resource set to XmDIALOG_ERROR)

Figure 8-11: MessageBox widget (XmNdialogType resource set to XmDIALOG_INFO)

Figure 8-12: MessageBox widget (XmNdialogType resource set to XmDIALOG_MESSAGE, the default)

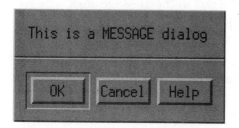

Figure 8-13: MessageBox widget (XmNdialogType resource set to XmDIALOG_QUESTION)

Figure 8-14: MessageBox widget (XmNdialogType resource set to XmDIALOG_WARNING)

Figure 8-15: MessageBox widget (XmNdialogType resource set to XmDIALOG_WORKING)

The MessageBox is one of Motif's simplest and most useful widgets. It is a BulletinBoard widget with a message display area, an optional representational icon, and three PushButtons: OK, Cancel, and Help. The text in the message area is set with the familiar XmNlabelString resource, and PushButton activation dispatches callbacks registered as XmNokCallback, XmNcancelCallback, and XmNhelpCallback.

You can change the MessageBox's appearance according to the kind of message being conveyed. A bitmapped icon, displayed at the left of the MessageBox's window, changes depending on the MessageBox type. There are six predefined MessageBox types, selected with the XmNdialogType resource. The illustrations show how the icon changes:

- XmDIALOG_ERROR
- XmDIALOG_INFORMATION
- XmDIALOG_MESSAGE. This is the default; it displays no icon.
- XmDIALOG_QUESTION
- XmDIALOG_WARNING
- XmDIALOG_WORKING

The XmString value in the XmNlabelString resource can be aligned on the left, centered, or aligned to the right by setting the XmNmessageAlignment resource to XmALIGNMENT_BEGINNING, XmALIGNMENT_CENTER, or XmALIGNMENT_END, respectively.

You also have considerable control over the buttons. The label text of the buttons can be changed with the XmNhelpLabelString, XmNokLabelString, and XmNcancelLabelString resources, freeing you to assign other meanings to the buttons. Also, you can select a default button by setting the XmNdefaultButton-Type resource to XmDIALOG_CANCEL_BUTTON, XmDIALOG_OK_BUTTON, or XmDIALOG_HELP_BUTTON. (The resource names stay the same even if you change the buttons' label text.) The default button appears with a sunken frame around it, and can be pushed from the keyboard by placing the keyboard focus in the MessageBox window, and pressing Return. The default default button (got that?) is XmDIALOG_OK_BUTTON, but, depending on the type of message you're presenting, you may wish to change it.

The MessageBox types permit you to express varying degrees of urgency without adding a lot of explanatory text to your message. Instead of saying, "This is only a warning," or "Pay attention—this is serious," in words, the

MessageBox's changeable icon lets the user see the severity of the condition at a glance.

The example is short and simple. It only instantiates the MessageBox, and lets the external resource file do the rest. The resource file has commented-out entries that let you see what each of the varying MessageBox types look like on your system, but the icon images are part of the standard Motif style. There shouldn't be any surprises.

The makefile template should be modified as follows:

```
PROGNAME=       messageb
OBJS=           messageb.o
CFLAGS=         -O -I.
LIBS=           -lXm -lXt -lX11 -lsocket
```

The resource file, MessageB, starts out like this:

```
# uncomment one of the following pairs:
#*dialogType:          DIALOG_ERROR
#*messageString:           This is an ERROR dialog

#*dialogType:          DIALOG_INFORMATION
#*messageString:       This is an INFORMATION dialog

#*dialogType:          DIALOG_MESSAGE
#*messageString:       This is a MESSAGE dialog

*dialogType:           DIALOG_QUESTION
*messageString:        This is a QUESTION dialog

#*dialogType:          DIALOG_WARNING
#*messageString:       This is a WARNING dialog

#*dialogType:          DIALOG_WORKING
#*messageString:       This is a WORKING dialog
```

Here's the source code for the example:

```
/* messageb.c: MessageBox Motif example for chapter 8 */
/* tabs are four spaces apart */

#include <X11/Intrinsic.h>
#include <Xm/Xm.h>
#include <Xm/MessageB.h>
```

```
#include <stdio.h>

/* define a handler for the "quit" convenience push button */
void QuitCallback(widget, client_data, call_data)
Widget              widget;
void                *client_data;
XmAnyCallbackStruct *call_data;
{
    exit(0);
}

main(argc, argv)
int     argc;
char    **argv;
{
    Widget       shell, message_box;

    /* Initialize the toolkit, set up top-level shell */
    shell = XtInitialize("shell", "MessageB", NULL, 0, &argc, argv);

    /* create instance of MessageBox */
    message_box =
        XtCreateManagedWidget("message_box",
            xmMessageBoxWidgetClass, shell, NULL, 0);

    /* wire our quit button callback into all the buttons in
        message_box */
    XtAddCallback(message_box, XmNcancelCallback, QuitCallback, NULL);
    XtAddCallback(message_box, XmNokCallback, QuitCallback, NULL);
    XtAddCallback(message_box, XmNhelpCallback, QuitCallback, NULL);

    /* make the whole thing appear */
    XtRealizeWidget(shell);

    /* run the event loop */
    XtMainLoop();
}
```

PanedWindow

Include file: Xm/PanedW.h
Class name (for resource file):   XmPanedWindow
Creation examples:

```
Widget     panedw;
Arg        *args;
int        argcnt;

panedw = XtCreateManagedWidget("widget_name",
    xmPanedWindowWidgetClass, parent_widget, args, argcnt);
```

or

```
panedw = XmCreatePanedWindow(parent_widget, "widget_name",
    args, argcnt);
XtManageChild(panedw);
```

Figure 8-16: PanedWindow widget with PushButton children

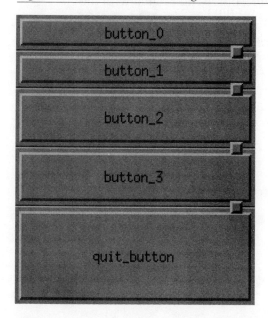

The PanedWindow accepts a number of child widgets, placing each one in its own subwindow. The subwindow's size can be adjusted by the user through the movement of a *sash*, a small control that sits between child windows. Placing the mouse pointer over the button on a sash changes the mouse cursor into a cross-hair. Holding down mouse button 1 and moving the mouse vertically will adjust the sash's position between windows. Holding the Shift key down while adjusting resizes the pane above the sash and all resizable panes below, while holding the Control key down adjusts the pane below the sash and all the panes above it.

The PanedWindow is a widget that makes the best of tight screen space. The example shows the effects of resizing panes on the widget children contained in them, but it is far from a typical use of a PanedWindow widget. It is most often seen in complex user interfaces in which a portion (or all) of the interface can sometimes be obscured in favor of more room to type, draw, or whatever. You could, for instance, build a PanedWindow with two children: A BulletinBoard full of PushButtons and other controls in the upper pane, and a multi-line editable Text widget below. You could create lots of buttons in the upper pane without worrying too much about how much space they take away from the editable area: The user can just push the sash up to allow for more room to type, or pull it down when access to one of the obscured buttons is needed, temporarily shrinking the amount of viewable text. There are several resources associated with the PanedWindow widget, but its default settings suit most applications. Therefore, there is no resource file associated with this example.

The makefile template should be modified as follows:

```
PROGNAME=    panedw
OBJS=        panedw.o
LIBS=        -lXm -lXt -lX11 -lsocket
```

Here's the example:

```
/* panedw.c: PanedWindow Motif example for chapter 8 */
/* tabs are four spaces apart */

#include <X11/Intrinsic.h>
#include <Xm/Xm.h>
#include <Xm/PanedW.h>
#include <Xm/PushB.h>
#include <stdio.h>

/* define a handler for the "quit" convenience push button */
void QuitCallback(widget, client_data, call_data)
Widget              widget;
```

```
void                  *client_data;
XmAnyCallbackStruct *call_data;
{
    exit(0);
}


main(argc, argv)
int      argc;
char     **argv;
{
    Widget       shell, buttons[4], quit_button, panedw;
    int          i;
    char         button_name[20];

    /* Initialize the toolkit, set up top-level shell */
    shell = XtInitialize("shell", "PanedW", NULL, 0, &argc, argv);

    /* create the PanedWindow instance */
    panedw =
        XtCreateManagedWidget("panedw",
            xmPanedWindowWidgetClass, shell, NULL, 0);

    /* create four buttons to show widget's behavior */
    for (i = 0; i < 4; i++) {
        sprintf(button_name, "button_%d", i);
        buttons[i] =
            XtCreateManagedWidget(button_name,
                xmPushButtonWidgetClass, panedw, NULL, 0);
    }

    quit_button =
        XtCreateManagedWidget("quit_button",
            xmPushButtonWidgetClass, panedw, NULL, 0);

    /* set up the quit button callback */
    XtAddCallback(quit_button, XmNactivateCallback,
        QuitCallback, NULL);

    /* make the whole thing appear */
    XtRealizeWidget(shell);

    /* run the event loop */
    XtMainLoop();
}
```

RowColumn

Include file: Xm/RowColumn.h
Class name (for resource file): XmRowColumn
Creation examples:

```
Widget     rowcol;
Arg        *args;
int        argcnt;
rowcol = XtCreateManagedWidget("widget_name",
    xmRowColumnWidgetClass, parent_widget, args, argcnt);
```

or

```
rowcol = XmCreateRowColumn(parent_widget, "widget_name",
    args, argcnt);
XtManageChild(rowcol);
```

Figure 8-17: The RowColumn widget showing vertical orientation and tight packing

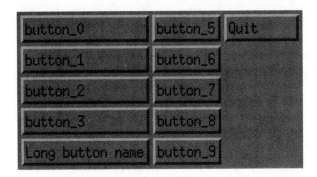

You've already seen the RowColumn widget in action behind the scenes in the popup and pulldown menu examples. The basic idea behind the RowColumn widget is that you occasionally need to display a large number of widgets, and that precisely setting the position of each one gets a little tiresome. The RowColumn widget manages a number of children, most typically PushButton widgets, and arranges them automatically, based on guidelines you set through the RowColumn's resources. There is a long list of RowColumn resources, but most of them are related to special instances of RowColumns used with menus.

When you use a RowColumn as a "plain" widget, the following resources are among the most important:

- **XmNorientation.** Determines stacking order of widgets. When set to XmVERTICAL, widgets are stacked top to bottom, wrapping around to subsequent columns as needed and permitted by the resource settings. XmHORIZONTAL orientation stacks widgets left to right, wrapping to subsequent rows as needed and permitted by the resources.

- **XmNpacking.** Determines how RowColumn packs widgets. When set to XmPACK_TIGHT, the RowColumn squeezes in as many widgets as possible before wrapping to the next row (XmNorientation set to XmHORIZONTAL) or column (XmNorientation set to XmVERTICAL). Widgets retain their original sizes, except as described in the XmNadjustLast resource description. When set to XmPACK_COLUMN, the widgets are arranged in the number of rows or columns specified by the XmNnumColumns resource, and all widgets are resized to match the size of the largest widget. A value of XmNONE for this resource turns off the RowColumn's automatic placement.

- **XmNnumColumns.** Specifies the number of rows (for XmHORIZON-TAL orientation) or columns (for XmVERTICAL) into which the widgets will be stacked. Meaningful only when XmNpacking is set to XmPACK_COLUMN.

- **XmNadjustLast.** When set to True (the default), widgets closest to the edges of the RowColumn are resized to fill in any blank areas between the widget edges and the RowColumn's edge.

- **XmNspacing.** Sets the spacing between widgets in pixels.

- **XmNmarginHeight and XmNmarginWidth.** Determines respectively the vertical and horizontal margins measured from the edges of the RowColumn to the nearest child widget edges. Specified in pixels.

Besides menus, the RowColumn is most useful for maintaining collections of PushButton widgets. When XmNpacking is set to XmPACK_TIGHT, resizing the RowColumn widget will cause the children to be rearranged to fit the new space.

The makefile boilerplate should be modified as follows:

```
PROGNAME=    rowcol
OBJS=        rowcol.o
LIBS=        -lXm -lXt -lX11 -lsocket
```

The initial default resource file, RowCol, is as follows:

```
*quit_button*labelString:    Quit
*row_column*numColumns:      3
#*row_column*packing:        PACK_COLUMN
*row_column*packing:         PACK_TIGHT
*button_4*labelString:       Long button name
```

Here's the example:

```
/* rowcol.c: RowColumn Motif example for chapter 8 */
/* tabs are four spaces apart */

#include <X11/Intrinsic.h>
#include <Xm/Xm.h>
#include <Xm/BulletinB.h>
#include <Xm/RowColumn.h>
#include <Xm/PushB.h>
#include <stdio.h>

/* define a handler for the "quit" convenience push button */
void QuitCallback(widget, client_data, call_data)
Widget              widget;
void                *client_data;
XmAnyCallbackStruct *call_data;
{
    exit(0);
}

main(argc, argv)
int     argc;
char    **argv;
{
    Widget      row_column;
    Widget      shell, buttons[10], quit_button;
    int         i;
    char        button_name[15];

    /* Initialize the toolkit, set up top-level shell */
    shell = XtInitialize("shell", "RowCol", NULL, 0, &argc, argv);

    /* create RowColumn widget */
    row_column =
        XtCreateManagedWidget("row_column",
            xmRowColumnWidgetClass, shell, NULL, 0);
```

```
/* create ten PushButton instances */
for (i = 0; i < 10; i++) {
    sprintf(button_name, "button_%d", i);
    buttons[i] =
        XtCreateManagedWidget(button_name,
            xmPushButtonWidgetClass, row_column, NULL, 0);
}

/* build the quit button */
quit_button =
    XtCreateManagedWidget("quit_button",
        xmPushButtonWidgetClass, row_column, NULL, 0);

/* set up the quit button callback */
XtAddCallback(quit_button, XmNactivateCallback,
    QuitCallback, NULL);

/* make the whole thing appear */
XtRealizeWidget(shell);

/* run the event loop */
XtMainLoop();
}
```

Scale

Include file: Xm/Scale.h
Class name (for resource file):   XmScale
Creation examples:

```
Widget     scale;
Arg        *args;
int        argcnt;

scale = XtCreateManagedWidget("widget_name",
    xmScaleWidgetClass, parent_widget, args, argcnt);
```

or

```
scale = XmCreateScale(parent_widget, "widget_name",
    args, argcnt);
XtManageChild(scale);
```

Figure 8-18: A vertical Scale widget

The Scale is a simple widget that lets the user adjust a numeric value between a minimum and maximum value by moving a slider with the mouse. The value is determined by the relative placement of a small rectangular region, the slider, along the length of the scale. The minimum and maximum numeric values are set by the Scale resources XmNminimum and XmNmaximum, and the XmNdecimalPoints determines where the decimal point will be placed, specified as the number of digits from last digit on the right. The XmNminimum and XmNmaximum values must be specified as integers. If you need to represent floating-point numbers, use XmNdecimalPoints to simulate them.

The widget's appearance is governed by these resources (among others):

- **XmNorientation.** Set to either XmVERTICAL or XmHORIZONTAL.
- **XmNprocessingDirection.** Determines which end of the Scale's line represents the maximum value. Set to XmMAX_ON_LEFT or XmMAX_ON_RIGHT for an XmHORIZONTAL orientation, or XmMAX_ON_TOP or XmMAX_ON_BOTTOM for XmVERTICAL.
- **XmNshowValue.** When set to True, the current numeric value is "floated" in text over the top or to the left of the Scale widget.
- **XmNvalue.** Specifies the slider's starting position on the scale. Can also be modified with XmSetArg()/XmSetValues() at any time to move the slider to a new position on the scale.
- **XmNscaleHeight and XmNscaleWidth.** Sets the length, in pixels (by default), of the scale on which the slider moves. The value of XmNorientation determines which of these resources is effective for setting the scale's length.

There are two ways to use the mouse to move the slider, and two callbacks that are associated with this movement. The user can move the slider by positioning the pointer over it, pressing and holding the mouse button, and dragging the slider to a new position. As the slider is dragged, XmNdragCallback is called multiple times with the changed values. The user can also click the mouse button inside the slider's track to move the slider toward the pointer. XmNvalueChangedCallback is dispatched each time the slider is moved this way. Both callbacks use the XmScaleCallbackStruct structure to return the data through the value member and the reason for the callback through the reason member. When the XmNvalueChangedCallback is dispatched, the reason member is set to XmCR_VALUE_CHANGED. When XmNdragCallback is called, the reason member is set to XmCR_DRAG.

The Scale is a convenience widget that lets the user specify numeric values visually, and without dropping the mouse to use the keyboard. It's not suitable for all forms of numeric input, and it can be downright frustrating to use when precision over a broad range of possible values is required. In general, broad ranges (large numeric distances between the minimum and maximum values) and short scale lengths (as specified by XmNscaleHeight or XmNscaleWidth) decrease the Scale's precision. The Scale widget drops intermediate values as needed to make a range fit on a scale of the specified length.

The makefile boilerplate for this example should be modified as follows:

```
PROGNAME=    scale
OBJS=        scale.o
LIBS=        -lXm -lXt -lX11 -lsocket
```

Here's the initial default resource file, named "Scale":

```
*showValue:        True
*scale.x:          50
*quit_button.labelString:    Quit
*scale.minimum:       0
*scale.maximum:      180


#uncomment one pair of lines below:
*scale.orientation: VERTICAL
*scale.processingDirection: MAX_ON_TOP
#*scale.orientation:    HORIZONTAL
#*scale.processingDirection:    MAX_ON_RIGHT
```

Here's the example:

```
/* scale.c: Scale Motif example for chapter 8 */
/* tabs are four spaces apart */

#include <X11/Intrinsic.h>
#include <Xm/Xm.h>
#include <Xm/BulletinB.h>
#include <Xm/Scale.h>
#include <Xm/PushB.h>
#include <stdio.h>

/* first, set up the callback routine */
/* one function is used for all four arrows. The client_data argument
   (set by the XtAddCallback function) will indicate which arrow
   was affected. */
void ScaleCallback(widget, client_data, call_data)
Widget                widget;
void                  *client_data;
XmScaleCallbackStruct *call_data;
{
    /* display the reason for the callback */
    if (call_data->reason == XmCR_DRAG)
        printf("DRAG: ");
    else printf("VALUE CHANGED: ");
    printf("%d\n", call_data->value);
}

/* define a handler for the "quit" convenience push button */
```

```
void QuitCallback(widget, client_data, call_data)
Widget                 widget;
void                   *client_data;
XmAnyCallbackStruct *call_data;
{
    exit(0);
}
main(argc, argv)
int     argc;
char    **argv;
{
    Widget      shell, bulletin_board, scale, quit_button;

    /* Initialize the toolkit, set up top-level shell */
    shell = XtInitialize("shell", "Scale", NULL, 0, &argc, argv);

    /* create instance of BulletinBoard container widget class */
    bulletin_board =
        XtCreateManagedWidget("bulletin_board",
            xmBulletinBoardWidgetClass, shell, NULL, 0);

    /* create scale widget instance */
    scale =
        XtCreateManagedWidget("scale", xmScaleWidgetClass,
            bulletin_board, NULL, 0);

    quit_button =
        XtCreateManagedWidget("quit_button",
            xmPushButtonWidgetClass, bulletin_board, NULL, 0);

    /* link in the callbacks for the scale */
    XtAddCallback(scale, XmNvalueChangedCallback,
        ScaleCallback, NULL);
    XtAddCallback(scale, XmNdragCallback,
        ScaleCallback, NULL);

    /* set up the quit button callback */
    XtAddCallback(quit_button, XmNactivateCallback,
        QuitCallback, NULL);

    /* make the whole thing appear */
    XtRealizeWidget(shell);

    /* run the event loop */
    XtMainLoop();
}
```

ScrolledWindow

Include file: Xm/ScrolledW.h
Class name (for resource file): XmScrolledWindow
Creation examples:

```
Widget     scrolled_win;
Arg        *args;
int        argcnt;

scrolled_win = XtCreateManagedWidget("widget_name",
    xmScrolledWindowWidgetClass, parent_widget, args, argcnt);
```

or

```
scrolled_win = XmCreateScrolledWindow(parent_widget, "widget_name",
    args, argcnt);
XtManageChild(scrolled_win);
```

Figure 8-19: The ScrolledWindow widget. The scrollbars can be used to reveal concealed portions of the child widget (in this case, a Form with PushButton children).

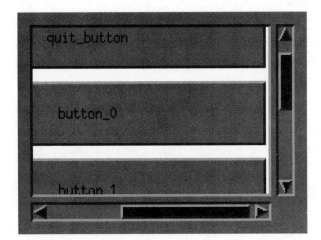

The ScrolledWindow defines a viewport through which a child widget, or a portion of it, can be viewed. If the child widget is larger than the viewport, the ScrolledWindow can use ScrollBar widgets to make an obscured portion of its child wiget visible. The ScrolledWindow is useful wherever there is more information to be presented than there is room to present. (Or, at least, you want to give the user the option of making the window smaller while still using the interface.)

The ScrolledWindow's child widget is typically a container (like a BulletinBoard or Form) that holds the component widgets of the interface. The easiest way to use the ScrolledWindow is to let it manage itself, and it is that configuration that is discussed here. The Reference Manual shows you how to configure a ScrolledWindow to permit you more precise control over its actions. The widget's automatic behavior is suitable for the majority of applications—you aren't likely to find it limiting.

To make the ScrolledWindow automatically manage itself and its child widget, the following resources should be set appropriately:

- **XmNscrollingPolicy.** For automatic management, this resource should be set to XmAUTOMATIC at the time the widget is created, since it cannot be changed later. Declaration in an external resource file, as in the following example, is sufficient. Automatic behavior means that the horizontal and vertical scrollbars are created for you, and built-in callbacks are registered that move the child widget under the viewport when the ScrollBar sliders are moved.

- **XmNvisualPolicy.** When XmNscrollingPolicy is set to XmAUTOMATIC, this resource is automatically set to XmCONSTANT. This setting causes the ScrolledWindow's viewport to change size only when its parent widget requests it, such as when the window containing it is resized. You do not need to change this value.

- **XmNscrollBarDisplayPolicy.** This resource can safely be changed without affecting automatic operation. It determines when the ScrollBar widgets will appear around the edges of the ScrolledWindow's viewport. When set to XmAS_NEEDED, scrollbars will appear only when the child widget is larger than the viewport. The vertical or horizontal scrollbar may appear alone if the child widget is larger than the viewport in only one dimension. The scrollbars will appear and disappear as the child widget and ScrolledWindow widget's size changes require. The other setting, XmSTATIC, causes both ScrollBars to be visible even when they are not needed. User adjustment of an unneeded scrollbar has no effect on the display.

In addition to these behavioral resources, there are a few that relate to the
ScrolledWindow's appearance:

- **XmNscrollBarPlacement.** Determines where the ScrollBars will be placed along the edge of the ScrolledWindow's viewport. XmTOP_LEFT, for instance, displays the horizontal scrollbar over the top of viewport, and displays the vertical scrollbar on the viewport's left side. Other settings are XmBOTTOM_LEFT, XmTOP_RIGHT, and XmBOTTOM_RIGHT.
- **XmNscrolledWindowMarginWidth.** Sets the distance (in pixels) from the left and right edges of the viewport to the corresponding edges of the ScrolledWindow widget's outer window.
- **XmNscrolledWindowMarginHeight.** Sets the distance (in pixels) from the top and bottom edges of the viewport to the corresponding edges of the ScrolledWindow widget's outer window.

The example declares a Form widget to be a child of a Frame, which is a child
of the ScrolledWindow. The Frame is used to give the Form its shape. The Frame
and Form widgets were used to show that the ScrolledWindow can be used with
most any kind of widget, but a RowColumn or BulletinBoard child might have
been more appropriate for this specific example. Try modifying the code to use
one of these widget types instead. Experiment with settings in the default
resource file, and resize the main window after it appears to see the effects.

The makefile boilerplate should be modified as follows:

```
PROGNAME=      scrollw
OBJS=          scrollw.o
LIBS=          -lXm -lXt -lX11 -lsocket
```

Here's the initial default resource file, which includes settings for both the
ScrolledWindow and Form widgets in this example:

```
# settings for ScrolledWindow widget example

*form.background:       White
*scrollingPolicy:       AUTOMATIC
*visualPolicy:          CONSTANT
*scrollBarDisplayPolicy:    AS_NEEDED
*frame*height:          300
*frame*width:           300
*scrolledWindowMarginWidth: 10
```

```
*scrolledWindowMarginHeight:     10

*form*XmPushButton.leftAttachment:   ATTACH_FORM
*form*XmPushButton.rightAttachment:  ATTACH_FORM
*form*XmPushButton.leftOffset:       5
*form*XmPushButton.rightOffset:      5

## top and bottom positions for each of the widgets
*form*quit_button.topAttachment:     ATTACH_FORM
*form*quit_button.topOffset:         5
*form*quit_button.bottomAttachment:  ATTACH_POSITION
*form*quit_button.bottomPosition:    18

*form*button_0.topAttachment:        ATTACH_POSITION
*form*button_0.bottomAttachment:     ATTACH_POSITION
*form*button_0.topPosition:          20
*form*button_0.bottomPosition:       38

*form*button_1.topAttachment:        ATTACH_POSITION
*form*button_1.bottomAttachment:     ATTACH_POSITION
*form*button_1.topPosition:          40
*form*button_1.bottomPosition:       58

*form*button_2.topAttachment:        ATTACH_POSITION
*form*button_2.bottomAttachment:     ATTACH_POSITION
*form*button_2.topPosition:          60
*form*button_2.bottomPosition:       78

*form*button_3.topAttachment:        ATTACH_POSITION
*form*button_3.bottomAttachment:     ATTACH_FORM
*form*button_3.topPosition:          80
*form*button_3.bottomOffset:         5
```

Here's the source code:

```
/* scrollw.c: ScrolledWindow Motif example for chapter 8 */
/* tabs are four spaces apart */

#include <X11/Intrinsic.h>
#include <Xm/Xm.h>
#include <Xm/Frame.h>
#include <Xm/Form.h>
#include <Xm/PushB.h>
#include <Xm/ScrolledW.h>
#include <stdio.h>

/* define a handler for the "quit" convenience push button */
```

```
void QuitCallback(widget, client_data, call_data)
Widget               widget;
void                 *client_data;
XmAnyCallbackStruct *call_data;
{
    exit(0);
}

main(argc, argv)
int     argc;
char    **argv;
{
    Widget       shell, buttons[4], quit_button, form, scrolled_win;
    Widget       frame;
    int          i, n;
    char         button_name[20];
    Arg          args[10];

    /* Initialize the toolkit, set up top-level shell */
    shell = XtInitialize("shell", "ScrollW", NULL, 0, &argc, argv);

    /* create the scrolled window */
    scrolled_win = XtCreateManagedWidget("scrolled_win",
        xmScrolledWindowWidgetClass, shell, NULL, 0);

    /* create a frame to give the form widget shape */
    frame = XtCreateManagedWidget("frame",
        xmFrameWidgetClass, scrolled_win, NULL, 0);
    /* create the Form instance */
    form =
        XtCreateManagedWidget("form",
            xmFormWidgetClass, frame, NULL, 0);


    /* create four buttons to show form widget's behavior */
    for (i = 0; i < 4; i++) {
        sprintf(button_name, "button_%d", i);
        buttons[i] =
            XtCreateManagedWidget(button_name,
                xmPushButtonWidgetClass, form, NULL, 0);
    }

    quit_button =
        XtCreateManagedWidget("quit_button",
            xmPushButtonWidgetClass, form, NULL, 0);

    n = 0;
    /* attach all widgets to left and right sides of form */
```

```
XtSetArg(args[n], XmNleftAttachment, XmATTACH_FORM); n++;
XtSetArg(args[n], XmNrightAttachment, XmATTACH_FORM); n++;
for (i = 0; i < 4; i++)
    XtSetValues(buttons[i], args, n);
XtSetValues(quit_button, args, n);

/* position widget top and bottom edges */
n = 0;
/* quit button at top */
XtSetArg(args[0], XmNtopAttachment, XmATTACH_FORM);
XtSetValues(quit_button, args, 1);
/* buttons stacked beneath */
XtSetArg(args[n], XmNtopAttachment, XmATTACH_WIDGET); n++;
XtSetArg(args[n], XmNtopOffset, 10); n++;
XtSetArg(args[n], XmNtopWidget, quit_button); n++;
XtSetValues(buttons[0], args, n);

for (i = 1; i < 4; i++) {
    n = 2;  /* reuse first two resources from above */
    XtSetArg(args[n], XmNtopWidget, buttons[i - 1]); n++;
    XtSetValues(buttons[i], args, n);
}

/* fix last button to bottom of form */
XtSetArg(args[0], XmNbottomAttachment, XmATTACH_FORM);
XtSetValues(buttons[3], args, 1);

/* set up the quit button callback */
XtAddCallback(quit_button, XmNactivateCallback,
    QuitCallback, NULL);

/* make the whole thing appear */
XtRealizeWidget(shell);

/* run the event loop */
XtMainLoop();
}
```

Text

Include file: Xm/Text.h

Class name (for resource file): XmText

Creation examples:

```
Widget    text;
Arg       *args;
int       argcnt;

text = XtCreateManagedWidget("widget_name",
    xmTextWidgetClass, parent_widget, args, argcnt);
```

or

```
text = XmCreateText(parent_widget, "widget_name",
    args, argcnt);
XtManageChild(text);
or
text = XmCreateScrolledText(parent_widget, "widget_name",
    args, argcnt);
XtManageChild(text);
```

*Figure 8-20: A pair of text widgets. On top, a
one-row Text widget with its XmNeditMode resouce set to
XmSINGLE_LINE_EDIT. Below, a widget created with XmCreateScrolledText.*

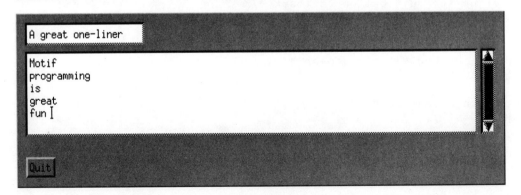

Of all the widgets in the Motif arsenal, none is more versatile or complex than the Text widget. As its name suggests, it is a general-purpose widget for displaying and editing text. A Text widget can be editable or not, display a single line or multiple lines of text, and is almost infinitely tunable in terms of configuration and behavior. In the interest of keeping things simple, I won't discuss all the possible settings of the Text widget here. I do recommend, however, that you consult your Reference Manual and Programmer's Guide to learn more than just these basics of using the Text widget.

The Text widget displays all of its text in a single font and color, and a Text widget's attributes affect equally all of the characters contained in the widget. A Text widget maintains its entire contents in memory. This buffer is manipulated as an ordinary array of characters, *not* as an XmString value. It can, therefore, be read from and output to ordinary files without conversion.

There are several convenience functions associated with the Text widget (you'll find them in the Reference Manual with the prefix XmText), but two are most important: XmTextSetString() and XmTextGetString(). XmTextSetString() loads the Text widget's internal buffer with the null-terminated string passed as the second argument (the widget ID is the first argument). XmTextGetString() copies the string's internal buffer—all of it—to a temporary storage area, and returns a pointer to that temporary storage. The storage allocated for this buffer should be deallocated with the XtFree function once you've copied the buffer's contents to an area under your application's direct control, or when you have otherwise finished manipulating the returned string. Since new storage is allocated every time XmTextGetString() is called, failing to free that storage with XtFree() can cause your application's memory usage to expand out of control.

A single-line Text widget, a type determined at creation time by setting the XmNeditMode resource to XmSINGLE_LINE_EDIT, accepts a single line of text, up to a maximum size set by the XmNmaxLength resource. The text is displayed in a window sized, by default, to fit a single line of text and display the number of characters specified in the XmNcolumns resource. The text can be longer than the Text widget can display all at once; arrow keys can be used to scroll the text horizontally in the window. The text in this type of widget cannot contain new-line characters. When Return is pressed, the callback registered with the XmNactivateCallback is dispatched. Prior to this callback, the current contents of the Text widget's string can be retrieved with XmTextGetString(). You can also register other callbacks, including XmNvalueChangedCallback, which calls a function every time a change is made to the text. More on this callback in a moment.

A multi-line Text widget (XmNeditMode is set to XmMULTI_LINE_EDIT) creates an editable text window XmNcolumns wide by XmNrows deep. Text can be entered past the right or bottom edges of the window. If the XmNwordWrap resource is set to True, the Text widget will move any word that would go off the right edge of the visible window to the next line, and it will move the cursor so that continued typing will be added to that new line. As with the single-line Text widget, XmTextGetString() can be called at any time to retrieve the entire string contained in the widget's edit buffer. The returned string is not affected by the XmNwordWrap setting; newline characters appear in the string only where they were entered by the user. However, unlike the single-line Text widget, there is no default key that triggers the function registered as XmNactivateCallback.

If you want your application to be notified of changes to a Text widget's single- or multi-line contents as they happen, you should register an XmNvalueChangedCallback, or an XmNmodifyVerifyCallback. The XmNvalueChangedCallback doesn't return much information, just the callback reason (which is set to XmCR_VALUE_CHANGED), and a pointer to the X event that caused the callback. You'll still need to call XmTextGetString() to get the edited string, and there are times when that may not be very efficient. If you're modifying a file, for example, you will either have to write the entire string to the file each time the callback is triggered, or figure out where the change was made and write only that portion.

For more detailed reporting of changes as they occur, you can register the XmNmodifyVerifyCallback. This callback is dispatched every time the user tries to change the widget's text. It returns detailed status to the application through the XmTextVerifyCallbackStruct structure:

```
    {
        int             reason;    /* reason for callback */
        XEvent          event;     /* raw X event */
        Boolean         doit;      /* permit change? (true/false) */
        XmTextPosition  currInsert, newInsert;
        XmTextPosition  startPos, endPos;
        XmTextBlock     text;
    }
```

The currInsert and newInsert members are most useful with XmNmotionVerifyCallback calls, but their values are also updated for XmNmodifyVerifyCallbacks. Text widget positions are always offsets from the first character in the string. These XmTextPosition members hold the position of the insert cursor (currInsert), and the position to which the user wants the cursor moved (newInsert). The other two XmTextPosition members, startPos and endPos, hold the starting and ending character positions of the text the user is asking to modify. Usually these are both the same number, reflecting the addition or deletion of a single character. However, it is possible, through selection, to affect a range of characters in a single operation.

Motif Text Selection

Motif Text widgets support a selection mechanism through which portions of text can be marked and deleted, copied to another location in the same widget, or copied to another Text widget. This cross-widget copying can take place even if the destination of the copy is under the control of another application, or executing on a different machine. Also, other X Window applications, like the xterm terminal emulator, that support the same kind of text selection can participate equally in this method of transferring text data.

Like many facilities in X and Motif, the selection mechanism is very capable, and can be adapted to perform a number of functions beyond the most obvious. Because this book's scope is limited, we will deal only with the highest level interface to text selection. That interface is really no interface at all, at least from a developer's point of view: Text selection is part of every Motif Text widget you create, and you don't have to write any code to support it. You can, however, retrieve a Text widget's currently selected text at any time with the XmTextGetSelection function. This returns a pointer to an internal buffer that must be deallocated with XtFree() when no longer needed.

Through the selection mechanism, your application can perform special functions on user-selected portions of text. A word processor, for instance, could do a thesaurus lookup on a selected word. An appointment scheduler could bring up a contact record based on a selected phone number, or person's name. A help facility could pop up a help window based on a topic name highlighted through selection. There are plenty of potential uses for the Text widget's selection, but to use any of it, you need to understand how to select text.

Text selection in the Motif Text widget is governed by translation table entries that define what combination of actions select what quantity of text. As mentioned before, the translation manager is beyond the scope of this book. Fortunately, the default translations for selection are sensible, easy to remember, and (most importantly) expected by users.

Dragging (moving the mouse with the left button pressed) over characters in a Text widget selects those characters. As the mouse is moved vertically, entire lines of text are selected. Each full line selected will include a newline character at the end. Mouse button presses also have a default effect: one click positions the text cursor, two clicks selects the word under the cursor, three clicks selects the entire line, and four clicks selects all the text in the Text widget, including text that is not visible. A fifth click in rapid succession restarts the sequence, clearing the selection, and positioning the text cursor.

Text selected in any Text widget can be "pasted" into any compliant X Window application, including other Text widgets, with the middle mouse button (mouse button 2). A full copy of the selected text will be pasted each time the button is pressed.

There are other user actions that have an effect on the contents of a Text widget; these actions are listed in the Reference Manual under "Behavior".

There is a special variety of Text widget called ScrolledText. By design, ordinary Text widgets scroll both vertically and horizontally as needed, but the keyboard must be used to position the text cursor to bring obscured text into the viewing area. The ScrolledText version of the Text widget, which is created by the XmCreateScrolledText convenience function, makes the Text widget a child of a ScrolledWindow widget, adding scrollbars and built-in callbacks that manage the repositioning of text in the viewing area as the scrollbars are used. The ScrolledText variety only makes sense with multi-line Text widgets, but a single-line Text widget will work as well; the scrollbars will simply never appear. If you wish to address resources associated with the ScrolledWindow widget created by the XmCreateScrolledText call, reference the widget name you supplied with a suffix of "SW". The example's resource file shows this.

The makefile boilerplate for the example should be modified as follows:

```
PROGNAME=      text
OBJS=          text.o
LIBS=          -lXm -lXt -lX11 -lsocket
```

The default resource file, Text, should start out:

```
# resources for Text widget example

*XmText.background:      white
*text1*y:                10
*text2SW*y:              40
```

```
*text1*editMode:        SINGLE_LINE_EDIT
*text2*editMode:        MULTI_LINE_EDIT
*text2*rows:            6
*text2*columns:         80
*quit_button.labelString:   Quit
*quit_button.y:         150

# The following are optional:
*text2*wordWrap:        True
*text2*scrollVertical:  True
*text2*scrollHorizontal:    False
```

Here's the example:

```
/* text.c: Text Motif example for chapter 8 */
/* tabs are four spaces apart */

#include <X11/Intrinsic.h>
#include <Xm/Xm.h>
#include <Xm/BulletinB.h>
#include <Xm/Text.h>
#include <Xm/PushB.h>
#include <stdio.h>

/* callback routine for single-line Text widget */
void Text1Callback(widget, client_data, call_data)
Widget                  widget;
void                    *client_data;
XmAnyCallbackStruct *call_data;
{
    char    *ptr;
    /* we asked to be notified only when activated (Return key
        press by default */
    /* note that the string is not stored as an XmString */
    printf("Activate called for text1\n");
    printf("String: %s\n", ptr = XmTextGetString(widget));
    XtFree(ptr);
}


void Text2Callback(widget, client_data, call_data)
Widget                  widget;
void                    *client_data;
XmTextVerifyCallbackStruct  *call_data;
{
    /* called only for modification */
    printf("MODIFYING_TEXT_VALUE callback. Start=%d, end=%d\n",
        call_data->startPos, call_data->endPos);
```

```
    /* the string is NOT null-terminated! */
    printf("String: '%*.*s'\n\n", call_data->text->length,
        call_data->text->length, call_data->text->ptr);
}
/* define a handler for the "quit" convenience push button */
void QuitCallback(widget, client_data, call_data)
Widget              widget;
Widget              *client_data;    /* pointer to text widgets */
XmAnyCallbackStruct *call_data;
{
    char    *text_ptr;

    printf("\n\n** Quit button activated **\n");
    /* grab the values for both strings and display them */
    text_ptr = XmTextGetString(client_data[0]);
    printf("Text1: '%s'\n\n", text_ptr);
    XtFree(text_ptr);    /* be a good citizen (a little silly now) */
    text_ptr = XmTextGetString(client_data[1]);
    printf("Text2: '%s'\n", text_ptr);
    exit(0);
}

main(argc, argv)
int     argc;
char    **argv;
{
    Widget      shell, bulletin_board, quit_button, text1, text2;
    Widget      call_array[2];

    /* Initialize the toolkit, set up top-level shell */
    shell = XtInitialize("shell", "Text", NULL, 0, &argc, argv);

    /* create instance of BulletinBoard container widget class */
    bulletin_board =
        XtCreateManagedWidget("bulletin_board",
            xmBulletinBoardWidgetClass, shell, NULL, 0);

    /* create two Text instances */
    text1 =
        XtCreateManagedWidget("text1", xmTextWidgetClass,
            bulletin_board, NULL, 0);

    text2 =
        XmCreateScrolledText(bulletin_board, "text2", NULL, 0);
    XtManageChild(text2);

    /* give it some default text */
    XmTextSetString(text2, "Motif\nprogramming\nis\ngreat\nfun");
```

```
/* declare callbacks */
XtAddCallback(text1, XmNactivateCallback,
    Text1Callback, NULL);
XtAddCallback(text2, XmNmodifyVerifyCallback,
    Text2Callback, NULL);

quit_button =
    XtCreateManagedWidget("quit_button",
        xmPushButtonWidgetClass, bulletin_board, NULL, 0);

/* fill call array with Text widget IDs so their text can be
    displayed when the Quit button is activated */
call_array[0] = text1;
call_array[1] = text2;

/* set up the quit button callback */
XtAddCallback(quit_button, XmNactivateCallback,
    QuitCallback, call_array);

/* make the whole thing appear */
XtRealizeWidget(shell);

/* run the event loop */
XtMainLoop();
}
```

ToggleButton

Include file: Xm/ToggleB.h
Class name (for resource file): XmToggleButton
Creation examples:

```
Widget     toggleb;
Arg        *args;
int        argcnt;

toggleb = XtCreateManagedWidget("widget_name",
    xmToggleButtonWidgetClass, parent_widget, args, argcnt);
```

or

```
toggleb = XmCreateToggleButton(parent_widget, "widget_name",
    args, argcnt);
XtManageChild(toggleb);
```

Figure 8-21: Two collections of ToggleButton widgets. On the left, buttons arranged as chidlren of a RowColumn widget that permits any number of buttons to be selected at once. On the right, the buttons are chidlren of a RowColumn defined as a RadioBox, a type which permits only one ToggleButton at a time to be selected.

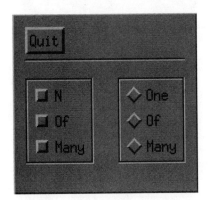

The ToggleButton widget is, as its name suggests, a button that reverses state each time it is pressed. If the button's shading shows it to be "pressed in," then it represents a True state. If its shading makes the button looked popped out, then the button's value is False. This makes the ToggleButton something like a check box on a handwritten form, in that its appearance immediately reveals its state.

Used alone, a ToggleButton widget is a bit different from its PushButton cousin. There is no XmNactivateCallback, because the button's action is not momentary like the PushButton. Instead, the worthwhile callback is the XmNvalueChangedCallback. The widget's value (boolean True or False) is passed to the callback routine through the set member of the XmToggleButtonCallbackStruct structure. A ToggleButton's value can also be obtained at any time with a call to XmToggleButtonGetState(), which returns a True or False value for the ToggleButton passed as an argument.

ToggleButtons are not usually seen alone, but in groups. In Motif, RowColumn widgets are used to contain groups of ToggleButtons. A group of buttons that can be independently set or reset is managed by an ordinary RowColumn widget, and this type of group is referred to as "N of many," because any, none, or all of the buttons can be selected at once. The other type, "one of many," is covered by a special flavor of the RowColumn widget called the RadioBox. The RadioBox RowColumn is created with the XmCreateRadioBox convenience function. Each ToggleButton widget pressed in a RadioBox pops up any other selected button; only one button at a time can be selected. The shape of the ToggleButton differs according to which selection mode is active: "N of many" ToggleButtons are square, and "one of many" ToggleButtons (children of RadioBox RowColumn widgets) are diamond-shaped.

While not shown in the example, ToggleButtons can also be used in menus. They can be a little awkward to press, particularly on spring-loaded menus, but they provide a needed service.

Each ToggleButton has an XmNlabelString resource associated with it. By default, the label is displayed to the right of the button. Another resource, XmNset, shows a button as selected if set to True.

The makefile boilerplate should be modified as follows:

```
PROGNAME=    toggleb
OBJS=        toggleb.o
LIBS=        -lXm -lXt -lX11 -lsocket
```

The default resource file, ToggleB, contains this text:

```
# ToggleB: default resources ToggleButton example in chapter 8

*geometry:              150x140
*quit_button*labelString:    Quit
```

```
#resources to place the separator
*separator.orientation:     HORIZONTAL
*separator.y:                    35
*separator.width:                130
*XmFrame.y:                 50

*frame_2.x:                 85

#get button labels under control
*n_of_many_0.labelString:       N
*n_of_many_1.labelString:       Of
*n_of_many_2.labelString:       Many

*one_of_many_0.labelString:     One
*one_of_many_1.labelString:     Of
*one_of_many_2.labelString:     Many
```

Here's this chapter's final example:

```
/* toggleb.c: ToggleButton Motif example for chapter 8 */
/* tabs are four spaces apart */

#include <X11/Intrinsic.h>
#include <Xm/Xm.h>
#include <Xm/RowColumn.h>
#include <Xm/BulletinB.h>
#include <Xm/Frame.h>
#include <Xm/ToggleB.h>
#include <Xm/ToggleBG.h>
#include <Xm/Separator.h>
#include <Xm/PushB.h>
#include <stdio.h>

/* handler for the toggle buttons */
void ToggleCallback(widget, client_data, call_data)
Widget                          widget;
void                            *client_data;
XmToggleButtonCallbackStruct    *call_data;
{
    printf("Button %s is now %d\n", client_data, call_data->set);
}

/* define a handler for the "quit" convenience push button */
void QuitCallback(widget, client_data, call_data)
Widget              widget;
void                *client_data;
XmAnyCallbackStruct *call_data;
```

```
{
    exit(0);
}

main(argc, argv)
int     argc;
char    **argv;
{
    Widget      shell, bulletin_board, quit_button, separator;
    Widget      one_of_many[3], n_of_many[3];
    Widget      frame_1, frame_2, rowcol_1, rowcol_2;
    int         i;
    char        button_name[20], button_names[6][20];
    Arg         args[3];

    /* Initialize the toolkit, set up top-level shell */
    shell = XtInitialize("shell", "ToggleB", NULL, 0, &argc, argv);

    /* create instance of BulletinBoard container widget class */
    bulletin_board =
        XtCreateManagedWidget("bulletin_board",
            xmBulletinBoardWidgetClass, shell, NULL, 0);

    /* build a pair of frames to hold RowColumn widgets */
    frame_1 =
        XtCreateManagedWidget("frame_1",
            xmFrameWidgetClass, bulletin_board, NULL, 0);
    frame_2 =
        XtCreateManagedWidget("frame_2",
            xmFrameWidgetClass, bulletin_board, NULL, 0);

    /* two RowColumn widgets for buttons--one created as a RadioBox
       so that buttons are managed in a "one of many" fashion */
    rowcol_1 =
        XtCreateManagedWidget("rowcol_1",
            xmRowColumnWidgetClass, frame_1, NULL, 0);
    rowcol_2 =
        XmCreateRadioBox(frame_2, "rowcol_2", NULL, 0);

    /* create two sets of three buttons each */
    for (i = 0; i < 3; i++) {
        sprintf(button_name, "n_of_many_%d", i);
        n_of_many[i] =
            XtCreateManagedWidget(button_name,
                xmToggleButtonWidgetClass, rowcol_1, NULL, 0);
        strcpy(button_names[i], button_name);
        XtAddCallback(n_of_many[i], XmNvalueChangedCallback,
            ToggleCallback, button_names[i]);
```

```
        sprintf(button_name, "one_of_many_%d", i);
        one_of_many[i] =
            XtCreateManagedWidget(button_name,
                xmToggleButtonGadgetClass, rowcol_2, NULL, 0);
        strcpy(button_names[i+3], button_name);
        XtAddCallback(one_of_many[i], XmNvalueChangedCallback,
            ToggleCallback, button_names[i+3]);
    }
    XtManageChild(rowcol_2);

    /* create a separator */
    separator =
        XtCreateManagedWidget("separator",
            xmSeparatorWidgetClass, bulletin_board, NULL, 0);

    quit_button =
        XtCreateManagedWidget("quit_button",
            xmPushButtonWidgetClass, bulletin_board, NULL, 0);

    /* set up the quit button callback */
    XtAddCallback(quit_button, XmNactivateCallback,
        QuitCallback, NULL);

    /* make the whole thing appear */
    XtRealizeWidget(shell);

    /* run the event loop */
    XtMainLoop();
}
```

What Now?

While we've covered most of the interesting Motif widgets, this chapter has barely scratched the surface of Motif and X Window programming. Important concepts, like proper handling of colors and use of multiple fonts, were necessarily omitted. You can write good Motif programs with just the material in this book's chapters, but you may find that you'll reach the limits of your knowledge fairly quickly. Now that you understand the basics, the *Programmer's Guide* and *Reference Manuals* for the X library, X toolkit, and Motif are all good sources for additional information. The optional source code disk (see the order form in the back) also contains example X/Motif code that illustrates important concepts not covered here.

Becoming good at X and Motif applications programming isn't something you can do by watching or reading. Since the objective is a visually effective result, a reasonable way to proceed with your own projects is to start small. Build your interface in pieces, getting each small group of widgets to look right and work properly before you link them into your application's main widget tree. Use external resource files to save yourself, and your users, time and frustration. Remember, too, that the objective of a graphical user interface is to make the user's work easier. If a graphical interface takes more time to learn and operate than a corresponding text interface, do it in text.

Index

Source Code License

All of the source code examples in this book (the material that appears in monospaced type), plus any additional examples on the source code disk, are Copyright © 1991, Tom Yager. No portion of this book's source code may be reproduced or redistributed in any form without the author's written permission, except under the terms of the license which follows:

The original purchaser of this book is granted a single, non-transferable license to use this book's source code examples on a single machine. Others who wish to use the source code may do so only after purchasing a license (there is a form in the back of this book) or a copy of this book.

Licensees may use portions of the source code in any number of original products, provided no portion of this book's source code is made available to those without valid licenses. The Motif resource files in Chapter 8 and shell script programs are excepted from this. All other code may only be redistributed in binary form as part of an original binary program. There are no royalties for the legitimate redistribution of this book's source code in binary form, and no mention of its origin is required.

Source Code Order Form

The examples in this book may be purchased on magnetic media. Diskettes and tapes are available, along with licenses for additional users of the source code and additional systems.

The diskettes are available in both DOS and UNIX tar formats, in 3.5 and 5.25 inch sizes. Tapes are 150MB QIC-standard UNIX tar format.

Full payment must accompany the order. Orders paid in money order or other certified funds will be processed immediately. Personal and business checks will be held until they clear the bank.

This page (the original, not a copy) must accompany your order to waive the license fee. Each additional user of the source code, and each additional machine on which the code resides, must be covered by a separately purchased license. Orders including licenses will be acknowledged in writing; if you have not purchased a book, you may not use the source code until you receive the license acknowledgment.

Allow up to 4 weeks to receive your order. Thank you.

- -

Media/License Order Form

Product	Qty	Description
Media type:	____	3.5" UNIX tar diskette (1.44MB) 15.00
(mark	____	5.25" UNIX tar diskette (1.2MB) 15.00
quantity for	____	3.5" DOS diskette 15.00
each type)	____	5.25" DOS diskette 15.00
	____	150MB QIC tape cartridge (UNIX tar). . . . 50.00
License:	____	Additional right to use license for
		one individual on one machine 10.00
		Total ____

Make check or money order payable to Tom Yager and send it, along with this original completed order form, to:

Tom Yager
ATTN: Media Orders
P.O. Box 467
Peterborough, NH 03458

Correspondence regarding this book, including requests for site licenses and other special situations, may also be directed to the above address.